CW00547653

Writing Your Master's Thesis

Sara Miller McCune founded SAGE Publishing in 1965 to support the dissemination of usable knowledge and educate a global community. SAGE publishes more than 1000 journals and over 800 new books each year, spanning a wide range of subject areas. Our growing selection of library products includes archives, data, case studies and video. SAGE remains majority owned by our founder and after her lifetime will become owned by a charitable trust that secures the company's continued independence.

Los Angeles | London | New Delhi | Singapore | Washington DC | Melbourne

Lynn P. Nygaard

Writing Your Master's Thesis

From A to Zen

Los Angeles | London | New Delhi
Singapore | Washington DC | Melbourne

Los Angeles | London | New Delhi
Singapore | Washington DC | Melbourne

SAGE Publications Ltd
1 Oliver's Yard
55 City Road
London EC1Y 1SP

SAGE Publications Inc.
2455 Teller Road
Thousand Oaks, California 91320

SAGE Publications India Pvt Ltd
B 1/I 1 Mohan Cooperative Industrial Area
Mathura Road
New Delhi 110 044

SAGE Publications Asia-Pacific Pte Ltd
3 Church Street
#10-04 Samsung Hub
Singapore 049483

Editor: Jai Seaman
Assistant editor: Alysha Owen
Production editor: Ian Antcliff
Copyeditor: Rosemary Campbell
Proofreader: Thea Watson
Indexer: David Rudeforth
Marketing manager: Sally Ransom
Cover design: Shaun Mercier
Typeset by: C&M Digitals (P) Ltd, Chennai, India
Printed in the UK

© Lynn P. Nygaard 2017

First published 2017

Apart from any fair dealing for the purposes of research or
private study, or criticism or review, as permitted under the
Copyright, Designs and Patents Act, 1988, this publication
may be reproduced, stored or transmitted in any form, or
by any means, only with the prior permission in writing of
the publishers, or in the case of reprographic reproduction,
in accordance with the terms of licences issued by
the Copyright Licensing Agency. Enquiries concerning
reproduction outside those terms should be sent to
the publishers.

Library of Congress Control Number: 2016947450

British Library Cataloguing in Publication data

A catalogue record for this book is available from
the British Library

ISBN 978-1-4739-0392-0
ISBN 978-1-4739-0393-7 (pbk)

At SAGE we take sustainability seriously. Most of our products are printed in the UK using FSC papers and boards.
When we print overseas we ensure sustainable papers are used as measured by the PREPS grading system.
We undertake an annual audit to monitor our sustainability.

CONTENTS

FIGURES

ABOUT THE AUTHOR

Since moving to Norway from the US in the late 1980s, Lynn P. Nygaard has provided editorial support, writing instruction, and coaching for researchers in a wide variety of disciplines. A native English speaker, Nygaard started as a freelance copyeditor and translator for Norwegian academics aiming to publish their work in international journals. In 2000, she became the editorial advisor at the Center for International Climate and Environmental Research – Oslo (CICERO). This position allowed her to view researchers and the writing process from close quarters, and she discovered that language was seldom the main explanation for what was going wrong. After several years of leading workshops on academic writing that focused on developing an awareness of audience, formulating the core argument, and structuring the story, she published *Writing for Scholars: A Practical Guide to Making Sense and Being Heard* (originally published by Universitetsforlaget in 2008, and published in a second edition by Sage and Universitetsforlaget in 2015). In 2008, she became a special advisor at the Peace Research Institute Oslo (PRIO), and continues to develop her expertise in how to support scholars through the writing process. With an undergraduate degree in women's studies from the University of California at Berkeley and a graduate degree in political science from the University of Oslo, she is currently pursuing a doctorate in education from the Institute of Education, University College London, focusing on research productivity, academic writing, and gender gaps in academia.

PREFACE

Imagine that you are an orthopaedist. For years you've specialized in setting bones, coaxing them to grow the right way after an injury, secure in your knowledge of what must be done to help the patient. And then one day, you break your ankle. The first thing you discover is that breaking your ankle hurts. So much that you do all the wrong things – neglect the ice and put weight on it before you're ready, all the while cursing up a storm as if you were the first person in the world to experience this particular pain.

But then you pull yourself together, remember your training, and do what needs to be done to fix the break. You get help, even though it galls you to have to rely on others to do something you know how to do yourself. As you heal, you monitor your own progress, alternating between the curious intellectual observation of the expert ('Ah, yes, we are now entering the phase of stiffness and itching') and the gloomy self-pity of the patient ('This is no fun at all. What if my ankle never gets better?'). And occasionally you have flashes of insight: you begin to understand how being a patient can make you a better doctor, and being a doctor can make you a better patient.

This is what it has been like for me to write this book. I wrote my first graduate thesis in political science many years ago, and since then I've been an editor and writing coach. Recently I returned to being a student: I enrolled in a part-time doctor in education (EdD) programme, focusing on the topic of academic writing and publishing among faculty. Because the programme is aimed at practising professionals, we write two shorter theses rather than one long one. The first focuses on our own practice and has the scope of a Master's thesis (about 20,000 words); the second, about twice as long (45,000 words), has a more academic focus. I wrote this book in between writing the two theses. You can imagine the number of conversations over the past year that went something like this:

Friend: So, how's your thesis going?

Me: A bit slow right now. I'm taking some time off to write a book.

Friend: Really? What's the book about?

Me: How to write a thesis.

         [Awkward silence.]

Writing a book about thesis writing when I am knee deep in my own thesis has been, in the words of a colleague, 'very meta'. Putting aside the irony for a moment, I like to think that both the thesis and the book have emerged all the better for it. As breaking an ankle and being treated for it was for the orthopaedist, writing this book has been for me a mind-bending experience. I was wearing all my hats at once: writer, writing coach, researcher of writing, and student. As a student, the book I was writing was the one I actually needed to read. As a writing coach, I knew what I needed to do to carve out time for writing this book in an otherwise busy schedule, but the writer in me balked. Did I really have to get up at 6 a.m. and write for an hour before I went to work? 'I can't write unless I have heaps of time all to myself with no distractions. An hour a day just won't work for *me*', I would whine to myself. The writing researcher in me countered with, 'But the evidence is really clear. Writing in short bursts on a regular basis whether you are inspired or not has been proven to increase productivity'.

OK, I said to myself. Writing this book will be an experiment in trying to follow all the advice I give everyone else. Knowing that my own medicine was good for me made it only marginally easier to swallow. At least in the beginning, it took a tremendous amount of self-discipline to make myself get up every morning and write. But I kept doing it because the coach in me knew it would work. And it did. An hour a day gradually led to a rough draft, and then a second draft, and a third draft.

During the course of this writing, I would sometimes forget which hat I was supposed to be wearing at that moment. I would find myself writing something like, 'You need to figure out what conversation you are taking part in', and then my next thought would be 'In my own thesis, should I position my work in the context of research on gender balance at the professor level or the gender gap in research productivity?' At first I was frustrated at my seeming inability to focus on the task at hand, but then I realized that this illustrated one of the main points I was trying to make: that understanding the purpose of academic writing in general is one thing, but understanding how to apply it to your own research and context is quite another.

Juggling all these hats also made me acutely aware that writing a thesis actually requires several different skills: writing skills in general, academic writing skills in particular, and research skills. They are all related (and all require you to be able to translate general principles to your specific context), but they are not the same thing. You can be a very good writer in some ways (fluent in the language, adept at grammar and style, and gifted with words), but have a hard time discovering your voice as an academic. You can excel at one kind of academic writing (such as the essays you wrote in your coursework), but struggle when you have to write a thesis. Or you may both understand the thesis genre very well and be a highly competent writer, but still struggle because you don't actually know what you want to say (yet) as a researcher. And of course you can be a brilliant researcher but lack the ability to tell the story of your work in such a way that the reader might hope to understand it. As a coach, it was easy for me to say, 'Tighten up your research question!' But when I became a student again, I'd look at my own frustratingly bloated research question and realize I couldn't tighten it up until I understood my own research better.

So while I was writing this book, I tried to be continually mindful that while some of the struggles involved in writing a thesis might *feel* like writing-related challenges, they may actually come from something else. Not finding the right word is only very occasionally a vocabulary problem; it's usually because you don't really know what it is you are trying to say. Writing your literature review can be painful not so much because you can't write good sentences as because you don't yet understand the point of a literature review.

This is where being in the middle of my own thesis was actually an advantage – the struggles of writing a thesis were no longer simply a distant memory. I know *exactly* how difficult writing a thesis can be because I'm doing it right now. And being an experienced writer, even one who knows a lot about academic writing in general, hasn't necessarily made writing my own thesis any easier – simply because I'm young as a researcher, still trying to figure out what my research is about. In the process of working on my own thesis I think I have blithely stumbled into almost every trap a student can possibly stumble into – and because I have not yet finished there is plenty of time to stumble into the few traps I've missed, as well as possibly invent some new ones. So although my knowledge of writing has not kept me from sometimes getting stuck, it has made it possible for me to get out of these traps a bit faster than most other students. Because I'm familiar with them from the outside, I know what triggers them and where to find the hidden release buttons. So instead of getting stuck and thinking 'Why am I here?' I usually end up thinking 'OK, I'm here now. So this is what it feels like from the other end'. It's still a lot of work to get out, but at least I know it's possible. Just knowing that there is a way out, even if I can't quite manage it at the moment, makes all the difference and has saved me from despair countless times already. This is why I agreed to write this book; if I can't get you unstuck, I hope I can at least give you a better understanding of the trap you might be stuck in.

The title of this book comes as a direct result of having to think about my own thesis while I was writing about thesis writing: it's not a book about how to write *a* Master's thesis, it's a book about how to write *your* Master's thesis. It's easy to write a recipe for writing the ideal Master's thesis, but real research very seldom conforms to a recipe. I suppose it is the difference between making a meal plan based on what you ideally would like to eat compared to opening up your refrigerator and seeing what you actually have to work with. Both in general throughout the book but also specifically in the section called 'Points for reflection' at the end of each chapter, I try to direct your focus to thinking about how you can apply the general advice on writing a Master's thesis to your own situation. I've also included some vignettes illustrating how different students might choose different solutions to give you an idea of how individual your thesis can be.

The subtitle of the book, 'From A to Zen', refers to the process of moving away from thinking of academic writing as a list of rules you have to follow (a, b, then c) and towards developing such a good understanding of the purpose of writing your thesis that the rules become superfluous. You don't have to remember them because you know what you are doing and why. Back to the cooking metaphor, it's like moving from being someone dependent on a recipe (measuring everything to the nearest gram) yet still making a lumpy, tasteless sauce, to becoming someone who follows no recipe at all (measuring by feel), but is guided by experience and an ability to taste how things are developing so far. When you *know* something, you don't have to remember all the details because it makes sense to you and you can think through it. Each chapter begins with a kind of metaphor and ends with a Zen proverb. Both have been chosen to give you a feel for the deeper purpose of a particular aspect of academic writing: not the rules, but the reasons behind the rules.

I'm not promising that reading this book will make writing your thesis easier. Zen is supposed to be a work in progress. According to one Zen proverb, 'If you want a certain thing, you must first be a certain person. Once you are that certain person, obtaining that thing will no longer be a concern of yours'. Reflecting on the purpose of your thesis will take you much further in the long run than just trying to write something as quickly as possible so you can add another diploma to your list of accomplishments: it will help you become a scholar.

ACKNOWLEDGEMENTS

Anyone who thinks they can write a book completely on their own is either deluded or still pecking away at a manuscript that will likely never be submitted (let alone published). Getting feedback along the way is essential, and providing feedback on a manuscript that is only just beginning to take shape requires a special level of diplomacy. I would like to thank especially Unn Målfrid Rolandsen and six anonymous peer reviewers who took on that daunting task. I would like to thank my editor at SAGE, Jai Seaman, and especially my developmental copy editor, Susanna J. Sturgis, for helping me navigate the early feedback, to find my voice and my path, and seeing me through safely to the end.

I would also like to thank my colleagues at PRIO for helping me develop some of the content. In particular, the PhD network group read and commented on some early versions of the chapters on theory, method, and analysis. Rojan Tordhol Ezzati and Marta Bivand Erdal took additional time to share their thoughts about theory, particularly theory about how things should be. Kristoffer Lidén provided valuable insight into what it is like to write a theoretical work, as well as giving some good examples. Ragnhild Nordås gave me some important feedback on the analysis and conclusions chapters. Lectures given by Jørgen Carling and Gudrun Østby provided the inspiration for the figures in chapters 3 and 4 respectively; Gudrun also helped me shape the character of Amina. And Jonas Nordkvele generously designed the figure in Chapter 11 showing how the same data can be visualized in different ways.

And of course, special thanks to the Master's students who let me know what it was they wanted to understand better. Students in the Peace and Conflict Studies programme and from the Center for the Study of Human Rights at the University of Oslo, as well as students from the Peace Studies programme at the University of Tromsø were regular contributors to the process. Because writing a Master's thesis is not unlike writing a doctoral thesis, students in my other writing workshops also contributed valuable thoughts. Nina Irene Jon provided the inspiration for the character of Emma, and Kine Haugen gave me the concrete example of 'criminal addiction' as a term that deserves to be coined. Finally, everyone in my own doctoral programme at the Institute of Education who shared with me their struggles to understand theory and the genre of the EdD thesis, especially those who came from very different countries or disciplines with very different conventions, gave me added insight into the situated nature of thesis writing.

Other individuals who deserve special thanks are my husband Harald Nygaard who watched me alternate between elation and despair seemingly without reason, and was still brave enough to offer comments on the entire manuscript; my friend and colleague Tora Skodvin who had no time for this but gave some anyway; and my doctoral supervisor Lesley Gourlay, who very diplomatically swallowed questions about my own thesis progression and gave some useful feedback on one of the chapters and the character of Keiko. My children, Marlena and Johan, wisely did not try to offer feedback on the manuscript, but were willing to listen when I needed to talk.

Finally, I would like to show my gratitude to our dog, Sasha, who died the week before this manuscript was finished. Not all the help and inspiration we get as writers is verbal. For 13 years Sasha was a natural Zen master, showing us all how to be relaxed in the midst of chaos and how to make the most out of what life puts in your path. I wrote most of this manuscript on our sofa at home with her offering gentle encouragement by lying next to me and just being. I would like to dedicate this book to her.

YOUR MASTER'S THESIS AND YOU

Moving towards academic Zen

....

....

'Zen' and 'academic writing' are not normally said in the same breath – let alone experienced in the same universe. Most people would say that writing their thesis was as un-Zen-like as it is possible to get. That's because we usually think of Zen as a state of blissful relaxation. The only person I know who was blissfully relaxed while writing his thesis had copious amounts of medicinal assistance, and he is probably still sitting in some corner of Berkeley, staring peacefully at his unfinished manuscript. That's not what I mean by Zen. What I am talking about here is enlightenment – the kind that is based on simplicity and intuition, and direct experience with the world. And it's not only possible to achieve this kind of Zen, it's necessary if you want to get more out of your thesis than just the ability to say you survived it.

It's tempting to go into survival mode when you are faced with something like a Master's thesis: it's going to be difficult, but you'll never have to do again, so hunkering down and powering through it as quickly as possible looks like a good strategy. On the other hand, no matter what you intend to do afterwards, writing is likely to be a big part of it. Writing a Master's thesis offers you the opportunity to develop skills you can carry with you wherever life takes you: how to organize and plan a project, how to think critically, how to read a large amount of material and make sense of it, and how to write something that is intentionally targeted at a specific audience in a specific context for a specific purpose.

If you want to continue in academia, and you want your career to be personally satisfying, coming to grips with writing and your relationship to it is essential. Academic life at all levels revolves around research and writing – doing it, reading it, and teaching it. Weekends and holidays are often less about having time off from writing, and more about having time to write without interruption from students or colleagues. If you don't understand the purpose of all this writing, it is hard to feel any sense of fulfilment. And if you feel unsure of yourself, it is hard to feel any joy. But if what you are doing feels meaningful, and you know what you are doing, then spending a few hours of your holiday polishing a manuscript will not feel like torture. (And perhaps more important, if you know what you are doing, then you will only need a few hours to do it and your holiday will not be completely ruined.) The more that the writing you do feels like it is *yours* – where you feel in control of both the process and the product – the more satisfying it becomes. If you want a career in academia, this is the state you want to be in.

Thus in this book, I use the concept of Zen to mean the intuitive insight that comes from understanding what it is you want to do with your writing and why. This means understanding that academic writing is always a matter of asking a question grounded in an academic discussion, and supporting your answer to that question with reasons and evidence. It also means understanding that the way you frame that answer, what counts as support for it, and how much you need to explain will depend on who will be reading it and what you are trying to achieve. This does not (unfortunately) mean that every moment you spend writing will be filled with deep meaning and profound joy, but it does mean that you will be able to say, 'I get what I'm supposed to be doing – and why'.

Knowing what you are aiming for with your writing is not the same thing as knowing what you are doing every single moment. Many scholars, even at the professor level, quite regularly feel like they have no idea what they are doing; they are afraid they don't know nearly as much as they should know, that their accomplishments are just a matter of luck, and that they do not deserve to be where they are. Regardless of how much they have achieved, they can't shake the feeling that they do not belong. This is what is known as 'Impostor Syndrome'. Feeling as if you don't know enough is almost inevitable in academia: by definition, researchers quite literally re-search – exploring the unknown, and sometimes the unknowable. What makes something original is that we push the boundaries of what has been done before, which means that at times we just have to make it up as we go along – not sure whether we have chosen the best approach or the most correct way to interpret something. To thrive in academia, or at least survive, you need to start getting used to the idea that not only do you not know everything, but you will *never* know everything, and you will *always* be wondering if there is some better way to do the things you do. Some self-doubt is healthy: it makes you think twice about what you write, and helps you develop your critical thinking abilities. But too much self-doubt will paralyse you. A basic intuitive understanding of what you are doing, combined with the ability to think through the demands of your particular situation, should give you the confidence to think, 'I may not know enough *right now*, but I know what I need to do to figure it out'.

This book aims to help you better understand the task that lies before you when you write a Master's thesis – both the process you are going through and the product you need to deliver – and how this all fits into the larger picture of academic writing and knowledge production. Rather than seeing the Master's thesis as something to get over with as quickly as possible, this book sees it as an essential step in your development as an independent researcher and academic writer. The focus is on what you can be learning now that will help you build an intuitive understanding of writing and research that should not only help you feel more confident as a student, but also better prepare you for the kind of writing you will do afterwards, whether you choose to continue in academia or not.

The audience for this book is anyone writing a Master's thesis in the social sciences. It is aimed primarily at those writing within one academic discipline, but it also discusses challenges for those writing an interdisciplinary thesis, a professional thesis, or an industry-based study. The point of departure is an Anglo-Saxon style of writing, and as such this book will be particularly relevant for students in North America, Western Europe, and Australia. Since one of the main aims of this book is to explain *why* we do things the way we do, I also hope this book will be helpful for students coming from different disciplinary or geolinguistic contexts who are having to grapple with expectations different from what they are used to.

The remainder of this introductory chapter explores in more detail the conversational nature of academic writing and the specific genre of the Master's thesis, the kind of variations you might experience, and the organization of the rest of this book.

ⓐ WRITING AS A RELATIONSHIP BETWEEN YOU AND THE READER

When you can see someone – when you can register their facial expressions, when you can learn something about the way they think just by looking at them – it is much easier to say what you want to say because you automatically (and almost unconsciously) tailor your argument to suit that person. This is very hard to do if you cannot see them, or even envision them in your head. Likewise, it is much easier to write something if you know what it will be used for. Imagine right now that you are asked to write a 200-word autobiographical statement but you are not told why. What should you put in there? Should you focus on your academic achievements? What about your professional background? Should you say something about where you live? Your hobbies? Imagine your frustration if you decide to play it safe and just mention your academic background, then your piece appears in a pamphlet emphasizing the cultural diversity of your workplace – and you didn't mention that you speak four languages.

Writing is a form of communication. It involves more than just the writer: audience and context matter too. When you write academically, you are not simply typing up some results from your research, downloading your thoughts onto paper, or composing grammatically flawless sentences. You are communicating with a particular audience in a

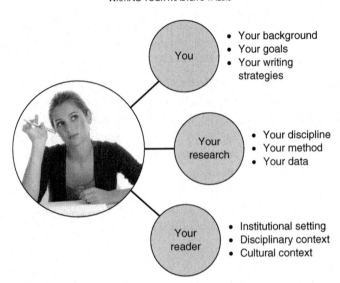

Figure 1.1   Getting to thesis Zen: Getting to thesis Zen means striking the right balance between what you want to do, what you are able to do given your research design, and what your reader (who is also your evaluator) expects from you.

particular situation, which means understanding what you want to say as well as how to say it so your readers will respond the way you hope they will. Brilliance may be in the eye of the beholder – but it's your job to make them see.

Your research skills will help you find the buried treasure; but your communication skills will help others see its value. Explain badly, and all they will see is a dusty, broken old urn; explain well, and they will see history, a missing piece of our heritage, and a vital clue to understanding how people lived two thousand years ago. Looking at your screen and wondering 'Is that introduction long enough? Do I have an appropriate number of para- graphs?' misses the point: you have the right number of paragraphs when you have said what you need to say to the audience you want to reach, in the way you want to reach them. (See Figure 1.1.)

ⓑ UNDERSTANDING YOURSELF: WHAT DO YOU WANT FROM THIS?

Reaching your audience successfully depends on how you define success, which means knowing what is important to you. Individual writers vary tremendously when it comes to what they fear, what they desire, what they feel they are good at, and what feels meaning- ful to them. When it comes to writing a thesis, some people just want the external approval and the degree that comes with it. Others want to feel that they have created something uniquely theirs. Some find writing painful and fear 'getting it wrong'. Others want to play with words and 'challenge the genre'. Think for a minute about who you are and what you want. You may even want to jot down your thoughts about the following questions:

- **What brings you joy?** Collaborating with others? Exploring the freedom of your own thoughts? Starting a new project? Finishing something?
- **What feels meaningful to you?** Saving the world? Solving an intellectual puzzle? Exploring the unknown? Fixing a practical problem?
- **What do you feel you are good at?** Understanding what others are saying? Seeing significance where others do not? Thinking of new ways to do something, or applying old knowledge in new ways?
- **What worries you the most?** The prospect of an insecure future? The possibility that you might not have anything important or original to contribute? Being wrong? Being overlooked?
- **What interests you?** If you were walking through a crowded place, overhearing snippets of other people's conversations, what conversation would tempt you to stop, listen, and maybe even say something?
- **What do you imagine yourself doing when you finish your thesis?** Continuing on to a doctoral degree? Working in the corporate world? Providing services in the public sector?

All of these thoughts and feelings will – consciously or unconsciously – affect the choices you make as a student researcher and writer. If what makes you happy is to have things under control (including having a secure source of income), the choices you make about your research and writing should probably be pragmatic and aimed at allowing you to finish on time. But if you want to contribute an original idea to a complex academic discourse, then you will probably be willing to take more risks. Finishing on time might be less important to you than creating something you can be proud of. Because the definition of successful communication depends on your achieving what you want to achieve, knowledge about what *you* really want is essential.

And keep in mind that identity is neither static nor singular. Your priorities are likely to change over time – particularly during such a rich experience as writing a thesis. Things that were important to you when you started may be less important as you progress, or vice versa.

ⓒ UNDERSTANDING YOUR AUDIENCE: WHAT DO YOUR READERS EXPECT?

Once you know what you want out of all this, you can start thinking about your readers. In the context of your Master's thesis, your readers are primarily your examiners, the ones who will be deciding whether you get to move to the next level. Gatekeepers are present at all levels in academia: even after you finish your doctorate, you will face them regularly every time you submit an article, book, or book chapter for publication and it goes through a form of peer review. In each of these contexts, the gatekeepers will ask, 'Is this good enough? Can we let this through?' They have an exceptionally difficult job. Academia is about building knowledge and developing individual researchers who are capable of thinking critically and working independently. But it isn't always easy to know whether someone is being uniquely brilliant and creative or has simply lost the plot. It also isn't all that easy to instantly know whether a particular set of findings should be trusted or not. The task of the gatekeepers is to ensure that the academic writing put before them meets the required standards for both the writing and the research behind it.

The thesis thus marks a rite of passage between one stage of academia and the next: from undergraduate, to graduate, to postgraduate. At each level you are expected to demonstrate an increasing ability to think critically, work independently, understand the field you are in, and contribute something original to it. The thesis is supposed to represent your competence in three main areas:

- **Knowledge of the discipline**: When you are granted a degree, you are granted a degree in a particular discipline. The examiners want to see that you are engaging with the core ideas of the discipline, even if you are importing ideas from other disciplines.
- **Ability to conduct research**: At each stage you should be learning more about applying critical thinking to an investigation that is designed to answer a particular question. The examiners want to see that you have made good choices in your research design and methods, as well as about ethics.
- **Competence in writing academically**: The examiners want to see that you can formulate an academic argument and provide sufficient support, as well as follow the specific writing conventions in your context.

Essentially, you are demonstrating a set of skills to an audience that is evaluating whether you are ready to continue to the next stage of your academic career. And at each stage, you will be expected to demonstrate these abilities at higher levels. For an undergraduate thesis, the demands for independent research are minimal, but by the time you finish your doctorate you should be ready to work on your own.

 KEIKO

I studied English language and literature in Japan, but I never lived in an English-speaking country before I came to Australia for my Master's in education. The English they speak here is very different from the English I studied! It took some time before I got used to the accent and some of the expressions I had never heard before. I was terrified of saying something wrong at first, and was really unsure about how I should write. It helped to read some of the other Master's theses in my field.

Throughout this transition, your stance as a writer is shifting from speaking as a student to speaking as a full-fledged contributor to an academic conversation. The more you make academic writing your own, the more difficult it becomes to follow a rigid set of rules, and the further you move from using the formulas you have been taught to figuring out what works for you in your context. As a Master's student, you are somewhere in the middle of all this – perhaps the rules you followed as a Bachelor's student are still a good fit for your current work, or perhaps you have already started adapting them to your context. As you move away from thinking in terms of rules and absolutes, your focus changes from 'getting the answer right' (i.e., getting your answer as close as possible to what the examiner is looking for) to arguing for an idea that is uniquely yours and convincing the examiner that you have a valid point. Getting to that point will require you to read extensively beyond whatever reading was required in your coursework, and while your supervisor will probably be able to point you in the right direction, you will have to search for much of this literature on your own. When you start writing, you will discover, quite possibly for the first time, that you know more than you can comfortably write about within the page limits you are given. So rather than forcing yourself to think about how to fill the pages (which is fairly typical for an undergraduate student), you will find yourself worrying about how to cut them down (which is more typical for professional academic writers). And particularly if you are entering your Master's programme as a mature student after working some years outside the university, you might find that you know more about your topic than your supervisor (and possibly your examiners), although you will probably still be a novice with respect to the related theory and method.

🅓 WHEN A ROSE ISN'T A ROSE: VARIATIONS IN THE GENRE

The format of a Master's thesis varies considerably from setting to setting. In some educational contexts, particularly in programmes with a large number of taught modules, a Master's thesis is only slightly longer than a typical term paper. In other contexts it is a book-length document. And while most students write their Master's thesis firmly within one identifiable academic discipline, this is far from the only way to do a graduate degree. Different variations of the Master's thesis genre present different challenges.

ⓘ The interdisciplinary degree

Each discipline or sub-discipline has its unique brand of ontology and epistemology, its own understanding of what phenomena are worthy of study and how to study them. And each discipline tends to develop its own language and culture, populated by the theories and concepts that make up its 'vocabulary'. Choosing an interdisciplinary approach allows the student to combine ideas, approaches, and themes from more than one discipline. For example, if you picked as a topic 'adaptation to climate change in a remote northern fishing village', you would be required to have a fundamental understanding of both climate change and social processes, perhaps combining human geography, economics and insights from the natural sciences. While you are most likely to be based primarily in one discipline that will grant your degree, some programmes allow you to receive degrees from both disciplines. The challenge of writing this kind of thesis is related to aiming at two very different audiences, often with different expectations of what constitutes good research and good academic writing.

EMMA

I'm writing my thesis in criminology, but some of the main concepts I'm using come from sociology and psychology. My supervisor didn't understand why I needed those concepts, so I had to spend a lot of time explaining, comparing them to similar concepts in criminology and showing how they were different.

(ii) The professional degree

Some graduate programmes are tied more closely to a professional field – such as education, healthcare, or social work – than to academic disciplines like sociology, political science, or history. This means that the examiners do not just want to see your ability to conduct research and write about it, they want to see if you understand the significance of your research for a particular profession. For example, if you are undertaking a professional degree in education, you might explore research questions such as 'How can classrooms be better organized to facilitate learning?', rather than their more academic variations such as 'How does learning take place?' While there is considerable overlap between these types of questions, if you are doing a professional degree, you will be asked to reflect on your own practice in a way that other students will not. This means that you will be asked to draw on your own experience and professionalism in a way that might feel strange if you have only ever previously taken purely academic degrees. The challenge of writing this kind of thesis is thus to comfortably straddle writing for the profession and writing for academia.

ROBERT

I was involved in different kinds of social work for about fifteen years before I went back to school to get my Master's degree, and my topic is based directly on things I work with in my job. I wanted to make sure that whatever I wrote about would make a difference in the real world.

(iii) The industry-based study

Like the professional degree, a thesis designed in collaboration with a business or industry means that you have close ties to 'the real world' and are expected to produce something directly relevant for the business or industry with which you are partnering. Sometimes this means that you are expected to produce something that isn't even a written product, such as a management tool or a new kind of software. The challenge is that the university granting your degree will generally want a thesis *in addition* to whatever else you have produced.

SAMIR

I was hired by a multi-national telecommunications company to analyse the feasibility of expanding to remote villages of India. When I started, I wasn't that interested in the topic; I just wanted to improve my chances of getting a job when I finished. But I ended up writing something I'm quite proud of.

Each of these variations will have different formal requirements: what they want your thesis to look like, how you are supposed to submit it, and what will happen to it after you have submitted it. Some of the requirements you will be expected to follow are purely cosmetic, such as double-spacing, printing on only one side of the page, and how you are expected to bind your work. Other requirements have a far more profound effect on the way you will approach your writing: how long the dissertation is supposed to be, what the component parts are, and the timeframe for submission. Becoming familiar with these requirements before you start writing will help you visualize where you need to end up when you finish. Although you might feel that the most important thing for you to pay attention to is your research (and rightly so), becoming familiar with the requirements for submission – long before you are ready to submit – might save you from some nasty surprises at the end.

e   WHAT A DIFFERENCE A PLACE MAKES: CULTURAL AND DISCIPLINARY DIFFERENCES

Sometimes the different requirements for a dissertation are related to what country you are in. Geolinguistic differences affect both explicit conventions about what a Master's thesis is (for example, how long it is supposed to be, how much weight it is given compared to coursework, and how much independent research you are expected to carry out) and what constitutes good writing style. The implicit conventions of 'good writing' can be particularly tricky to navigate.

The Anglo-Saxon style of writing emphasizes a straightforward, no-frills language with minimal adjectives and adverbs, transparent premises, and a clear line of reasoning. A more continental style allows for more expressiveness and a looser structure, but may demand more from the reader (for example, through tangential lines of reasoning). And within these general styles there are variations: US English is a less cautious and more informal language than UK English, for example.

What might make this difficult for students is that most people are generally not aware that they have adopted a regional style; they simply think that this is what good writing is.

So if you have attended university in one country and over the years absorbed the myriad comments from your teachers and built up a tacit understanding of what makes good academic writing, you may well find that understanding challenged – if not shattered – should you continue your education in a completely different part of the world. The language might be the same, but the way it is used might be very different.

SAMIR

My previous degree was in engineering. Now I'm doing a degree in business administration, and the writing is very different. And even though I consider English to be my first language, at least when it comes to writing, the style of writing in the UK is different from the style I was used to in India.

Similar differences can be found between disciplines. Not only are there different expectations related to language and writing, but there are also differences in how much importance they place on language and writing. Some fields (those dominated by the natural sciences, for example, or even quantitative research in the social sciences) place less emphasis on the unique authorial voice and more on standard expressions. Or, expressed another way, you might feel less pressure in the natural and quantitative sciences to play with the language and find your own voice.

You may not notice this unless you move from one discipline to another, or even from one sub-discipline to another. For example, say you did your undergraduate degree in international relations but switched to the field of education for your Master's degree (after having had a few years of classroom teaching experience). You might have been taught previously that you cannot use the pronoun 'I' because it will make your writing subjective. This might have been unproblematic in your Bachelor's thesis on neoliberalism and the Eurozone, where there was no reason to refer to yourself, but it will be very difficult to avoid in your Master's thesis on teaching international politics in a multicultural classroom, which requires you to discuss your own positionality and relationship to your participants. It is a difficult transition to move from thinking that using 'I' makes you a subjective writer (and therefore a bad academic) to not only using 'I' but also actively exploring how you might have inadvertently had some influence on what your informants told you just because of who you are. Even if you theoretically understand the different way of thinking about objectivity and subjectivity, it might take you some time before writing about it ceases to feel awkward.

🔒 COMING IN FROM THE OUTSIDE: ENGLISH AS AN ADDITIONAL LANGUAGE

The subtle differences in regional variations and disciplinary conventions when it comes to writing can be particularly frustrating if you have English as an additional language. Not only will you have to contend with the inexplicable small differences between varieties of English (such as punctuation conventions, what gets capitalized, and how you spell things), you will also have to try to pick up the differences in voice. And if you have worked very hard to develop one way to write in English (say, UK English suitable for everyday conversation), making the adjustment to another style (for example, American English suitable for writing academically as a sociologist) can be bewildering. Native English speakers have a closer relationship with the language and thus sometimes feel freer to play with it, to challenge conventions intentionally. Non-native speakers are often more focused on not making 'mistakes' or sounding like a foreigner. Trying to 'get it right' can be very difficult if what is 'right' changes whenever you move from one context to another.

 AMINA

I grew up in the Democratic Republic of Congo, but received most of my education in Brussels and the Netherlands, so English is actually my fourth language. It helps that everything I read is in English, and since I am doing a quantitative study, the vocabulary is pretty standard.

This might make it tempting to write your thesis in your native language – and indeed, there are very good reasons to do so: some people feel very strongly about preserving local languages also as a medium for academic conversation. But the dominant role of English means that much of the research you are likely to be reading will be published in English, and if everything you have read is in English, regardless of your native language, you might find it difficult (if not impossible) to talk about the topic in any other language but English. Some will argue that for precisely that reason it is important to write in local languages: attempting to explain the material in your own language when you have read about it in another language will force you to think through what you are writing because you do not have comfortable jargon to fall back on.

Just be aware that changing the language changes the nature of the conversation. Say you are a Norwegian writing about child care. Norway has a system of early child care (*barnehage*) that does not easily translate to 'day care', 'preschool' or 'kindergarten'. It is all of these things and none of them. Thus it is not just a question of finding the 'right' word in English, it is also a question of explaining the entire concept because there is no equivalent in English. This would not be necessary for a Norwegian audience. Sometimes having to explain and contextualize for a different audience gives you greater insight; sometimes it just means you have a very long background section.

The decision to write in English when it is not your native language is not a trivial one. Globalization and internationalization have meant that English is increasingly becoming the lingua franca of academic conversation. So, on one hand, if you write in English, you have a greater chance of having your work read by a larger number of people – not just native English speakers, but everyone else whose second language is English. This can give you a much greater voice in the conversation than if you write in a language that very few people speak. On the other hand, writing in a second language might be more difficult and stifling for you. Writing your thesis can be hard enough without feeling constrained by a lack of fluency. It is worth spending some time thinking about this decision; input from your supervisor can be valuable in this respect.

🅖 ORGANIZATION OF THIS BOOK

This book has two main sections: one that focuses on the process, the behind-the-scenes journey you take as a student learning to carry out research; and one that focuses on the product, the written work you submit for evaluation. We will look at these two separately because although the final product should look organized and rational, getting to that point is seldom an organized and rational process. Focusing merely on the end product without looking at what goes on before you get there would only further give the impression that writing a thesis is mostly about producing a document and not about learning how to conduct research and write about it. Below you'll find an overview of the focus and key message of each chapter.

PART I: The Process

- **Chapter 2. From topic to question to design: Planning your journey.** There is more than one path to good research. This chapter looks at different research approaches and which one(s) might apply to the question you want the answer to. The key message here is to better understand the connections between your general topic, a specific question, and research design – and how to move between them.
- **Chapter 3. Ethics: Making good choices.** It is tempting to treat research ethics as a checklist – items you can simply tick off. This chapter looks more deeply into the sometimes difficult choices you have to make as a researcher, and how to think through what is 'right' when you are in an unfamiliar situation without guidance, or when fulfilling one criterion seems to threaten another.
- **Chapter 4. You are what you read: Building a foundation of knowledge.** If academic writing is a conversation, then reading is how you listen to what others have said. The reading you do shapes both your foundation of knowledge and your implicit understanding of what academic writing should be like. This chapter talks about how to know where to start, how to know when to finish, and how to remember what you have read and incorporate it into your writing.
- **Chapter 5. Writing as thinking: From rough draft to final document.** Writing a document as long and difficult as a thesis is a daunting task. This chapter discusses how writing is not something you do all at once, but something that must become a regular part of a sustainable lifestyle.
- **Chapter 6. Supervision and guidance: Getting help along the way.** Although research can be a lonely undertaking, you needn't be completely on your own. This chapter looks at the important role your supervisor can play, as well as how you can get help from others, including your peers.

PART II: The Product

- **Chapter 7. Structure and argument: What's the logic of your story?** As rewarding and interesting as the process may be for you, the product you deliver needs to be designed with others in mind. This chapter looks at how to organize and tailor your structure to strike a balance between the argument you want to make and the way your audience expects that argument to be organized and supported.

- **Chapter 8. Your introduction: How do you fit into the conversation?** Academic writing is ultimately meant to represent a contribution to a discourse, and this chapter looks at how you present the conversation for the reader and position yourself within that conversation.

- **Chapter 9. Your theoretical and conceptual framework: What ideas are you using?** It is not enough just to give the reader a detailed account of your fieldwork; we need to see how you connect your thinking with what others are thinking. Showing your reader how you relate to existing ideas – including concepts, mechanisms, and normative assumptions – provides insight into how your work connects to the ideas of others.

- **Chapter 10. Your method: What did you do to answer your question?** There is a big difference between designing research, conducting it, and then explaining what you did to the readers. This chapter looks at how to explain your methodological approach to a critical audience.

- **Chapter 11. Your results and analysis: What are you building your argument on?** The bulk of your dissertation should consist of showing the reader what you found, and how these findings create the foundation for your overarching argument. This chapter discusses how to present your findings and analysis, for both qualitative and quantitative research.

- **Chapter 12. Your discussion and conclusion: So, what does all this mean?** After you have presented your research you need to bring your reader back out to the academic discourse you presented in your introduction and reflect on the implications of your findings. This chapter addresses the kinds of things you can talk about in your discussion and conclusion.

- **Chapter 13. The finishing touches: Polishing and submitting your work.** Even when you have a draft you are happy with, there are still things you need to pay attention to before you submit. This chapter covers the things you should think about when editing for clarity, language, and style (including your references), as well as double-checking the rules for formatting, binding, and submission.

Each chapter is illustrated with short vignettes that represent concrete (fictionalized) experiences of students I have worked with to show how they have addressed a particular challenge in the context they found themselves in. At the end of each chapter I give you a taste of Zen, knowing full well that achieving insight is always a work in progress, but it helps to know what you are aiming for. This is followed by some points for reflection that can help you to focus on how to make the general points of the chapter relevant for your thesis in particular.

Finally, I give you some tips for exploring these ideas further through additional reading. So take a deep breath, lower your shoulders, and focus: use this book as a way to think about what you want to put into your thesis and what you what to get out of it.

'You should spend 20 minutes meditating every day – unless you are really busy, then you should spend an hour.'

With the greater pressure on universities to push graduate students through the system as quickly as possible, it is easy to think of writing a Master's thesis as being more about producing a document than about learning how to conduct research, think critically, and write academically. But if your education is going to be a sound investment, when you hand in your thesis and walk away with another diploma under your arm you should also be leaving with an intuitive knowledge about research, writing, and communication that will serve you for the rest of your career – long after you have forgotten (or repressed) the actual topic of your thesis. Reflecting on what you are learning needs to be part of your everyday work – unless you become truly overwhelmed and then it should become your main focus.

Finding your path: Points for reflection

What do you want to get out of writing your Master's thesis?
- What aspects of writing your thesis feel meaningful to you?
- How does the thesis fit into your long-term career plans?

What do you think your readers (examiners and supervisor) will be expecting from you?
- How is good academic writing defined in your context?
- What are the expectations for the specific type of thesis you are writing?
- How much do you want to challenge these expectations?

FURTHER READING

Becker, Howard (1986) *Writing for Social Scientists: How to Start and Finish Your Thesis, Book, or Article*, 2nd revd edn. Chicago, IL: University of Chicago Press. Chapter 2 'Persona and authority' challenges old myths about what academic writing is, and Chapter 3 contests the notion of 'one right way'.

Curry, Mary Jane and Lillis, Theresa (2013) *A Scholar's Guide to Getting Published in English: Critical Choices and Practical Strategies*. Bristol: Multilingual Matters. Although focused on academic publishing, the dilemmas for non-native speakers of English that Curry and Lillis identify are equally relevant for MA students.

Kamler, Barbara and Thomson, Pat (2014) *Helping Doctoral Students Write: Pedagogies for Supervision*. London: Routledge. Although aimed at supervisors, the book is useful for getting an idea of how academic writing can be different from context to context, and the identity work involved in writing a thesis.

Murray, Rowena (2011) *How to Write a Thesis*, 3rd edn. Maidenhead: Open University Press. Murray provides a nice overview of what writing a thesis is all about, including some thoughts on how disciplinary context matters.

Paltridge, Brian and Starfield, Sue (2007) *Thesis and Dissertation Writing in a Second Language: A Handbook for Supervisors*. London: Routledge. Aimed mostly at supervisors, the book sheds light on some of the essential challenges for those who are writing their thesis in a second language.

Reid, Natalie (2010) *Getting Published in International Journals: Writing Strategies for European Scientists*. Oslo: Norwegian Social Research (NOVA). Written specifically for non-native speakers of English, the book focuses on the sentence level and explains the Anglo-Saxon style of writing.

Sword, Helen (2012) *Stylish Academic Writing*. Cambridge, MA: Harvard University Press. Using her own research as a point of departure, Sword shows how different disciplines have different styles of writing.

PART I
THE PROCESS

FROM TOPIC TO QUESTION TO DESIGN

Planning your journey

....

   a Choosing a topic

   b From topic to question

   c From question to design: Fitness for purpose

   d Methodology, methods, and materials: What approach will best help me answer my question?

   e Theory: Which ideas will I use to help me make sense of my material?

   f Quality checks: The art of critical thinking

....

Like planning a holiday, planning research is all very exciting when you are just dreaming of things you want to do. But then reality happens. At some point you have to make some tough decisions about what you realistically can do with the time and resources available. Certainly, the better your plan is from the beginning, the fewer nasty surprises you will get – just like reading up on your holiday destination will save you from showing up with the wrong currency. Even with careful planning, however, you will often find that things don't turn out the way you thought they would. Maybe some of the data you planned on using turned out to be unreliable. Maybe some of the interviews you counted on couldn't be carried out. But as with any good holiday, sometimes disappointment leads to unexpected opportunities: perhaps you were unable to interview the CEO, but it turned out that the secretary was happy to talk to you – and had access to information that shed new light on your question.

What makes you a good researcher is not necessarily how well your final product resembles your original idea, but how well you are able to anticipate challenges you are likely to face, respond appropriately to the challenges you did not anticipate, and embrace the fortuitous surprises. This chapter looks at the process of planning your research: moving from topic to question, and from question to research design.

ⓐ CHOOSING A TOPIC

Not everyone joins a Master's degree programme with a clear idea of what they want to write their thesis on. And, furthermore, your interests are likely to change throughout the programme. Sometimes you get inspired by a course you take, a lecture you hear, or something you read. Other times, your supervisor might steer you in one direction or another. Most often, however, you become clearer about what you want to focus on as you start reading, writing, and thinking – perhaps even gathering data. In other words, the more you do stuff, the more you figure out what you want to do.

It is also true that the more you do stuff in a particular area, the more of an expert you become in it, and the more you are expected to continue working there. This is a good reason to spend some time contemplating the topic of your thesis: it may stick with you for many years, whether or not you want to stick with it. The topic of your Master's thesis could grow into a topic for doctoral work; if you publish anything on the basis of your Master's thesis you could be asked to become a peer reviewer for others writing about that topic; if you present your topic at a conference, you may meet others interested in that topic who wish to collaborate with you, and so on. So choosing a particular topic just because your supervisor wants you to, or because you think it will guarantee you a job afterwards, might not be a good idea in the long run if you do not also find that topic interesting. One of the most powerful tools researchers have is curiosity about and passion for their field of study: they are frequently wondering 'what if … ?' or 'what about … ?' This will only happen if you find your topic so interesting that it tickles your mind even when you are not 'at work'.

 **EMMA**

I got the idea for my thesis from something I read in a course I took about how women are involved in violent crimes in different ways than men, and that they are treated differently than men, both when they are arrested and when they are imprisoned. I just kept thinking about it. So in my thesis I looked critically at how this might be related to how gender is understood and performed in society.

You might also want to consider your topic's possible relevance in other contexts. Depending on where you end up in the next phase of your career, your ability to pursue your ideas could be influenced by whether funding agencies think your ideas are worth pursuing. Thinking about how your topic might be relevant for other contexts – within both academic and 'real-world' discourses – might help you sharpen not only your research focus but your ability to persuade others that your work is relevant. Funding cycles are fickle; the better able you are to see your area of interest in a wider context and to argue its relevance, the more likely it is that you will be able to secure funding for future research projects as the priorities of the funders shift.

b FROM TOPIC TO QUESTION

Once you have an idea about your general topic, you can start thinking about how to turn it into a researchable question. Any given topic can give rise to an almost infinite number of research projects. Settling on the right one for you involves knowing enough about the field to ask an insightful question, then balancing what should be done with what is possible to do given the constraints of time, money, and other resources. The best questions spring out of a genuine puzzle, perhaps a social problem that has yet to be resolved, or a disagreement in the literature that needs teasing out.

Unfortunately, at this stage in your academic career, you are unlikely to know enough about the topic – at least in an academic context – to see that puzzle right away. It's like planning a holiday without really knowing anything about the place you're travelling to (or perhaps even worse, relying only on your preconceived ideas based on what you have seen in films). Sometimes you have to poke around a bit before you know where you want to go, which requires doing some reading (see Chapter 4) and a lot of thinking. Ask yourself what it is about this topic that makes you angry, frustrated or curious. The more deeply you engage with the literature, the more clearly you can see how much is known about the topic and what is still unresolved.

 ROBERT

As a social worker, I had seen that immigrant teenagers have a harder time beating addiction, but I wasn't really sure why – although I had some ideas. So I thought I could just do a smaller qualitative study focusing on the challenges that teenage addicts with an immigrant background face when they try to get clean. My starting research question was 'What are the main challenges that teenage addicts with an immigrant background face on their road to recovery?' One of the themes that came up early on was about the role of the church, and it turned out to be so interesting that I wanted it to be the main focus of my thesis, so the final research question ended up being 'What role does religious community play in the lives of teenage immigrants struggling to overcome addiction?'

Once you are able to identify a puzzle, you can start formulating your question (see textbox 'Research questions and the quest for originality'). A challenge that many researchers face is that the puzzle or problem they identify is not firmly rooted in their discipline; for those who are pursuing professional degrees or carrying out industry-based studies, the puzzle may not be rooted in academic research at all. But even in these circumstances researchers need to frame their questions in a way that makes them relevant to the discipline in which they are based. How your question relates to your field is something you might have to revisit several times during the research process.

Research questions and the quest for originality

Academic research is about generating new knowledge. So the questions you ask as a researcher should help you generate knowledge that is original – not necessarily so new that it will change the research agenda as we know it, or be based on data so fresh that they are still steaming, but something that is uniquely yours. Originality comes in many forms, and the further you go in academia, the more important it becomes to find your form of originality. Below I describe some of the main types of questions you can ask as a Master's student and the ways in which they can produce original work (see Nygaard 2015; Petre and Rugg 2010: 14).

Descriptive questions: If you rely on your own data or observations, rather than simply summarizing what other people have said, even questions that seek to codify the obvious or describe a single phenomenon can lead to highly original work: 'What are the religious practices and beliefs of second-generation North African migrants living in multi-ethnic communities in Paris?' If this is a topic about which we know very little – or assume a lot about without actually checking – then this can be an exciting research question. But descriptive questions can also go beyond simply summarizing your observations: you can also attempt to create a taxonomy of observed phenomena (such as categorizing these religious practices and beliefs), or make tacit knowledge explicit (for example, by describing everyday religious practices in detail).

Analytical questions: Analytical questions aim to go beyond describing a phenomenon; they attempt to explain it in some way by finding patterns, trends, or causal mechanisms. Instead of 'what' questions, these are often 'why' or 'how' questions: 'Why do the Nordic countries have so few female professors compared to other OECD countries, despite having a greater degree of gender balance in other areas of society?' Many original analytical questions are based on using old theory in a new context, such as 'How can Bourdieu's concept of *habitus* explain how administrative practices in higher education are gendered?'

Predictive questions: Usually the domain of researchers with access to large datasets or formal models, predictive questions aim to forecast the likelihood of a phenomenon, given a specific set of circumstances and a specific theoretical proposition: 'Given the proposition that the more fragile the state, the more likely environmental stress will lead to conflict, what is the prognosis for intrastate conflict in sub-Saharan Africa over the next 50 years?' This same logic can sometimes be used for hypothetical questions, such as 'What is the likely economic impact on European trading if melting sea ice leads to new shipping routes in the Arctic?' Originality for predictive questions seldom lies in the answer itself (because anyone can say 'I think wars will increase' or 'I expect economic trade to improve in some areas but decline in others'), but rather in your methodological approach to getting that answer. Since you cannot test your claims against a reality that has not yet occurred, the way that you derive your answer will be subject to intense scrutiny by your readers: if you can develop a novel approach to answering a predictive question, one that stands up to such scrutiny, then regardless of your answer, you will have made an original contribution. It is unlikely you will work with this type of question as a Master's student unless you are part of a larger project.

Problem-solving questions: If you are working on a professional degree or an industry-based study, you may well choose a question that is practical in nature – one that aims to solve a particular social problem or improve a given situation. Originality can come from developing or demonstrating the usefulness of a concept ('How can the concept of "criminal addiction" improve post-prison care?'), providing a new solution to an existing problem ('How can treating crime as an addiction reduce recidivism?'), evaluating a programme ('How can the treatment of repeat offenders be improved?') or developing a technology or tool ('What kind of intervention can be developed based on treating criminality as an addiction?'). If you are based in a purely academic context, however, you might want to exercise caution around these types of questions because they can easily become normative and directed at a non-academic audience.

Theoretical questions: The aim of a theoretical question is to develop theory (rather than test it), usually by building on an existing theory ('How can social cognitive theory be improved by conceptualizing the social environment as multi-layered?'), falsifying, contradicting, or critiquing existing theory ('How does the notion of stereotype threat challenge the assumption of agency in social cognitive theory?'), or joining two theoretical ideas together ('How can understanding of research performance be improved if academic literacies theory takes into account notions of agency and feedback loops from social cognitive theory?'). In the context of a Master's thesis, theoretical questions often mean that you do not have to do fieldwork or gather data in the traditional sense, but they very rarely make the writing process easier – quite the contrary. The more you work theoretically, the more your argument is likely to develop during the course of writing, sometimes shifting your focus to a very different place from where it started.

In principle, almost any kind of question can work – provided it is possible to answer through the research you can feasibly do. In practice, however, some types of questions can be problematic, particularly in specific research settings (see, e.g., Bui 2009: 34). Questions that involve a moral or ethical judgement, for example, require a very transparent discussion of premises and assumptions, and will be difficult to answer without resorting to 'because I think so'. Unless you are in the field of philosophy, ethics, or law, you probably want to avoid such questions.

....

You might also find that your question is less answerable than you had hoped. In the early stages of research it is natural to focus more on what you want to do than on what is possible to do – like planning your holiday without looking at your budget. You may find that the data you are able to access will not help you answer your question as it is currently formulated, and you might have to think about what kind of questions *can* be answered with the data you have access to. (See textbox 'Doing it backwards'.)

....

Doing it backwards

Logically it makes most sense to start with a question and then find a method that is best suited to answer that question. But there might be good pragmatic reasons to start with a method and then find a question you can ask using that method. Say you are part of a massive public health project that has been gathering longitudinal data about people's eating habits, exercise habits, health profiles, personal income, and residence. Although you are interested in why some people are able to maintain a regular exercise regime while others quit after a short period, you realize that you cannot actually answer that question with the data you have access to. The method of gathering the existing data is beyond your control, but you can formulate your question so that it can be answered with the available data. For example, you could settle on 'What is the relationship between income and regular exercise habits?'

....

But most likely your greatest challenge will be that your initial question is simply too vague. Because most programmes ask you to come up with a question very early in the process, before you have had a chance to explore the literature more fully, your question will naturally tend to be overly broad. As you dig more deeply into the literature, and indeed once you begin writing, your question will become more focused. Because your Master's thesis probably represents the first original piece of research you've carried out and the first document of any real length you've ever written, you might be surprised to learn that this is a dilemma you will often face as a researcher: your focus will sharpen while you do your research, so the question you start with may not be the question you end up with. (See also Chapter 4.) Nevertheless, you have to start somewhere. When you think you have found an intriguing puzzle and formulated a good question as a starting point, your next step is to start thinking about how you are going to go about answering it.

C FROM QUESTION TO DESIGN: FITNESS FOR PURPOSE

Moving from question to design marks the transition to thinking about what, exactly, you plan to do when you go about answering your question. To return to the holiday metaphor, this is when you start planning your itinerary – where you will be and what you will be doing each day. For research, this means thinking about not only the specific activities you will undertake during your research, but also the logic that will connect these activities to what you want to find out. Even if you are planning to answer a theoretical question and 'just read stuff and think about it', you still need to think about what you will read and what ideas will guide your thinking.

 KEIKO

I used a flexible approach. I wanted to look at how English teachers in Japanese schools saw their roles as teachers and how they did things in practice. At first I thought I would use mostly filming, but it didn't give me insight into what they were thinking about, so I ended up adding interviews, too. After I did the first analysis of my data, I decided it would be a good idea to also have a group interview.

It is not always obvious which approach you should use to answer your question. A common distinction is between quantitative and qualitative design: a quantitative design is usually deductive in nature (hypothesis-testing) and based on numbers and statistics, while a qualitative design is usually inductive (hypothesis-generating) and based on words and ideas. However, while it might be meaningful to describe individual methods and data as quantitative or qualitative, you can also use qualitative data and methods deductively, and quantitative data and methods inductively. Perhaps a more meaningful distinction is the one Robson (2011) makes between *fixed* designs and *flexible* designs. He describes fixed designs as those in which the researchers draw from a particular theoretical framework to decide beforehand which variables they will include and which procedures they will follow. In flexible designs, the methods for collecting and analysing the data develop as the research progresses, as does the choice of theory that will be used in the interpretation. Although fixed designs are commonly associated with quantitative methods and flexible designs with qualitative methods, each type of design can use either kind of method, or a combination of both. What is important for you to think about is whether you are using a fixed approach to test a hypothesis or a flexible approach to develop a hypothesis.

AMINA

My supervisor was doing a survey study on how access to maternal healthcare throughout Africa is affected by conflict, and I did some fieldwork in South Kivu to add to that data. For my thesis, I tested a hypothesis that I could answer based just on the data that I helped gather and code – which meant I had to use a fixed design and think carefully about what exactly I needed to know before I went into the field.

Two things will guide your decision. The first is the context in which you are doing your research. One practical consideration is the methodological orientation of your supervisor or department. Although all methodological approaches have something to offer, if you happen to be in a department that believes that the only real science is experimental or quasi-experimental in design, then you might want to think twice about doing, say, autoethnography. If you deliberately set out to do something entirely different than those around you, you might cut yourself off from an important source of learning.

The second, and ultimately more important, thing you need to think about is the research itself. Research design is the framework for your entire study, and as such is only as good as its ability to help you answer your question. There are three aspects to research design that are particularly worth spending time thinking about:

- **Methodology and methods:** What approach will best help me answer my question? What kind of data do I need, and how can I best go about getting it?
- **Theory:** What ideas will help me relate what I'm doing to other research? What assumptions am I making, and what ideas will help me make sense of what I am seeing?
- **Quality checks:** How will I know if I'm going about this the right way? How will I know if I've actually found what I think I've found? How can I think critically about my work?

Whether you start with a question and find a method, or have a method and find a question, the most important criterion for success is 'fit for purpose'. Is the approach you are considering well suited to actually answering your question? Almost any kind of method is useful under the right circumstances, and even very respectable methods can be inappropriate under the wrong circumstances. Fit for purpose also means that you have a logical connection between your overall approach, assumptions, tools, and ideas. And periodically revisiting your method, theory, and quality checks for fitness for purpose will help you make sure that if your research changes course you will not plunge into the abyss.

(d) METHODOLOGY, METHODS, AND MATERIALS: WHAT APPROACH WILL BEST HELP ME ANSWER MY QUESTION?

Integral to your overall design are your choices about methodology, methods, and materials. Although some people think that methodology is simply a fancy way of saying 'method' they are different things (see Figure 2.1). 'Methodology' encompasses the general ideas about what kinds of things constitute data, how you should go about getting that data, and how such data can be analysed (including how to think through the limitations of that process); 'methods' are the specific techniques you use within that approach, and 'materials' are the concrete items you use to carry out the method. As with the choices about research design, choices about methodology and methods go far beyond 'qualitative versus quantitative'. Very generally speaking, the social sciences have three main types of methodological approaches, or paradigms: positivist, interpretive, and critical (see, e.g., Hennink et al. 2011; Willis 2007).

> **Positivist approaches** are usually associated with fixed designs and quantitative methodologies such as experimental, quasi-experimental, correlational, and survey methods. Taking a cue from the natural sciences, these approaches assume objectivity is possible and desirable, and normally (but not always) follow the logic of deduction: where you start with a general theory, derive a testable hypothesis from it, and then gather data that can test that hypothesis. After the data is gathered, you can analyse it

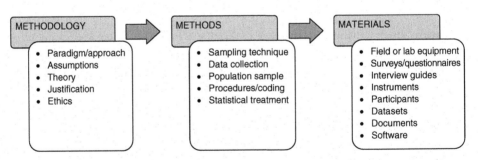

Figure 2.1 Methodology, methods, and materials: As you move from the more abstract questions of methodology to the more concrete questions of methods and materials, there are a number of things you need to think about to ensure that your research design is logically coherent (adapted from Paltridge and Starfield 2007: 123).

statistically in various ways and discuss the extent to which your findings support your hypothesis, and thus the extent to which your findings strengthen or weaken the overarching theory.

Interpretive approaches are normally associated with flexible designs and qualitative methodologies such as Grounded Theory, narrative research, phenomenology, case study and ethnography. These approaches assume that because human behaviour is inherently different than the phenomena studied in the natural sciences, the methods used to conduct research in the social sciences should also be different. Likewise, objectivity is considered to be more problematic – and the closer you are to the subject of study, the more difficult objectivity is assumed to be. These approaches are generally associated with an inductive logic that attempts to generate propositions about social phenomena (why people do what they do) based on in-depth exploration.

Critical approaches are similar to interpretive approaches, but they do not take what they see for granted: they aim to look beyond what they see to consider the larger social structures and distribution of power behind them. They criticize positivist approaches for being oblivious to context, and interpretive approaches for taking things at face value. Critical approaches are also aimed not just at explaining the world as it is now, but also at trying to bring about social change – particularly with respect to hegemonies of gender, race, class, sexuality, or geopolitics. While traditional ethnographic approaches, for example, would strive to present the world exactly as the participants see it, a critical ethnographic approach would aim to find underlying power structures that the participants might not even be aware of.

Each of these general methodological approaches allows a variety of methodological tools, or methods, to gather and analyse data. Most methodologies have a set of methods associated with them, and depending on your particular research question, you may want to draw on more than one. Positivist methodologies generally rely on large datasets, and thus need tools to gather a large number of observations – perhaps in a number of different sites or settings if you are using survey, experimental or quasi-experimental methods. The data can be already available in an existing dataset, you can supplement existing datasets with data you have gathered yourself, or you can build your own dataset. Techniques used to gather the data can include questionnaires, structured interviews, or experiments. But you can also gather quantitative data from documents: you could, for example, analyse newspapers for articles on gang violence, code the occurrences of the term 'gang violence' and its related terms, and see if media attention is associated with an increase in the number of gang violence convictions. Interpretivist and critical methodologies rely more heavily on semi-structured or unstructured interviews, focus groups or group interviews, life histories, participant observation, and document analysis. The most important criterion for guiding your choice of methodological tools is, again, fitness for purpose: Which tools will give you the data you need to help you answer your question? (See textbox 'Getting the data you need'.)

Getting the data you need

How do you know which methods and methodological tools are useful for what it is you want to know? Robson (2011: 232) provides some useful rules of thumb:

- To find out what people do in public, use *direct observation*.
- To find out what they do in private, use *interviews* or *questionnaires*.
- To find out what they think, feel, and/or believe, use *interviews*, *questionnaires*, or *attitude scales*.
- To determine their abilities, or measure their intelligence or personality, use *standardized tests*.

Related to the question of thinking through your choices about methodological tools is thinking about your sources of data. If you plan to have direct contact with people, questions you need to ask yourself include how many people you need to have in your sample, how you contact them, and what kind of questions you ask them. But people are not the only sources of data we have at our disposal in the social sciences. Other typical sources are documents (official or unofficial reports), media (including social media), and observation of activities. What makes a good (or bad) source of data depends on your research question and methodology: if you want to see how the American presidential election is portrayed in social media, then Facebook memes are a natural source of information. If you want to understand what candidates actually said, then memes circulated on Facebook are a poor source of information. Likewise, if your methodological approach is based on an assumption that people do not always understand themselves as well as they think they do, then posing direct questions to your participants may not be sufficient; you might also need to observe their behaviour as they interact with others or to examine another source of data.

Some research questions within the social sciences, especially theoretical questions, do not require you to gather any empirical data at all – at least not in the traditional sense. For example, you can approach the question 'How do normative theories about liberal democracy conceptualize diversity within a multi-cultural society?' purely by referring to existing theories on liberal democracy, definitions of multi-culturalism, and logical inference. If you do use empirical data (such as texts, existing datasets, or secondary research), it will most likely be simply to illustrate your ideas. But be warned: skipping the laborious collection of data does not make the research any easier. Being left alone with nothing but your thoughts and no clear path forward might make you yearn for the apparent simplicity of straightforward statistical analysis.

(e) THEORY: WHICH IDEAS WILL I USE TO HELP ME MAKE SENSE OF MY MATERIAL?

Underlying your choice of method should be your theoretical perspective – the assumptions you make about what things are, what things should be, and how things work. The purpose of theory is to provide a vocabulary and set of ideas for expressing the concepts (ideas about phenomena), norms (ideas that explain how things should be) and mechanisms (ideas about how or why things happen) you use in your research to make sense of your material. (See Chapter 9 for more about how to explain your theoretical framework to your reader.) Drawing from existing theory gives you a language to connect your work with other people's work; it allows you to look at a certain event and say 'What I'm seeing is x, which is similar to/different from what Jones describes'. If we all invented our own words for things, and came up with our own explanations for why things happen, it would be very difficult indeed to connect our work to someone else's.

In the early stages of planning research, the idea of developing a theoretical framework can be intimidating. You are not alone if you are worried about whether you understand theory correctly, whether you are using it in the right way, or even whether the ideas you are drawing from can be considered 'theory'. In your particular context, there might be some very strong ideas about what is considered appropriate theory, or even theory at all. But generally speaking, a theoretical framework can be built from any number of existing ideas – everything from philosophical ideas about the nature of research itself, to theories that are easily identifiable ('social cognitive theory', 'regime theory', 'organization theory', and 'game theory', to name just a few), to ideas teased out from a larger collection of ideas (such as Bourdieu's concept of *habitus* or Foucault's concept of governmentality), to simple propositions derived from empirical observations.

 SAMIR

Because I was doing an industry-based study, I didn't feel like I had much choice about my topic. I had to write about whether or not the company should expand into remote areas of India. But I did get to choose my own approach to the study, and one of the things I chose to do was to look critically at how to define 'success', and the role of corporations in sustainable development. So I drew a lot from theory on Corporate Social Responsibility to help me frame these ideas.

Theoretical ideas about the nature of research itself do not always need to be addressed in your thesis, but part of your journey may involve thinking about where you stand philosophically: Am I a social constructivist? A critical realist? A post-structuralist? You might find that all of these philosophies sound so reasonable in some ways, but completely absurd if you take them to their logical extreme. It is not uncommon to get lost in theory at this point and spend hours reading, writing, and thinking – only to emerge at the other end thinking it was a waste of time. But it wasn't – even if not a single word from your reading makes it to the final draft of your thesis. What this exercise does is confront you with the assumptions you have about the world and the things in it, and how we obtain knowledge about those things – ontology and epistemology, in other words. These assumptions permeate every aspect of your research. For example, if you assume that people are not capable of full self-knowledge, then conducting a survey will not be consistent with your understanding of the world. Being aware of the assumptions you make about the world, the things in it, and how you acquire knowledge about these things will help ensure that all the elements of your research design are internally consistent.

Finding theory that applies more directly to your topic is perhaps something you should spend a little more time on. As a rule, theory does not come to you tailor made for your specific case or research question. If you are writing about the rise of blue frog worshippers in Nevada, you are unlikely to find a book conveniently titled *The Theory of Blue Frog Worshippers in Nevada*. Instead, you will probably have to pick your topic apart to look at its components and then go theory shopping. Theory shopping means looking around at what's out there, trying some of what you find on for size, and then selecting the theories with the best fit. Perhaps you want to start with theories about cults or new religions. If the blue frog worshippers are a modern offshoot of an indigenous group, you could look at works on Native American religion. Or do you think geography plays a role? Maybe some-one out there has written something like *Desert Regions and Faith as an Oasis*. Does Nevada in particular have a history of attracting peripheral religious groups? Maybe you could be inspired by Kerfuffel's work, *Nevada: A Magnet for the Weird?* Like shopping for clothing, you will be happier in the long run if you select things that suit you – not things that everyone else has, that someone assures you is the latest trend (but you don't dare admit you don't understand), or that are simply on sale – that is, handy and requiring little effort to under-stand. Construct your theoretical framework based on ideas you will use in your analysis: how to understand the rise of a peripheral religious group; how to understand the signifi-cance of blue frogs; how to understand the general role of geography, or maybe the specific role of Nevada.

Regardless of the type of theory you use – whether it is grand formal theory, abstract ideas that you have to interpret, or more situated propositions – one of the biggest decisions you need to make is about what this theory is doing in your thesis. Theory can be used to help you understand and explain what you are seeing in your data, or it can be a point of depar-ture for deriving a hypothesis. It can also be something you intend to build on, add to, or challenge. It can be something you start with, or something you end up with. Essentially you need to ask yourself whether the purpose of your research is to use theory (without challenging it), verify theory (without adding to it) or to build on or generate theory. Sometimes the role that theory is playing in your work will not be entirely clear until you are almost finished. So plan on thinking actively about theory throughout the entire pro-cess of carrying out your research and writing your thesis, rather than just summarizing a few theoretical concepts, putting them in a chapter, and never thinking of them again.

🅕 QUALITY CHECKS: THE ART OF CRITICAL THINKING

Through all this process of sifting, sorting, and trying on ideas for size, you need to be able to step back every now and then and ask yourself some hard questions about what you are trying to do in your research because any claim you make, or want to be able to make, has to be backed up by your findings. And your findings are only as good as the method that helped you gather your data, and the theory that helped you make sense of it. How do you know whether your method and theoretical framework are good enough? This is where critical thinking and quality checks come in. A solid research design – with logical connections between all of the elements – is essentially a systematic way to help you think critically through what you are doing at all stages of research, including how to avoid the things that can go wrong in the kind of research you are doing, or at least deal with them if they happen.

A lot of critical thinking is commonsensical, regardless of research design, and helps you think through your own biases. Even if you are doing Grounded Theory, you seldom approach your research with absolutely no idea of what you expect to find, especially if you are building on something related to your work as a professional. Your interest in the topic is what drew you to it, and it is difficult to imagine a situation where at the graduate level you are researching something you find interesting, and yet know nothing whatsoever about. The chances are that you already have some idea about what you will be arguing even before you start your systematic research. This is not a problem. What could be a problem is an inability to see that you might be wrong. So one of the most important quality checks you can perform is to ask yourself questions that challenge whatever biases you bring with you:

- **How will I know if something is true?** Merely believing something is true and informing your reader that it is true is not enough – you have to be able to demonstrate the strength of your claims. The way you do this will very much depend on what constitutes evidence within the tradition you are working in: positivist approaches support claims in different ways than interpretive or critical approaches. For example, an anecdote (properly analysed) might well constitute evidence in an ethnographic study, but it will seldom be considered more than a colourful distraction in an experiment.
- **If it were not true, what would I expect to find?** How do you make sure you do not ignore evidence that would challenge your claims? Thinking through what might constitute evidence that would disprove the claims you might be making will help you avoid seeing only what you want or expect to see. If, for example, you are looking at gender roles in informal organizational hierarchies, before you start describing the role that gender plays, you might want to think carefully about what might constitute evidence that gender plays no role whatsoever.
- **If I find something, how do I know it means what I think it means?** Are there alternative ways to interpret your evidence? Even if you find things consistent with your argument (and apparently inconsistent with the opposite argument), it is not always easy to know whether you have interpreted what you found in the most reasonable way. For example, if you are doing an experiment, it is not always clear whether the effect you observed was caused by the treatment or by something else, or whether you would see the same thing if the circumstances were different. Or if you are conducting interviews,

it is not always obvious how to interpret what people tell you – especially if you suspect that they might be telling you what they think you want to hear.

Thinking through all these questions while you are still in the design phase can make your design more robust: maybe you will add participant observation in addition to interviews so you can see how people behave, and try to see whether what they do matches what they say. Maybe you will collect data on another control variable. Three specific concepts that can help you operationalize this kind of critical thinking are validity, reliability, and generalizability (see Cresswell 2003: 157).

- **Validity:** Are you measuring what you think you are measuring? For example, if you want to look at how 'risk aversion' affects investment decisions, how do you know that a decision to not invest is 'risk aversion' and not something else? Quantitative methodologies often address this issue by using so-called validated instruments, which are (for example) questionnaires or tests that have been demonstrated to measure a particular concept. But if you are not using an instrument that has already been validated, you will have to think carefully about whether or not you are observing what you think you are observing.
- **Reliability:** If you do this again, are you likely to find the same thing? Or if other people were to look at your data, would they see what you see? There are a number of ways to test the reliability of your findings, depending on the type of research you have done. For example, if you are coding qualitative material, you can develop a coding manual and see whether two different coders will code the same material in the same way. (This may be a bit ambitious for a Master's thesis, but you can certainly talk to your supervisor about your coding decisions and perhaps have them check a random section of your data and see whether they would have coded it the same way.)
- **Generalizability:** To what extent is what you found likely to be true in other contexts? Even if you have investigated a very specific phenomenon in a very particular context, think about what would make some aspects of your work also true for other contexts. Similarly, even if you have done as much as possible to make your findings generalizable to a larger population, think carefully about to what extent your sampling, or the responses you got, might keep your findings from applying to as large a population as you would have liked.

Carrying out research seldom feels like taking a holiday. But like a holiday, you are more likely to be able to relax and enjoy what you are doing if you have taken the time beforehand to plan. You are also more likely to avoid getting into situations which could well have been avoided had you thought things through a little more carefully. You cannot plan for everything, but you can learn how to envision research as a process from beginning to end, and take the entire process into account while you are proposing what you would like to do.

'Do not seek to follow in the footsteps of the men of old. Seek what they sought.'

A research design is not an end in itself, but only a path that you follow to find something out about the world. Rather than copying someone else's research design, think about what it is you want to find out and design your research accordingly. While you can certainly be inspired by what other people have done, generating original work also means having your own research question, and thus your own approach to answering that question. Regardless of how exciting and innovative any given method might be, for you it is only as good as its suitability for answering the question you want to ask.

Finding your path: Points for reflection

Think about your general topic:
- Brainstorm at least three or four different research questions (try to vary between descriptive, analytical, predictive, and theoretical questions).
- What kinds of methods and data would you need to answer them?
- Which questions are most interesting to you?
- Which questions are the most feasible to answer?

Think about how you will answer the current version of your research question:
- What overall approach (positivist, interpretive, critical) will you be using?
- What is your general methodology (e.g., correlation study, ethnography, case study)?
- What specific methods will you use (e.g., semi-structured interviews, document analysis)?
- What particular materials do you need (e.g., questionnaires, databases)?
- How are each of these fit for the purpose of answering your question?

Imagine yourself carrying out your research from beginning to end:
- What will present the greatest challenges?
- What steps can you take to make sure that your data will tell you what you want to find out?

REFERENCES AND FURTHER READING

Booth, Wayne C., Colomb, Gregory G., and Williams, Joseph M. (2008) *The Craft of Research*, 3rd edn. Chicago, IL: University of Chicago Press. This book describes step-by-step how you can move from topic to question, to problems, to sources.

Bui, Yvonne N. (2009) *How to Write a Master's Thesis*. London: Sage. Although very specifically aimed at empirical (and largely quantitative) research, this book provides a helpful guide for thinking through your research questions and research design.

Cresswell, John W. (2003) *Research Design: Qualitative, Quantitative, and Mixed Methods Approaches*, 2nd edn. Thousand Oaks, CA: Sage. Cresswell discusses how qualitative, quantitative, and mixed methods approaches differ, as well as giving an overview of what kind of quality assurance is relevant for each approach.

Hennink, Monique, Hulter, Inge, and Bailey, Ajay (2011) *Qualitative Research Methods*. London: Sage. Provides a good overview of qualitative research, particularly ethnographic approaches.

Lunenburg, Fred C. and Irby, Beverly J. (2008) *Writing a Successful Thesis or Dissertation: Tips and Strategies for Students in the Social and Behavioral Sciences*. Thousand Oaks, CA: Corwin Press. With an entire chapter dedicated to picking your topic, the book provides excellent guidance on research design, particularly for quantitative research.

Nygaard, Lynn P. (2015) *Writing for Scholars: A Practical Guide to Making Sense and Being Heard*. See Chapter 5 on things to think about in developing your research question.

Paltridge, B. and Starfield, S. (2007) *Thesis and Dissertation Writing in a Second Language: A Handbook for Supervisors*. London: Routledge. The book gives a very good overview of the basics of methodology, particularly on the relationship between methodology, methods, and materials.

Petre, Marian and Rugg, Gordon (2010) *The Unwritten Rules of PhD Research*, 2nd edn. Maidenhead: Open University Press. Packed with good advice (including a discussion on critical thinking), this book is equally relevant for Master's research.

Robson, Colin (2011) *Real World Research*, 3rd edn. West Sussex: John Wiley and Sons. Robson's book explains the differences between fixed and flexible designs and gives some great tips for thinking through both your methodology and research questions.

Willis, Jerry W. (2007) *Foundations of Qualitative Research: Interpretive and Critical Approaches*. London: Sage. Willis provides in-depth background about paradigm development in the social sciences.

3

ETHICS

Making good choices

....

a Ethics related to the research

b Ethics related to the informants

c Ethics related to the profession

d Ethics related to the writing

e Relating to guidelines and procedures

f Real (academic) life is messy and ambiguous

....

Knowing the right thing to do is not always as easy as it sounds. Intentionally causing injury to another person is wrong, of course, but what if you accidentally break someone's rib while giving them CPR? Most would say that the life-saving intent outweighs the injury. But what if the person had merely fainted and didn't need heart compressions? The picture becomes even more complicated if the victim dies or is permanently injured as a result of your actions. When are good intentions not enough to outweigh the damage caused by an action?

When it comes to research, ethics are usually presented as a list: distinct activities that you can check off one by one. Obtain informed consent? Done! Protect my participants? Absolutely! Fully inform the reader about the research process? No question! It's hard to imagine any academic saying to herself: 'Why, yes, I think I will cut corners, mistreat my informants, and outright make things up. That's my plan'. And yet many well-meaning academics end up crossing the line into unethical behaviour because it's not always easy to see where the line is (for example, storing files without encryption might be considered unethical), or they simply find themselves in a situation that the guidelines do not cover.

This is really the main lesson to be learned about ethics: making good ethical choices is less about checking boxes and more about learning how to think through the possible repercussions of your actions, weigh concerns against each other, and make good decisions when something unanticipated happens or the guidelines fail you. This chapter discusses the main ethical considerations that social scientists need to take into account, and some of the dilemmas that typically arise.

ⓐ ETHICS RELATED TO THE RESEARCH

When it comes to research, fabrication and falsification are the two most serious forms of ethical misconduct. 'Fabrication' means you invent data that never existed – for example, quoting informants that don't exist and creating data out of thin air. 'Falsification' means intentionally misrepresenting what people say or misreporting results of your data to suit your hypothesis. You don't need a book on ethics to tell you that these things are wrong. They go against everything social science (indeed, all science) is supposed to be, and we feel collectively betrayed every time they happen. The scandalous 2011 discovery that a noted Dutch psychologist had both falsified data and invented entire experiments is a case in point. Ironically, one reason that he was able to continue for a decade without discovery is that he was the only one who had access to the raw (and presumably not yet anonymized) data; so the principle of protecting the confidentiality of participants might have made it easier for scientific misconduct to go unchecked.

Because you are not setting out to hurt or deceive anyone, you probably feel pretty confident that what you are doing is fine. But as a Master's student, you probably don't have enough experience to anticipate all the potentially troublesome aspects of research. There are any number of ways your research can be ethically questionable without involving outright fabrication or falsification – and most of them can be traced to poor research design. Indeed, it is often difficult to tell whether a researcher has been unethical, or simply sloppy and short-sighted (or perhaps just naïve). If you are unclear about your procedure, it is very easy to not follow it. And if you do not quite understand the limitations of your method, you may overgeneralize from too small a sample, or mishandle incomplete data.

 SAMIR

At first I didn't think the ethical statement was very relevant for me because I wasn't doing research on people. But after talking to my supervisor, I realized there were a lot of things I hadn't thought about – especially the ethical impact of the research findings and my relationship with the company. I had to think about how to design the research in such a way that I wasn't just telling the company what they wanted to hear, and about the general ethics of multinationals doing business in developing countries.

To avoid such problems it is important to remember what social science research is all about: investigating people and social systems, and reporting honestly what you actually see – not what you want to see. This sounds quite obvious, but in the crush to finish your thesis, with looming deadlines and high pressure, it is all too easy to forget. Imagine that your supervisor advises you to refer to a particular source; you do not have time to read it but you refer to it anyway. This moves you subtly into a situation where you are reporting on something that you wish you had read, but haven't (yet). Being ethical about your research, then, means being honest with others – and with yourself – about the data you have in front of you and how you went about getting it.

🅑 ETHICS RELATED TO THE INFORMANTS

A second set of ethical concerns relates to how you treat the people you are researching. Because social science is generally about doing research on people – as individuals or as groups, or both – many of our ethical dilemmas will be related to how we interact with the people we study and write about. Many of the ethical principles in place today have resulted from the fallout of studies such as the Stanford Prison Experiment (a role-play experiment conducted in 1971 that randomly assigned each participant to the role of prisoner or guard to see how they would behave), which did not let the participants leave the experiment before it was finished, and many complained of psychological trauma as a result. As a community, social scientists have become more sensitive to the ethical rights of informants that we face not only in designing the research, but also in carrying it out and writing about it (see Figure 3.1). The following text details some of the things we need to think about.

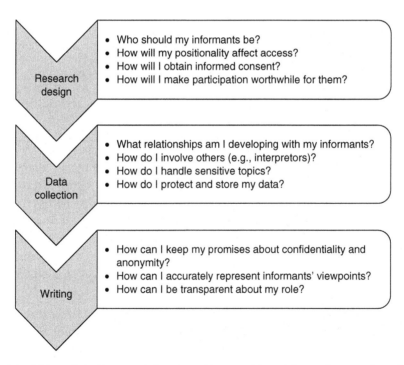

Figure 3.1 Ethics related to your informants: Your work is not done when you have finished filling out the ethical clearance forms. You need to think about your ethical relationship with your informants through all stages of research (based on lecture by Jørgen Carling, PRIO Research School, 3 May 2016)

Respect for individuals and groups: Social science is driven by both curiosity and the need to address social ills. For that reason, we often research people we think of as different from us – different ethnicities, nationalities, sexualities, age groups, social classes, and so on. Because researchers and college students have historically been members of privileged groups, this often means that the more privileged are researching the less privileged. Although the 'scientific racism' of the late 1800s that was used to justify imperialism is now clearly seen as wrong by modern standards, it is still easy to find examples of social science research that makes sweeping statements about less privileged groups. Ethical research means remembering that the people you are researching are individuals – with a right to privacy and dignity – as well as members of a group. Being respectful does not mean pretending differences do not exist if your findings suggest they do, but it does mean being mindful about where those differences might come from, what they might mean, and what your conclusions about them might imply. For example, if you find gender differences in students' maths scores, you might think through the extent to which these differences might be an artefact of the testing procedure or a result of girls and boys being treated differently, rather than one gender having a biological aptitude for succeeding in maths.

 AMINA

I was gathering sensitive data about women and their pregnancies, so I definitely needed ethical clearance. When I coded the data and added it to the larger dataset, I was careful to anonymize the individuals as much as I could, but it still might have been possible to identify some women based on their village and date of pregnancy. So I had to be very careful about the way I stored and described the data.

Respect for individuals also applies to public figures. The lives of public figures (political leaders, celebrities, and so on) are often subject to scrutiny from the press and general public, which might give the impression that anyone in public life has no right to privacy. A general rule of thumb is that anything related to their public role – decisions they make and possible reasons for those decisions, for example – is fair game, but regarding anything not related to that role (such as medical records) you need to exercise extreme caution. Even if the figure you are researching is no longer living, the person's reputation and relatives can both suffer undue harm from irresponsible speculation.

Personal safety: Sometimes in our zeal to find out more, we fail to see that participating in our research might put the participants (or ourselves – see textbox 'Personal safety applies to you, too') in danger. Sometimes the danger is acute – for example, by simply interviewing someone in an authoritarian country about their political views, you might be putting them at risk of imprisonment or worse. Or if you want to talk to individuals about crimes they may have committed, you might be putting them at risk of arrest by authorities or reprisals from former partners. Sometimes the danger is less physical than psychological: interviewing victims of sexualized violence, for example, might retraumatize them. Sometimes the danger is 'merely' to someone's reputation. To avoid possibly putting your participants in harm's way, ask yourself how the act of participating in your research might affect them. This means thinking about more than just your research when you are planning your research design. Do you need to avoid talking to some people altogether? Can you ally yourself with a psychologist or some support network to handle possible retraumatization? Are there other ways you can protect your informants? These are questions that your supervisor, or a senior researcher in your area of research, can advise you on.

Personal safety applies to you, too

It's not just your participants you have an obligation to protect. Think about your own personal safety and the safety of those working with you. Will you be establishing contact with people who might perceive you as a threat? Do you have research assistants who will be carrying out a survey in a dangerous area? What actions would be reasonable to take to ensure your safety and the safety of others?

Informed consent: Ethical guidelines are full of procedures for how to establish informed consent. What this essentially means is making sure that your informants know what they are getting themselves into. It is common procedure to give informants an information sheet describing the research and the purpose of their participation, and then to ask informants to sign a consent form that specifies the ways in which they agree to participate: Do they agree to be interviewed? To be videotaped or voice recorded? To have excerpts of the interview quoted in your research? To have excerpts of the interview published? It is also common procedure to assure informants that they can withdraw their consent at any time, without stating a reason.

Going through the motions mindlessly is far too easy: write a quick description, download a boilerplate consent form, and effusively promise that withdrawal is non-problematic. But what if your research is based on videotaping the interaction between members of a group? If one person wants to withdraw, how will you delete their data? Is it even feasible? And think about how capable your informants are of giving informed consent. Young children, for example, are not likely to fully understand what they are agreeing to, but it is difficult to know at what age you can safely assume they understand the implications of what you are asking. Interviewing teenagers, for example, is particularly tricky. While you might want to play it safe by asking for parental consent, the mere act of describing the research objectives to the parents might put your participants in an awkward position. What if you wanted to interview teenagers who have had abortions, but some of them had not told their parents about their pregnancies?

 KEIKO

One of the reasons I decided to focus on teachers instead of students was because of the ethics and getting informed consent. I had to think through the videotaping part carefully because I wanted to avoid filming the children.

Compensation: In some fields it is standard practice to compensate informants for their time by offering them a small honorarium – often in the form of a meal, a lottery ticket, or a small amount of cash. But in other fields this is considered highly unethical. The challenge here is to strike a balance between having respect for someone's time, particularly if the interview is lengthy and they have come far out of their way to meet with you, and not influencing the research by offering a reward for participation. If the honorarium is too small, then you have arguably taken advantage of your informants' time; if it is too large, then you have to wonder whether participants were motivated by the promise of reward and whether this might have skewed your findings. To complicate matters further, what might be a purely nominal amount to you might mean disproportionately more to someone else. Having extensive and localized knowledge of the group you intend to interview, particularly if you have participants who live outside your community or country, can help you find the right balance.

Professional boundaries: Finally, working with individual participants also means remaining cognizant of your role in relation to them: how you are perceived, whether you are in a position of power over them, and how their perception of your role might change the way they interact with you. Say you are interviewing refugees waiting for approval of their status, for example: if they think that you might have influence over the outcome of their case, this might affect what they tell you – or even influence their decision to speak with you at all. Moreover, you might be tempted to promise more than you can deliver. It is not easy to listen to one heart-wrenching story after another without wanting to take action – such as helping feed a hungry child, or approaching authorities on their behalf. Boundaries can become further blurred if you develop personal feelings for a participant, even simple friendship. Even if you do not act on these feelings, it might affect the way you interpret their story. But it is difficult to know where the line is between being a researcher and being an activist, between being human and being unprofessional – and whether you have crossed it. This might also depend on the kind of research you are doing: long-term participant observation in ethnographic fieldwork, or insider research where you conduct a study in a community to which you already belong, will necessarily entail some blurred boundaries between your professional identity as a researcher and your identity as a human being, and thus require a high degree of reflexivity (see Chapters 7 and 10).

ROBERT

The issue of drug addiction is obviously sensitive, especially for teenagers with an immigrant background. I had to make sure I could promise my informants full anonymity, which meant not only using a pseudonym but also leaving out any other information that could identify them. I was careful to not mention their ages or the specific country they came from, although when it mattered I mentioned the general region, like 'Middle East' or 'Western Europe' and the religious community they belonged to.

c ETHICS RELATED TO THE PROFESSION

Professional behaviour is not limited to how you treat your informants. It also encompasses how you treat your colleagues, fellow students, and the institution of academia. Harassment of others (sexual or otherwise), misrepresentation of your credentials, cheating or helping others to cheat, sabotaging the work of others, and overlooking the unethical behaviour of others are all threats to academia as a profession. Academia is built on a foundation of trust, and even seemingly innocuous deception – such as telling your supervisor you won't be able to hand in your draft chapter as promised because you are sick, when you are as healthy as can be – poses a fundamental threat to this trust. Part of the problem is that mild deception can grow quickly out of control. What starts as an attempt to bolster your chances of getting a job by manipulating a grade point average to show only the courses with the best scores may quickly lead to a fabricated CV. Sometimes you might not even be aware that you are headed down this path: you start by hiring a tutor to help you develop your essay-writing skills, but before you know it, the tutor is writing the essay for you; this well-written essay then helps you get into graduate school, but since you have not developed these skills yourself, you feel forced to steal the work of others – which brings us to the next point.

d ETHICS RELATED TO THE WRITING

Plagiarism comes up a lot in discussions of ethics. Most of us know that you cannot simply copy verbatim something that someone else has written and then take credit for it. Each time we hear about established professors stealing the work of a promising young PhD student and then publishing it under their own name, we are understandably horrified and outraged. But not all plagiarism is so clear-cut, or intentional.

Sometimes it is difficult to tell plagiarism from poor referencing or self-plagiarism. Poor referencing occurs when, for example, you provide a citation after summing up someone else's argument, but in the sentences that follow you keep paraphrasing that same source, thus giving the impression that the argument is your own. Surprisingly, where this seems to happen the most is in background sections – presumably because students think the background section is not that important, and the actual words do not matter very much. It might be easy to think that there are only so many ways to say 'Nevada is a state in the Western, Mountain West, and Southwestern regions of the United States. Nevada is the 7th most extensive, the 35th most populous, and the 9th least densely populated of the 50 United States', and since it is only background material it shouldn't really matter. But if you copy and paste sentences, whether they are background or not, then you need to treat those sentences like any other quoted material. The better option is to rewrite it completely in your own voice, taking care to think through which elements are important and which are not: 'Located in the western United States, Nevada is one of the largest and relatively least populated states'. Because this sentence now contains generally accepted truths written in your own words, no citation is necessary. But as soon as you start including facts that could be in dispute, or that change from time to time, then citations are again necessary to establish where you got those facts from: 'In 2014, the estimated population of Nevada was 2.8 million (US Census Bureau)'.

 EMMA

My biggest ethical challenge was pinpointing where my ideas came from – which wasn't always easy because sometimes I couldn't tell whether I was remembering something I read or thinking of an idea myself. I also felt that it was important to say straight out that I am a feminist who believes that gender is a social practice and not necessarily related to biology, because I am sure that this affected how I interpreted the things I read.

Unintentional plagiarism that stems from sloppy referencing is a particular hazard for those writing in a second language. One of the ways people learn languages is by mimicry, and it is quite common for a student to copy out sentences that are especially well written. But even if you are writing in a second language, you need to distinguish the information and ideas transmitted through the words you are reading from the words themselves. Writing academically requires you to transform that information and those ideas into your own words. You might reasonably wonder how much of the sentence you have to change in order for it to be considered paraphrased: 10 per cent, 15 per cent, 20 per cent? But avoiding plagiarism is not simply a matter of changing a certain number of words. Even if you use entirely different words but build up your argument in exactly the way someone else did, using their ideas without attribution, you are engaging in intellectual dishonesty. Even using an example the way someone else has used it might be problematic if the other person's use of that example was original.

A second form of unintentional plagiarism is self-plagiarism. It is quite natural to think, 'Well, they are my words. Why can't I use them again?' But if you have published them in another context you need to treat those words just as you would anyone else's published words. All good scholars build on their previous work, and you will too; you just need to show the reader how you've done it. When you're writing a Master's thesis, however, it isn't always clear whether your earlier work counts as 'published' or not. The early draft of a chapter of your thesis that you circulated among fellow students and your supervisor clearly has not been published; it is rather an early version of the current work. An essay that you submitted for a particular course, on the other hand, might well need to be cited as previous work. Here, you might need the guidance of your supervisor because there are different expectations about this in different universities. Some programmes are organized so that the courses require shorter papers that are meant to be built on and incorporated into your thesis. Others are not. Your supervisor should be able to tell you how to deal with this particular dilemma.

Potential plagiarism becomes even harder to identify when you are not sure whether it is your idea or not. Was this something that you read a long time ago but forgot? Or is this genuinely a new idea that you came up with all by yourself? Not many of us are born with photographic memories, and it is entirely possible to read something and not think much of it at the time, only to have it surface in your mind some months later – feeling very much like your own idea. If you have been careful about keeping track of what you have read and your thoughts about it (see Chapter 4), then you have a better chance of tracing those ideas back to their origin.

Borrowing ideas and inspiration from other authors is a cornerstone of academia. There is no shame in reproducing a sentence or two from Smith if he said something in a way that quite simply cannot be improved upon, or borrowing the example he used if you think it is brilliant, but you have to let the reader know that that's what you did. If you think that not giving credit where it is due cannot matter all that much, imagine what it would feel like if the words and ideas you sweated and cried over suddenly appeared in someone else's work (see textbox 'Protecting your own research'). The way to avoid unintentional ethical transgressions is to take referencing very seriously. This isn't always easy when rules for referencing differ so much from setting to setting (see Chapter 13), but it helps to remember that the purpose of referencing is transparency – showing your readers where your ideas and words come from. When the rules are unclear about how you should reference a certain type of document – personal diary, YouTube video, unpublished manuscript – think about your ethical obligation to the reader. If you got an idea by listening to a lecture or participating in a conversation with someone, and you are unable to find anything in which the speaker describes that idea in writing, then the most ethical thing you can do is to simply refer to the lecture or the conversation. For example, you can make a footnote and write 'Personal communication between Professor N.O. Ittall and author, 2 April 2015' or 'Lecture at the University of Nevada, Sociology of Cults and Mind Reform, 2 April 2015'.

Protecting your own research

One of the worst things that can happen to you as a young researcher is to have your research 'stolen' – that is, your ideas are used by others without attribution. Whether you present an idea at a conference that later shows up in someone else's paper without reference to your presentation, or several paragraphs from your unpublished thesis show up in a book written by one of your examiners without reference to you, the best way to demonstrate the origins of an idea is to establish a paper trail. Keep dated copies of earlier versions to establish when you wrote something, record the dates of public presentations and submissions to journals, and report transgressions to the appropriate venue in your department as soon as you can, with multiple copies to all interested parties. While some claim that the best way to protect your research is to show it to as few people as possible, this also leaves you vulnerable. If no one else has heard you talk about your work, it is harder to prove that you had an idea first.

(e) RELATING TO GUIDELINES AND PROCEDURES

Because the ethical landscape can be so confusing, most fields of research have developed ethical guidelines to help you. Some are relatively specialized, such as the guidelines for the British Education Research Association (BERA), while others are broader, such as the Guidelines for Research Ethics in the Social Sciences, Law, and the Humanities, produced by the Norwegian National Committee for Research Ethics (NESH). Why does it matter which guidelines you use? Because researchers in different fields face different dilemmas. If you are a social anthropologist, you are unlikely to face the same challenges as an experimental psychologist or a stem-cell researcher. Guidelines designed for the kind of research you will be doing, in the kind of field you will be doing it in, are far more likely to be useful to you than guidelines designed for a completely different setting.

Picking an appropriate set of guidelines thus requires you to think about your particular setting: your department, your university, and your discipline. Each of these levels may have its own set of procedures and ethical guidelines. As long as you are a student, you need to make sure that the procedures and guidelines of your specific department are the ones you follow. You can certainly use other guidelines for, well, guidance – but follow your local guidelines and procedures as closely as possible.

Some departments require you to go through a kind of ethical clearance before you start your research. Others do not. Some require you to discuss in writing the ethical dilemmas you are likely to face in your project; others just want you to check boxes. And some may simply expect you to work closely with your supervisor on these matters but not require you to discuss them explicitly. It is your responsibility (with help from your supervisor) to figure out what procedures you are expected to follow. If your research involves participants from other countries or a funder from a different country, you will need to know the procedures both for the country that is funding your research and the country where you are doing your research – as well as the procedures for the country or countries where your participants live. Some countries may require that you go through separate ethical approval procedures; others may accept the other country's approval in lieu of going through a separate process. Be aware that because the procedures are different, you might get mixed messages about the ethics of what you are doing.

🅕 REAL (ACADEMIC) LIFE IS MESSY AND AMBIGUOUS

Even if the procedures are clear and you have an obvious set of guidelines to follow, you might not get all the answers you need. As the world changes, new ethical dilemmas emerge. In the early 2000s, guidelines for the social sciences probably didn't discuss the ethics of lurking on web-based social networks for research purposes, but this emerging source of data presents unusual dilemmas: on one hand, social networking sites are effectively public, but, on the other hand, participants believe their conversations to be private, and if they are unaware of the presence of a researcher they cannot give informed consent. For this reason, guidelines and procedures can only take you so far. Even if you fill out all the forms and gather all the appropriate signatures, you are still required to use your head and think through what you are doing – particularly when the situation is ambiguous.

A classic case of ethical ambiguity that is worth reading up on is the so-called Tearoom Trade project from the 1970s. The doctoral researcher was trying to understand the phenomenon of anonymous sex between men in public restrooms. He positioned himself as a lookout, and took note of who participated. He then located the individuals by tracking down their licence plate numbers, before contacting them at home. Not disclosing his role as a researcher and violating privacy by contacting people at home seems a clear ethical breach. On the other hand, he played the role of an advocate, breaking down stereotypes and arguing that their activities posed no threat to anyone who did not wish to participate, and he protected the confidentiality of his sources. His defence for his deception was that he found that only a select (highly educated) group would talk to him when he informed them about the research. He believed that he improved the validity of his results by using deception and that no harm was done because he managed to protect confidentiality. To this day, the ethics of this case are debated (for a brief discussion, see the Wikipedia entry 'Tearoom Trade').

It is not uncommon to discover that you are doing something that is not described in the guidelines at all, or that by following one ethical principle you might be violating another. For example, the more transparent you are regarding your sources and data, the more difficult it becomes to protect the confidentiality of your participants. The more dedicated you are to ensuring informed consent and getting your participants to sign consent forms, the more you might put them in a vulnerable position if they are talking about sensitive subjects, and revelation of their participation in your research could put them in harm's way.

ROBERT

Getting informed consent was difficult in some cases because some were OK with talking to me but didn't want to sign anything that their parents might see. We solved that by getting on tape a discussion where I explained the research and they agreed to participate.

And as you move between different types of research, you might discover that what is ethically acceptable for one type of research is problematic for another. Among many quantitative researchers, it is common to make datasets available for public scrutiny and use by other researchers. This is a good way to ensure that you are not fabricating data (because others can double-check your work), and to ensure that the datasets can benefit as much research as possible. But making qualitative data publicly available is a different story altogether. Although validity might be improved if readers could have access to the original interview transcripts, this would be a tremendous breach of confidentiality, even if pseudonyms are used. In the average interview, people give away a lot of personal information that could be used to identify them – innocently describing a local shop, mentioning a neighbour by name, referring to a place of employment, and so on. Simply removing names is not enough to make it impossible to identify informants.

 AMINA

Because it was difficult to make the data completely anonymous, my supervisor and I decided not to put the dataset online, even though we know how important it is to make raw data available to other researchers.

Moreover, the principles of informed consent state that consent has to be given for each particular use of the data, so an interview given in one context cannot necessarily be used in another research context. Ironically, the principle of not re-using data to protect participants can backfire if a particular group becomes 'over-researched' – that is, they are contacted by multiple researchers, or the same group researches them multiple times. If the subject of research is sensitive, or forces them to relive traumas, then each time they are approached, they risk exposure or retraumatization.

Even pure quantitative data, or seemingly non-sensitive qualitative data, is not always safe to make freely available to other researchers – especially if it is in conjunction with other datasets. While an individual participant might not be identifiable with the one dataset alone, the combination of information in multiple datasets might reveal individuals. Juxtaposing data can reveal far more than each source of data alone.

Navigating this jungle of potentially mixed messages, ambiguous settings, and genuine dilemmas makes it difficult to approach ethics as a list of items to be checked off. Keep in mind the core principles: honesty about your research; regard for your informants; respect for your profession; and transparency to your reader. But put them into the context of your particular situation. There might be times when you have to do something that is 'unethical' in one way so you can be more ethical in another. Maybe you need to be less transparent in order to protect your participants. Maybe you need to be slightly deceptive about the purpose of your research in order to ensure valid results or protect your informants. Although it is tempting to say that regard for your participants should outweigh all other concerns, even this has its limits: even if your findings might damage the reputation of some of your participants, the potential harm to the individuals may not outweigh the need to honestly report what you find. You may decide that you can minimize the possibility of harm by taking a certain action: if your informants are too easy to identify no matter what, you might not be able to promise confidentiality, but maybe you can have them review and approve what you write about them. If you need to use some deception to ensure that your informants speak openly, perhaps you can debrief them afterwards and remind them again of their right to withdraw from the research. Even if you do not have to send in a form for approval, thinking through these dilemmas and considering how you can address them will make you a stronger researcher in the long run.

'He who asks a question is a fool for a minute; he who does not remains a fool forever.'

Because it may not be always evident what the most ethical course of action might be, being an ethical researcher means asking yourself some difficult questions: Where do these ideas come from? How can I get the data I need without impinging on the privacy or safety of my participants? How do I get informed consent from people who might be vulnerable? How much of the raw data can I show my reader without breaching the trust of my participants? What is the best action I can take here if I want to both carry out high-quality research and yet protect the people involved? Asking the questions is never wrong; assuming you know the answer might be.

Finding your path: Points for reflection

Think through all the people that will be touched by the research you are doing. What steps can you take to treat each of these groups as ethically as possible?
- The academic community in general (readers who want to trust your work)
- The authors whose ideas you are using (and who need to be credited)
- Your colleagues (your fellow students, your supervisor, and others)
- Those participating in your research (or whose personal data you will be using)

(Continued)

47

(Continued)

Are there any dilemmas that you are likely to face? For example, in providing information about your study, will you unduly affect the outcome?

- What are some different ways of resolving those dilemmas? (e.g., debriefing after the study rather than giving information beforehand vs trying to inform beforehand but as vaguely as possible)
- What are the advantages and disadvantages to each of these strategies?

REFERENCES AND FURTHER READING

Bloch, Joel (2012) *Plagiarism, Intellectual Property and the Teaching of L2 Writing*. Bristol: Multilingual Matters. Bloch examines how plagiarism is connected to different cultures of learning and writing.

British Education Research Association (BERA) (2011) *Ethical Guidelines for Educational Research*. www.bera.ac.uk/researchers-resources/resources-for-researchers (last accessed 19.05.16). Targeted at educational research, the BERA guidelines provide a good example of what discipline-specific guidelines look like.

Coleman, Allison and Williams, John (2006) 'Legal and moral issues' in Alan Bond (ed.), *Your Masters Thesis: How to Plan, Draft, Write and Revise*. Abergele: Studymates. This chapter focuses primarily on issues of copyright, particularly from a legal perspective, but also contains a good discussion of confidentiality.

Kirton, Bill (2011) *Brilliant Dissertation: What You Need to Know and How to Do It*. Harlow: Prentice Hall. Part 6 of this book has a special focus on ethics, with an emphasis on how to avoid plagiarism and reference correctly.

Miller, Tina, Birch, Maxine, Mauthner, Melanie, and Jessop, Julie (eds) (2002) *Ethics in Qualitative Research*. Thousand Oak, CA: Sage. This book is a collected volume that covers a range of ethical dilemmas associated with qualitative research, including research relationships and informed consent.

National Committees for Research Ethics in Norway (2006) *Guidelines for Research Ethics in the Social Sciences, Law and the Humanities*. Oslo: National Committees for Research Ethics in Norway. www.etikkom.no/en/ethical-guidelines-for-research/guidelines-for-research-ethics-in-the-social-sciences--humanities-law-and-theology. The NESH guidelines represent an example of a set of guidelines meant to apply to the social sciences in a wider sense.

Roberts, Carol M. (2010) *The Dissertation Journey: A Practical and Comprehensive Guide to Planning, Writing, and Defending Your Dissertation*, 2nd edn. Thousand Oaks, CA: Corwin Press. Chapter 3 covers ethical issues specifically, including a good discussion about how to avoid bias in your writing.

YOU ARE WHAT YOU READ

Building a foundation of knowledge

a Getting started

b How much reading is enough?

c Remembering and making sense of what you have read

d Transitioning from reader to writer

'We have two ears and one mouth for a reason!' is something your mother might have shouted at you just as a way to keep you from talking so much, but the point is well taken when it comes to academic discourse: we do ourselves no favours if we have no idea what we are talking about. If academic writing is a conversation, then the reading you do is part of the listening. Every time you read something, you get a better idea of what is going on in the conversation – what people are saying, how they are thinking, and what the points of contention are. As you learn more about what research has been done already, you gain a better idea of where your own research fits in. And as you read more about theory and methodology, the better you can see how your ideas and strategies compare to what others are thinking and doing. Reading provides you not only with explicit knowledge about theory and evidence, but also with examples of how these ideas are communicated. Reading introduces you to the norms and conventions of your field – what the core ideas are, what styles of argumentation are normally used, what kind of language is acceptable, and what terminology is common.

In this way, reading shapes your identity as a scholar: you are what you read. The language and style of argumentation you pick up from your reading will be reflected in your own voice as you write and signal to your reader where your theoretical and disciplinary homes are as a scholar (see Chapter 8). If you focus your reading within your field and consciously stick to your specific topic, you will more or less naturally reproduce the norms and language of your field when you write. If you read widely outside your field, you will pick up other language and terminology, other ideas, and other styles of argumentation. If you, consciously or unconsciously, import these other styles of thinking and writing into your work, it might be more difficult for others to place you as a scholar. Are you a political scientist or a psychologist? A geographer or an international relations scholar?

There is a very important trade-off to be considered here. Because a thesis is supposed to be grounded in a particular discipline, your examiners may penalize you for straying too far from home. But playing it safe by strategically reading only within your field may cut you off from the possibility of serendipity. Serendipity is when you see a connection between seemingly unrelated things, when you read an article on helicopter maintenance and suddenly understand why social welfare systems struggle to effectively give help to those who need it the most. It is when you are in the middle of writing your thesis on nursing practices and you remember something from a course you took on medieval literature that helps you explain the lack of communication you observe between nurses and doctors. Exposing yourself to ideas outside your discipline can be confusing, but it can also help your thinking become more original.

And ironically, one of the best ways to develop your own voice is to pay careful attention to the voices of authors you admire – not necessarily for what they say, but for the way they say it. You can almost hear their words being spoken out loud, ripe and fragrant, as you read. Just as some people bring out the best in you (just being around them makes you feel more intelligent and witty), some writers make you itch to start writing or simply inspire you to be a better writer. While you are reading for content, taking note at the same time of what kind of writing does (or does not) appeal to you will help you develop into the kind of writer you want to be.

This chapter discusses the process of reading to build a foundation of knowledge and find your voice as a writer: how to get started, what kinds of literature to look for and how to find it, how much reading is enough, how to remember what you've read, and how to start making the transition from thinking of yourself as a reader to thinking of yourself as a writer.

ⓐ GETTING STARTED

Some well-meaning experts will tell you to focus only on the literature that is directly relevant to your thesis. Sounds logical. It is logical. But it overlooks the problem that you don't necessarily know what is directly relevant to your thesis until you've read it (and sometimes not even then). When you are trying to figure out what might be relevant, it helps to consider that you have two main goals to accomplish: (i) building a foundation of core readings in your field (e.g., migration studies), discipline (e.g., anthropology), or method (e.g., ethnography); and (ii) building awareness of research on your specific topic (e.g., diaspora and transnational networks in Western Europe).

When it comes to building a foundation of core readings in your field, discipline, or method, the lectures and required reading that you do for your coursework (or that you have read for earlier coursework) should give you a good overview: the theoretical concepts, methodological approaches, and thematic foci. This means that if you have had courses within the discipline of your thesis, particularly if they are closely related to the topic, method, or theory of your thesis, you have a head start. For example, if you are in the field of political science or international relations, you should have a basic understanding of the notions of statehood, governance, democracy, realism, neoliberalism, regime formation, and so on. And if you are writing your thesis on state-building in the nations of the former Soviet Union, you have some concepts to start with. But this head start is just that: a start. You still have more work to do. For example, if you are planning to do phenomenological research, the one-hour lecture you might have had in your course on qualitative methods will seldom (if ever) be sufficient, but it will give you a clue about where to begin searching for literature. Based on the readings you had in your course, you can start looking for other, more specialized, texts on the subject – not only those that describe the method, but those that discuss the philosophy of the method, perhaps in comparison with other methods. After all, you will need to defend your choice of methodology, and if you have not considered the implications of your choice, it will be difficult for you to justify the path you have taken. You might also find it very helpful to find concrete examples of research that was carried out using a phenomenological approach, even if the research is on a different topic. This will give you an idea of how the method works in practice.

This is, of course, more complicated if you are changing disciplines. Those who move directly from a Bachelor's to a Master's programme in the same field can simply build on existing knowledge. But when you come from a different field, not only will you have blank spots to fill in your knowledge foundation, but you may also find that some of your new field's concepts simply do not map comfortably onto the knowledge you already have – and they may even directly challenge it. For example, say you have a BS in biology but are now pursuing a Master's degree in science and technology studies where you look critically at how available instrumentation affects the way scientists carry out their research, which may seem to not only go against what you have learned from before, but also to assume a strong background in philosophy that you may not have. If you are lucky, your coursework will provide you with a point of departure for filling in the blank spots in your knowledge. Even if you are not required to do coursework, you may want to at least look at the reading lists of courses in your discipline that are offered – even in other universities – to get a good idea of what the core readings of your new discipline are.

This brings us to the second kind of literature you need to track down: literature related to your specific topic. Two things can make this difficult: you are not exactly sure what your topic is because you are at a very early stage in the process, or you have settled on a topic but you are not sure what to call it. Both of these challenges will require you to be creative about which search terms you use. If you are not sure about what your specific topic will be (e.g., something about how the diaspora is involved in transnational networks, distribution of remittances, influence of diaspora on decision-making in the country of origin, etc.), you will have to read widely and note what you react to: what do you find particularly interesting, confusing, frustrating? Maybe you thought you knew what you were interested in but then realized that there was way more research on the topic than you suspected; now you are unsure how to find a new angle. Again, be aware of your reactions as you read: What surprises you? Do you see tensions in the literature suggesting different schools of thought? Although the literature answers the question you thought you had, does it raise another one? If you locate articles or books related to the topic that are outside your discipline or field, do they use theoretical ideas or methodological approaches that might be worth importing to your discipline?

Perhaps the most difficult challenge is if you are a mature student returning to academia after some years as a practitioner and the topic you want to research has sprung from things you have observed in your practice. The longer you have been outside academia, the longer you have built up your own well of tacit knowledge, and the more difficult it might be to map the vocabulary from disciplinary academic knowledge onto what you know first-hand. The things that you have observed and thought about in your practice might not be the same things that are talked about in the academic discourses. This might make it very difficult to figure out what to look for, or which search terms to use, when you are tracking down the academic literature. In my own research, I spent several months trying to find academic literature on why some academics write and publish more than others before I stumbled across the terms 'research productivity', 'research performance', and 'performativity'. None of these terms were in my working vocabulary as a teacher and coach of academic writers, and none of them mapped exactly onto the kind of thing I was trying to describe, but using those terms in my literature search gave me a good indication of how the academic discourse has unfolded so far.

 ROBERT

I had a hard time knowing where to start because I had been out of school for so long and because the things I wanted to talk about just were not in the readings we had for our coursework. Most of the stuff I had been reading is not really academic. So I had to start from scratch.

Regardless of how much (or how little) you know about your topic, it is always a good idea to assume that you are not the first person to have thought about whatever it is you are thinking about. Consider it your primary task to try to find the other people. Electronic searches can save you a tremendous amount of time, especially when you are not exactly sure what to search for or what terms to use. Although your university is likely to have specialized databases you can search, an initial search using Google Scholar could be helpful; it may not give you access to all the articles you need, but it will alert you to their existence. You can then use a more specialized database to track them down.

Electronic searches require that you type in one or more search terms. If you are building on an already established academic discourse, this will be relatively easy. But if your topic is based on an area of interest in the 'real world', finding the right search terms might take a while. If the terminology isn't obvious, brainstorm all the related terms you can think of. For example, if you don't find any obvious discourse on 'work-life balance among university faculty', then look for general articles about 'challenges for faculty in higher education' or 'university faculty with children', and so on. It might take several tries before you find something relevant. Once you find even one source that seems to be about what you are interested in, then move directly to scrutinizing the literature list of that source. This will give you other sources to track down and perhaps some key words that you can use for a new search. For example, in your search for literature on 'work-life balance', you might see articles with terms like 'professional identity' and 'ethics of care' in the titles; you can then try searching using those terms and see what you get.

Once you get a feel for the right search terms, your challenge will quickly change from having too little to choose from to having too much. So rather than broadening your search you will have to narrow it down. The first thing you can try is to focus on only the most recent years. Although older literature can be useful in establishing how the field has developed over time, or when the work in question is a classic that still shapes the field, you can get a better idea about the current state of knowledge by limiting your search to work published in the last few years. Second, instead of relying on one key word, you can string together a series of key words. For example, say you start off writing about the role of the Intergovernmental Panel on Climate Change (IPCC) in securing the future of small island states. You type 'IPCC' into Google Scholar and get about 380,000 hits, which are far too many to manage. If you type 'IPCC + climate negotiations' you cut the number of hits down to about 7000, which is still too many for any one person to read. If you narrow it down to publications after 2012, you are down to around 3000 – or about 1000 if you limit the search to those published after 2015. If you add another key word (in this case 'island states'), you are down to 163 hits – which is significantly more manageable than the initial 380,000 (see Figure 4.1). By experimenting with different time periods and key words, you can quickly build up a list of literature highly relevant to your topic. And when you start to read through this literature, it might point you in other fruitful directions.

If your search seems to have stagnated, you can also use electronic searches to view articles that are cited by or are related to some of the key articles you have already found. The 'cited by' function will produce a list of articles that have cited the article you were interested in. This can show you how other people have made use of it – sometimes in very different circumstances. 'Related articles' will bring up articles that have some of the same qualities as the one you found (see Figure 4.2). A similar tactic can also be used in libraries. Once you find a book that seems relevant, spend some time looking at the books in the immediate area – a couple of shelves up, down, right and left. You might find some unexpected treasures.

While you are poking around, expanding and contracting your searches, you will also want to consider the nature of your sources. Obviously, the most important sources for you will be well-respected academic works. But do not discount other sources as well. You might have

Figure 4.1 Narrowing down your electronic literature searches: Using multiple search terms on Google Scholar and limiting the search of publications to the most recent years can help you limit the hits you get to a more manageable number. In the figure above note that the first hit also has a pdf version of the article that you can download.

been told to avoid citing non-academic works, but this depends on what contexts you are trying to use them in. Take newspapers, for example, or social media. News sources and social media always operate on limited information and most are quite blatantly biased in one way

Figure 4.2 Expanding your electronic literature searches: If your search seems to have stagnated, then expand it by selecting the 'cited by' or 'related articles' links under the hits that seem particularly relevant and you will be directed to additional sources that might also be relevant.

or another. Citing the *New York Times* or Facebook rather than official police records as the definitive source for what happened in Charleston when nine people were shot to death inside a church would be inadvisable. But if your research happens to be on 'differences between how social media and mainstream media portray race-related violence', then both of these are valuable sources.

You might also want to keep in mind how your particular discipline views the difference between primary and secondary sources. Some disciplines, such as history, view primary sources as the original documents that constitute the data in their study such as memos, interviews, archived letters, medical records, personal diaries or journals, and any number of things that are not necessarily considered academic. But they comprise the body of material that will be analysed. Secondary sources in this respect are generally academic books or articles based on primary sources. In contrast, many other disciplines consider primary sources to be academic books and articles that make a particular argument, and secondary sources to be books or articles *about* the other books or articles. For example, in your discussion on gender identity, a primary source would be a book written by Judith Butler; a secondary source would be *Judith Butler for Dummies*. When you are considering what sources are important for you to read, think about what constitutes primary and secondary sources in your field, and what kind of sources are necessary to build the foundation you need.

🅑 HOW MUCH READING IS ENOUGH?

Once you find the right search terms, the right databases, and the right sources, you will probably find yourself with more articles, books, and other texts than you can possibly read in your lifetime. How much should you read then? There is no good answer for that. It's a bit like asking, 'How big is a house?' It is as big as it needs to be. You need to read enough to understand the shape of the conversation you want to take part in: what various people have said, how it fits in with similar discussions about related topics, how it has changed over time, how it relates to issues in the real world, what are the main points of contention, what is left that we really don't understand, and so on. You also need to read enough to make sure you understand the core concepts in your discipline, the nature of your methodology, and the key ideas you will be referring to. A rule of thumb in the context of a PhD might be about 150 articles (Petre and Rugg 2010: 16), but it will be much lower for a Master's thesis (perhaps about 30–50 articles). Eventually you will reach a point of saturation, where the new things you read add very little to what you already know. And at some point, you should begin to recognize the core literature for your topic, the 5–10 pieces that represent the main literature you want to respond to. Getting a good sense of the core pieces will make it easier for you to envision your conversation partners when you write (see Chapter 8). At this point you have probably read enough.

The total number of articles and books you need to read also depends on whether you are writing about something you already know a lot about, whether you are coming back to academia after a period of time in practice, whether you are changing fields, or whether you are trying to write interdisciplinarily. If you are writing a thesis on a topic you already know very well, you might not have to read as intensely, and you can afford to focus mainly on the newest publications. That being said, some core texts require several readings, and as you mature as a thinker you might understand them in different ways than you did only a few months ago.

 EMMA

I had already done a lot of reading on my topic because I did my Bachelor's degree in a similar subject, so a lot of the reading I did was re-reading. I was surprised at how different some of the books were when I read them a second time. I'm not sure whether this was because I'm older or because I was looking for something different, but the reading was way more interesting than it was the first time.

You might also have to consider the time factor. Most Master's programmes are relatively short, just one or two years of full-time study, which includes the time you have to write your thesis. Clearly, this will not give you enough time to read everything that you want to read, so you will have to make some choices and focus as quickly as you can. Talk to your supervisor about how much time you should spend reading, and figure out how to carve out room for that in your schedule. There will be a period where you are both reading and writing, so you might have to think about what makes sense to do at what time of day. For example, many people find it easier to read in the morning and write in the afternoon, while others prefer the opposite.

The truth is that you can never read enough, but at the same time you can absolutely read too much. It is very easy to get lost in the literature, especially if you read broadly. You can reach the point where things no longer make any sense, and you feel like you are drowning in ideas, concepts, facts, and just words. To avoid this, it helps to have a plan for processing and remembering what you've read.

ⓒ REMEMBERING AND MAKING SENSE OF WHAT YOU HAVE READ

Although, or probably because, reading is such an important part of being a researcher, we very seldom talk to each other about how we approach it. But reading is more than just moving your eyes across a page and registering the words written on it – it's also about making sense of what you have read and thinking about how it fits into your own research.

There is no one obvious way to organize, remember, and process what you have read. Finding the way that works for you may take some time. Some students simply write

Study	Research question(s)	Method	Key findings
Glueck & Jauch (1975)	Where do productive hard science researchers get their ideas?	In-depth interviews of 160 hard science researchers at US university, 1969–70.	Found that most ideas come from past work, then literature, then international colleagues, and finally local colleagues.
Wanner et al. (1981)	What are similarities and differences in research productivity between hard sciences, social sciences and humanities?	4-page questionnaire mailed to 108,722 faculty in 301 American universities and colleges. Analysis performed on 33% of total sample.	Differences in publication patterns based on discipline. Environmental factors more important for hard sciences, individual factors more important for humanities. Social sciences in the middle.
Kellogg (1982)	What is the relationship between work habits (writing sessions, tools, cognitive strategies, and frame of mind) and productivity?	Survey of 127 science and engineering professors.	Productivity correlated with frequent 1–2 hour writing sessions; working with noise; comfortable chair; detailed outlines; exercise and soft drinks; use of Dictaphone.
Boice & Johnson (1984)	What are the writing habits and attitudes of university faculty?	Questionnaire: 12 items. 400 responses out of 685 faculty from a US university.	Productive writers write regularly, have a positive attitude towards feedback, little anxiety about writing.
Boice & Jones (1984)	What factors discourage writing for publication for faculty in higher education?	Literature review.	Main obstruction is lack of momentum. Successful writers are not easily distracted. Recommends short sessions.

Figure 4.3 Making an overview of the literature you have read: In my own thesis on research productivity, I made a table that summarized the main focus of the previous research (this extract shows the first few entries, but the final table was several pages long). I organized it chronologically (rather than alphabetically), which allowed me to see how the research had changed over the last 30 years, both with respect to what kinds of questions were asked and how the researchers went about answering them, in addition to what the relevant findings were.

notes in the margins of paper copies. Others use reference management software (see textbox on 'Using referencing software' in Chapter 13) to collect electronic versions of the literature that they can then write memos about, classify, and code. The system you devise need not make sense to anyone other than you, but it does need to make sense to you (see Figure 4.3). The further along you move in academia, the harder it is to get away with 'desktop filing' – that is, piling all your reading on top of your desk. The more you read, the harder it is to remember what you read earlier. It is not wasted time if, while working on your thesis, you experiment a bit to find a system that allows you to keep track of what you've already read, remember what you read, and use those thoughts in your writing.

Those who make best use of the literature may use different referencing systems, but what they have in common is that they remember and understand the literature by *reacting* to it.

Instead of just trying to memorize what they read, they engage with it. Some students create an annotated bibliography: after summarizing the key points, they may jot down what they object to, what they find interesting, what conflicts with other things they've read, what makes them sceptical, what inspires them, what gives them ideas for their own work, and so on. Although many people think that emotion has no place in research, it can be quite helpful in this process. If you find something interesting, ask yourself why – perhaps it will lead you to dig further. If you find yourself getting angry at something someone has written, explore where that anger comes from: do you think the author is biased? Or are you angry because the author has touched on your own biases? As long as you are willing to explore your emotional responses to the literature honestly, and using tools of critical thinking, then responding emotionally to something you read will help you to both remember and understand it. It brings the literature to life in a way that a simple summary does not.

 KEIKO

At first I took too many notes. I would try to write down everything, copying a lot of sentences exactly to make sure I got them right. It was very time-consuming, and made it hard to think about the big picture. My supervisor told me 'Less note taking and more note making!' So I started making tables to summarize the main ideas instead.

(d) TRANSITIONING FROM READER TO WRITER

By far the most effective way to develop a deep understanding of the reading is to write about it, in one way or another. If you wait until you have read (and understood) everything before you sit down and officially start to write, you will probably have forgotten most of what you read. And because it is close to impossible to feel truly finished with the reading, you may end up never writing anything at all – ever. But if you start writing before you are done reading, you allow yourself an opportunity to clarify your thoughts, which helps you approach the next thing you read more critically. This, in turn may give you ideas about other types of literature to investigate, or how to rephrase your research question. You will be better able to see where the ideas of the other authors fit in with your own ideas if you actively try to think systematically about the reading as you go. The transition between 'reading' and 'writing' can be very messy indeed (see Figure 4.4). Most of the writing you do at this stage of the research will not be visible in your final draft – but it will help you get there.

It might help if you think of the writing that you do at this stage as 'thinking on paper' rather than 'writing the thesis', because when you think on paper you do not have to attend so closely to the needs of your audience. You can simply say what you want to say.

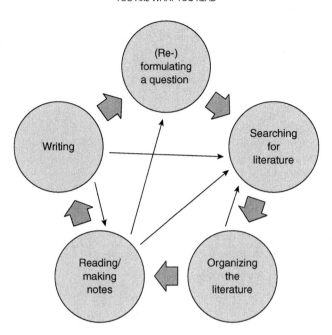

Figure 4.4   The reading and writing cycle: It might feel like almost every step forward can require a step back: formulating a question inspires a search for literature, and as you start to organize what you've found, you may get ideas for other things to search for. As you start to read and react to the literature, you may rethink your question, and continue to search for literature. As you start writing, you may need to go back to the reading, or even find more literature (based on a lecture by Gudrun Østby, Peace Research Institute Oslo, 3 March 2016).

If you get into the habit of regularly writing down your thoughts about what you have read, and of trying to describe how the literature you have read fits together, then you may find it easier to actually start the first draft of your thesis – because you already have lots of words on paper that you can draw from. Indeed, sometimes it is difficult to tell when you have made the transition between 'thinking on paper' to 'writing the thesis'.

What might be more difficult than making the transition from reading to writing, however, is making the transition between thinking of yourself as a listener in this conversation to thinking of yourself as a speaker. I started this chapter by saying that it is a good idea to listen to the ongoing academic conversation before you attempt to join it, but knowing when to start speaking can be difficult. Unfortunately, it sometimes feels as though the more you read, the less ready you are to start writing. This feeling will be compounded if you have not allowed yourself to react to what you have read, and instead have only focused on remembering it. The more you have critically responded to what you have read, however, the easier it will be to see yourself as a writer and not just a reader. The next chapter addresses in more detail how to make the transition to thinking of yourself as a writer and how to make writing a part of your everyday life – even before you start officially writing your first draft.

'It takes a wise man to learn from his mistakes, but an even wiser man to learn from others.'

While getting lost in the literature and never daring to venture your own thoughts on paper will make it difficult for you to produce an independent and original piece of research, the opposite might be true as well. If you are impatient to start your research right away and feel that taking the time to read what others have written might unnecessarily slow you down, you rob yourself of the collective wisdom of those who have gone before you – those who have also thought long and hard about how to define and describe what they are seeing, who have tried and possibly failed to see a connection between two things, and who have studied a phenomenon under less than ideal circumstances. By reading carefully what others who have come before you have thought, about how they have designed their research, and what they have learned, you can focus on making improvements – rather than starting over from scratch.

Finding your path: Points for reflection

What do you want and need from the reading?
- What kind of background on your topic do you need?
- What kind of empirical studies can you look at to give you an idea of what other scholars have done?
- What kind of discipline-based reading do you need?
- What kind of theory do you need?

How will you find these readings?
- What kind of key words can you use?
- How can you get help from a librarian?
- How can you use course readings or other readings to point you in the right direction?

If you skim through the material rather than reading every word, what kinds of things should you look for?

What will you do if there is something you do not understand?

How will you remember what you have read?

REFERENCES AND FURTHER READING

Bui, Yvonne N. (2009) *How to Write a Master's Thesis*. Thousand Oaks, CA: Sage. See Chapter 3, 'Using the literature to research your problem' for good tips on how to get started in your literature search.

Jesson, Jill K., Matheson, Lydia, and Lacey, Finona M. (2011) *Doing Your Literature Review: Traditional and Systematic Techniques*. London: Sage. Aimed primarily at Master's students, this excellent guide makes a point of describing approaches to the literature review from a variety of different disciplinary and methodological perspectives.

Kirton, Bill (2011) *Brilliant Dissertation: What You Need to Know and How to Do It*. Harlow: Prentice Hall. Part 3 of this book, 'Finding and using information', contains a number of useful tips for finding literature, reading, and note taking.

Petre, Marian and Rugg, Gordon (2010) *The Unwritten Rules of PhD Research*, 2nd edn. Berkshire: Open University Press. Although aimed at PhD students, this down-to-earth guide is highly relevant for Master's students as well. Chapter 6 focuses specifically on reading.

Ridley, Diana (2012) *The Literature Review: A Step-by-Step Guide for Students*, 2nd edn. London: Sage. A highly detailed and thorough guide to searching for, organizing, and writing about the literature that includes an excellent discussion of reading and writing critically.

Roberts, Carol M. (2010) *The Dissertation Journey: A Practical and Comprehensive Guide to Planning, Writing, and Defending Your Dissertation*, 2nd edn. Thousand Oaks, CA: Corwin Press. Chapters 8 and 9 both give some useful tips for using the internet to search for literature and developing your approach to the literature review.

Shon, Phillip Chong Ho (2015) *How to Read Journal Articles in the Social Sciences: A Very Practical Guide for Students*, 2nd edn. London: Sage. This book lives up to its title by not only discussing what to read, but also *how* to read it so that you get something out of it.

Single, Peg Boyle (2010) *Demystifying Dissertation Writing: A Streamlined Process from Choice of Topic to Final Text*. Sterling, VA: Stylus. Chapter 3, 'Interactive reading and note taking' does a particularly good job at explaining how reading involves engaging with what you read, and that writing notes is not so much about writing down what others have said, but rather about reflecting on what you have read.

5

WRITING AS THINKING

From rough draft to final document

Many of us approach writing like we have just been diagnosed with a terminal illness. First there is denial: 'I can't start writing now; it's way too soon. I have plenty of time. I must finish the collected works of Proust even though it is only marginally related to my work. Besides, the dog really needs shampooing'.

Then there is anger: 'They expect too much from us! My supervisor doesn't get me at all. I think it was a mistake coming to this university. The library doesn't have the one volume I'm sure will make all the difference. Everyone here is an idiot. And my coffee is cold'.

This is followed shortly by bargaining: 'Maybe if I just finish up my method section I'll be on track again. How about if I reformat all my references? If I spend all weekend thinking about my thesis that counts for something, right?' And depression – which hits most of us when we are about two-thirds of the way through. 'There is no way I will finish this. Everything worth saying about this has already been said. Everything I have written so far is terrible. Everyone else is almost done and I am seeing zero light at the end of my tunnel. I don't belong here'.

Unfortunately, a lot of people give up at the depression stage before they get to the most important stage of all: acceptance. 'Writing is a lot of work, and there is no way around it. I guess I'd better just sit down and do it. I hate the part when I think it won't come together, but it always does in the end – it just takes work.' And it is this stage that separates the amateurs from the professionals. All writers – good or bad, experienced or inexperienced – go through difficult phases during virtually every writing project. The longer and more important the project, the more likely you will go through the black pit of despair. But the more experienced writers know that this is normal, natural, and a phase that they can learn to get through – simply by continuing to write, even if they don't like what they are writing in that particular moment. They just know it is part of the process.

Less experienced writers, on the other hand, do not think of writing as a process that has its ups and downs but rather a performance where every word that is committed to paper will be there for eternity. The final version of your thesis should indeed be a well-structured written document, tailored to your audience, purpose, and context. But when you start writing, you are not necessarily producing *that* document. Much (if not most) of the writing you do at the beginning will not appear in the final version. A lot of the writing you do is for you, to help you figure out what you want to say and how you want to say it. It is normal to have many false starts and to occasionally get lost. Writers often take two steps back for every one step forward. But what will make it possible for you to finish, and end up with a product you can be proud of, is your willingness to keep writing, even – or perhaps especially – when it gets difficult. What makes this possible is learning to see writing as a tool for thinking, not just as a way to communicate fully developed thoughts to others.

This chapter looks at how you can incorporate writing into your daily life so that the transitions from reading to writing, and from writing-as-thinking to producing a final document, feel more natural.

ⓐ WRITING AS A LIFESTYLE

To effectively use writing as a tool for thinking, you have to make it part of your everyday life. This is the opposite of what most of us did when we were undergraduates and wrote only when fuelled by caffeine and deadline panic. The further up you move in academia, the harder it becomes to do everything in one determined sprint, and writing your thesis is not something you can do over a weekend, no matter how much coffee you drink. Think of it like exercising. If you do nothing for a month and then spend 10 hours in a gym, you are probably just going to injure yourself, setting yourself back even further. Likewise, writing irregularly makes it difficult for you to progress because you can't remember what you were trying to do when you left off: 'What was I talking about? Did I even write this? I can't imagine what I was thinking …'. Just as you are probably better off if you take a 30-minute walk every day rather than go on a four-hour hike once a week, you will benefit from carving out a specific part of your day – every day – for writing. If you do, writing will become as natural a part of your day as eating and sleeping.

ⓑ DEVELOPING A ROUTINE

When you set aside part of every day for something, it becomes part of your routine. When routines work well, they relieve us of some unnecessary decision-making. You never realize how routine your eating and sleeping are until your routine gets disrupted. Having to actively decide exactly when and where you will eat every meal or retire for the night would be exhausting if you had to do it all the time. So we fall into a routine – eating meals and sleeping at roughly the same time and place every day.

The same should be true with writing. Instead of starting every day asking yourself whether you have time to write, make room for writing on a regular basis so it feels more like the rule rather than the exception. Research shows that those who write regardless of whether they feel inspired end up having more ideas than those who wait for inspiration before they get started (Boice 1990; Silvia 2007). And the more regular your routine becomes, the easier it is to do it. An hour a day can make all the difference. Just an hour of writing a day. Some days, especially as a deadline approaches, you will probably want to put in more time. But that one hour should be something you do no matter what else you have scheduled that day.

 — **ROBERT**

I wrote my thesis while having a full-time job and two busy teenagers in the house, so finding the time to read and write was really difficult. I got into the habit of getting up early and writing for an hour before going in to work because I think best in the mornings.

If you write at roughly the same time every day, your brain will adapt to working well at that hour – although it is always a good idea to schedule that hour for a time of day when you are already likely to be at your best. For most people, but by no means all, this is early in the morning. And of course you have to schedule it around your other commitments as well. But take a good hard look at your regular routine. When can you carve out an hour? Or at least a half-hour? If you cannot do this now, as a student with only one main project to focus on, it will be virtually impossible when you become a professional and have to juggle teaching, multiple research projects, administrative duties, and family.

Knowing when (and how) to stop for the day is as important as getting started. Working too late into the evening might destroy not only your sleep that night, but also your productivity the next day. Sleep deprivation is seldom conducive to sharp thinking. So figure out how much sleep you need to be at your best (this varies from person to person), and how much time you need to wind down after working in order to fall asleep. For example, if you need at least seven hours of sleep to be at your best, your mind needs at least two hours to settle down, and you normally wake up at six in the morning, then you should make it a rule not to work past eight or nine in the evening.

Stopping writing at a predetermined time has another advantage: it allows you to feel good about what you have accomplished. When you stop because you got frustrated with whatever you were working on, you're likely to feel discouraged and guilty that you aren't writing. But when you stop because it's time to stop, you can use your time off to replenish yourself. When you get back to writing the next day, you are then more likely to feel motivated and even eager.

ⓒ INTENSIFYING YOUR FOCUS

Regular writing routines tend to erode over time, for any number of reasons. You can lose motivation, or other things steal your time and attention. A writing retreat can help you get back on track by letting you focus intensely on your writing for a period of time; usually three to five working days are enough to achieve maximum benefit. This is often called 'binge writing' – full immersion in the writing (see, e.g., Kellogg 1994; Murray 2013). After an interval of binge writing, it is much easier to get into a more normal routine of 'snack writing' (writing in short bursts of about an hour or so).

At a writing retreat, you *write*. You don't just think about writing, talk about writing, or make detailed plans to write. You get down to the business of writing. There are many different ways to do this, but following some sort of schedule for when to write and when to take breaks lets you focus your energy on the writing alone and not waste energy thinking about logistics. The less motivated you are to write, the more important the schedule becomes – and the more you might want to rely on shorter writing periods and more frequent breaks (such as the Pomodoro technique, which alternates 25 minutes of writing and five-minute breaks).

You don't have to travel far from home, but it is important to get away from your regular desk. Your usual setting is full of potential distractions. When you go somewhere else, taking with you only the project that you want to work on, you remove yourself from the things that pull your attention away from your writing. Be careful, though, that your chosen setting doesn't simply replace the old distractions with new ones. Settings that are simple (non-luxurious), quiet, and have some sort of natural view – trees, ocean, etc. – are ideal.

In addition to (or instead of) the multiple-day writing retreat, you can also indulge in a one-day retreat, or even just a few hours of structured writing. Again, what is important here is that you remove yourself from your regular setting and set a strict schedule. One increasingly popular format for this is called 'Shut Up and Write' (see textbox), which alternates intensive writing times with short breaks. The beauty of this format is that you do not need a professional to facilitate: all you need is someone with a timer (which most smart phones have) and a place where participants can write without sitting on top of one another.

'Shut Up and Write'

The 'Shut Up and Write' workshop was originally devised for fiction writers (see www.meetup.com/shutupandwriteSFO) but is becoming increasingly popular among academics (see the Thesis Whisperer blog at https://thesiswhisperer.com/shut-up-and-write/). Although under normal circumstances having people around you can be distracting, the opposite occurs when you are all following the same writing schedule. When you feel like giving up but see that everyone around you is writing, you can usually dig a little deeper and write a little more. Start the day by giving people 15 minutes to set up their work spaces and find a partner. Partners then tell each other what they will be working on that day, and specifically in the first session. There are two reasons for this: (1) saying your goals out loud to someone else makes you feel obligated to fulfil them; and (2) focusing on what you will do for the next hour helps you keep your goals specific and realistic. Instead of 'I will work on my thesis', a goal might be 'I will write the next section of my method chapter, focusing specifically on describing the relationship between my survey and case selection'.

After the preparation time, writing sessions and break times alternate throughout the day, with a longer break for lunch. The length of the writing sessions and breaks is mostly a matter of personal preference, but the less motivated you are, the more frequent the break times should be. A sample schedule might look like this:

9:00–9:15: Prepare your work space	Lunch
9:15–10:00: Write	13:00–13:45 Write
Break	Break
10:15–11:15: Write	14:00–15:00 Write
Break	Break
11:30–12:15 Write	15:15–16:00 Write

Enforced break times are what distinguish this kind of structured writing from the way we normally write, which is to take breaks only when we get frustrated or can't stand it anymore, in which case we try to make the break last as long as possible. Enforced breaks have a completely different dynamic. Even if during the writing session you looked at the timer a few times wondering how much longer the session would last, the buzzer always seems to go off when you are in the middle of a sentence. While finishing the sentence you are writing is perfectly fine, during the break you should make a point of getting up and physically walking away from the computer. Getting a fresh cup of coffee, using the restroom, chatting with colleagues, eating a snack, stretching: these are all acceptable break activities. A break is a break, and getting away from your computer is an important part of it.

When you are 'forced' to take a break, even a five-minute break feels refreshing. When you take a break out of frustration, it is hard to enjoy the time off because you're plagued by guilt and a sense of failure. When you take a break because the buzzer rings at a pre-determined time, you feel a sense of entitlement: I deserve this break! And because you started the break when you were in the middle of something, you look forward to getting back to work. When the break ends, you rush back to the computer with a renewed sense of purpose. And when the day ends, at the time agreed on beforehand, you feel like you can go home with a clean conscience.

ⓓ MOTIVATING YOURSELF

Retreats of whatever length work well because being surrounded by other people also working intensely provides a kind of positive peer pressure that in itself can be motivating. In addition, the tangible results of your writing efforts often increase your motivation to write more. Figuring out what motivates you, and making a conscious effort to do those things on a regular basis, might make the difference between finishing your thesis and *almost* finishing your thesis. In the long run, the single most important quality professional researchers need is the ability to motivate themselves and organize their writing time. This is because a lot of the writing we do is difficult or tedious. All the intelligence and creativity in the world will not help you if you cannot push yourself past the tough parts.

 **SAMIR**

I approached the writing very systematically. I don't think writing is fun, but I'm very practical. I made an outline very early on and just started trying to fill it in. I made a separate document for each chapter, and just tried to write everything I could think of that might go into each chapter – all the notes I had taken on all the literature I had read and classes I had attended. When all of the chapters had at least some thoughts in them, I went through them and put the thoughts in order, which gave me new thoughts. I then made a list of the questions each chapter was supposed to answer, which made me rethink my outline. Then I focused more deeply on one chapter at a time.

One thing that helps to maintain motivation is to change scenery now and then. You don't need to go on a retreat to do this. If you normally work in your room, try working in a café, or library. Take your laptop and sit outside. Some people work well while travelling on trains or planes. Although there might be other people around you, the point is that you can safely ignore them, which is much harder to do with colleagues. Working away from your usual physical space sometimes makes it easier to sink into the mental space you need to be in to think in a more focused manner.

Conversely, another way to motivate yourself is to seek out and talk to other people. Trying out your ideas on other people is a good way to regain the feeling that you are in a conversation, and not just drowning in your own research. In addition to cornering your fellow colleagues in the hall, or perhaps in the pub, conferences and seminars are excellent venues for talking about your work.

When things get really tough, a reward system can be a good idea. After you meet a certain goal (say, three half-hour sessions of writing), you can reward yourself with an activity you enjoy, such as taking a walk outside. Almost any kind of reward system will work, but you might want to avoid rewarding yourself with food – that can go really wrong if you do it too much. Notice that I've described work goals in terms of time. That is, working for a certain number of minutes or hours. You can also set goals in terms of pages or words – 500 words or two double-spaced pages a day, for example. This can be a difficult goal to measure, however: if you write 1000 words but delete 800 of them, have you done enough work for the day? Hours are much more straightforward, and measuring progress that way puts more emphasis on the thinking involved in writing rather than the concrete product that results.

e GETTING THE FLOW GOING

Just because the final document is meant to be read from beginning to end doesn't mean you need to write it that way. Using writing as a tool for thinking means that you can start anywhere. A typical place to start is the method chapter because this is what you know best. You can also put together a literature review that frames the problem you want to address. It doesn't matter where you start. You can make an outline, as long as you feel free to change it as often as you like. You can write a little bit in each chapter. You can write one chapter at time. It really does not matter.

When you find a place to start, the trick is to keep going: to establish flow and maintain it. I've already talked about the importance of sitting down and writing regardless of whether you feel like it. If you do this regularly, you are likely to develop enough momentum that you do not need a clock to make you sit down and start writing. And when you get really into it, you might find that you start writing things you didn't even know you knew: brand new ideas that you hadn't thought of before. This is what being in flow is about.

Maintaining this flow is key. There are dozens of ways to interrupt it: get up to check a reference, look up a word in an online dictionary … Don't do it. Perfectionism is rarely your friend, but at this stage you must consider perfectionism your mortal enemy. Simply make a note in your text: 'Add ref here', 'check word', or 'update figures?' You can go back and fill in those blanks when the flow comes to its own natural end.

Similarly, if you have a good idea for a different section than the one you are working on, jot down that idea somewhere as quickly as possible (maybe open the file for that other section and just write the idea at the top of the page) and then return to the section you were working on. Good ideas are too important to throw away, but if you're in the flow with one section, don't interrupt it by working any more than necessary on the other sections.

End your writing session by making a note to yourself about where to continue when you pick up the next day. You might think this would be obvious, but it is surprisingly helpful to start the next day by seeing a little note that says 'reread first three paragraphs and check for cohesion; continue paragraph about x'.

f REVISING, AND REVISING SOME MORE

The transition between just writing down your thoughts about what you've read and writing your thesis in earnest can be a very gentle one. A normal first draft includes incomplete sentences, meandering paragraphs, abrupt transitions from one subject to the next, long summaries of theory that you do not really understand but are trying to grasp, and too little detail about your actual research and ideas. This is fine, because what you are trying to do is give yourself something to work with.

Once you have something on paper, you can step back, see what you have, and start rewriting. Most of the writing you will do as an academic – not just as a student but for the rest of your professional career – is rewriting. A lot of participants in my writing workshops complain that they used to be good at writing, but when it comes to their thesis or dissertation they just don't feel like they have the knack anymore. When I ask them what they mean by 'good at writing', they say something like 'I used to be able to get it done in a single draft'. Writing a single draft only works when you are writing something short that you do not care much about. But high-stakes writing, like your thesis and all the professional writing you will do later, will necessarily involve quite a bit of rewriting. Sometimes a mediocre paper can be transformed into a really good one by all the drafts that happen in between. Each draft brings you closer to what you want to say. And it is not just the words and sentences that change: You can expect to adjust your core argument several times in the course of the writing. The more clearly you express your thoughts, the more clearly you are able to think, and the more your argument takes shape. So instead of thinking of rewriting as a sign of your failure to do it right the first time, start thinking of it as the power to change things – the power to try on words for size and tweak sentences until you find out what suits you, the power to hone an argument and develop your thinking.

g FINDING YOUR VOICE

It's in the process of rewriting that you start developing your own voice. This is difficult in first drafts because you are often too close to your source material. As I pointed out in the previous chapter, writing as you read helps you remember where you read things: if you don't write down key ideas from your sources right away – carefully referencing them, of course – you might find yourself frantically thumbing through one article after another muttering to yourself, 'I know I saw something on this somewhere, where was it?' However, writing as you read can also result in early drafts that are filled mostly with long quotes, especially if you are writing in a second language. This is fine for a first draft. In fact, it is much better to quote fully and include the source than to look at a partial quote and wonder where it came from.

As you progress beyond your first few drafts, you will need to move away from the words of the other authors and use more of your own words, which means more paraphrasing and interpreting – although you still have to be clear about where ideas came from. It is a good idea to save these early drafts that have the full quotes and the page numbers. As you start paraphrasing and interpreting, save each new draft under a new name and continue to edit. This way you can go back to an earlier draft if you inadvertently delete references or suddenly wonder whether you have cut too much out of the original quote.

KEIKO

It was really hard for me to feel comfortable using my own words. Even though I had studied English for many years, I just didn't feel good enough to use it as a language for writing, especially something so important as a thesis. My first draft was full of quotes from things I read, and my supervisor really pushed me to say things in my own words in the next drafts. This felt awkward for me because I felt like saying things in my own words was disrespectful to the original wording. Who am I to say it better? But towards the end I thought less about saying it 'better' and more about how what they said related to my study.

One thing to look out for in this process is undue influence from a particular source – that is, when you suddenly find that one particular author, book, or article dominates your writing and is quoted or referenced multiple times in a single page (or even paragraph). This sometimes happens when you are deep into the thinking process and project your half-formed ideas onto the words of another author. That is, you read something and think, 'That's exactly what I'm trying to say!' and then you want to quote half the book. But if you pick it up again a few weeks (or months) later, you may find yourself thinking, 'Why did I quote this? It doesn't really even make sense'. This is because when you first read it, you were probably grasping for your own way to describe something, and when you found something that was close, you jumped at it.

As you move away from the words of other authors and towards your own words, you might want to practise some freewriting. That is, in a new document (one that is not your thesis) spend about 15 minutes writing as if you were explaining your research to someone. This type of writing is not meant to be kept. It is more like a warm-up, a way of thinking on paper without having to be academic. You might even find that one or two of those thoughts can actually (perhaps with a little editing) be incorporated into your academic writing. But the important thing here is that these thoughts are yours, in your own words. Do this regularly and you will start to hear your own voice emerge.

h WRITING IN A SECOND LANGUAGE

Finding your own voice can be particularly difficult if you are writing in a second language. Through an accident of geopolitics, English seems to have emerged as the lingua franca for most academic discourse. There is increasing pressure on universities to make scholarly knowledge available to as many people as possible – which at this time in world history means writing in English, increasingly even at the Master's level. If you happen to have English as your first language, you can consider yourself a privileged minority.

If English is not your first language, you have some challenges ahead of you. Unless you are writing about a very local phenomenon (e.g., community-level politics), the chances are that most (if not all) of the literature you need to read will be in English. This will prove helpful if you also want to write in English. It is a much bigger problem if you want to write in your native language. If everything you have read is in English, you face the problem of trying to figure out what to call things in your own language. People who have never juggled more than one language fail to appreciate how tricky this can be. There is not always a one-to-one correspondence between words in different languages, and you may find that you know a concept very well in a second language but have no idea how to say the same thing in your mother tongue (see Chapter 13 on finishing touches).

 AMINA

I don't like writing very much. What I like best is analysing the statistics. I feel like there is so much you can do with numbers, and numbers make more sense to me. Although I feel like I can read English well, I don't feel like I find the words when I'm writing it. Sometimes I feel like I am just putting together phrases that other people use – groups of words that I see together a lot. What helped me the most was that a group of Master's students got together once a week and read through a few pages of each other's writing. It made me much more confident that what I was writing at least made sense.

If you are writing in English, you might avoid having to translate technical terms into your native tongue, but you still have to write everything else in a language that does not quite feel like yours. Before you use writing in a foreign language as an excuse for whatever problems you might be having with your writing, I should point out that most struggles with writing are related to thinking, not to vocabulary – the ideas behind the words, not necessarily the words themselves. If you decide to write in English, just do the best you can, and then get someone to give you some help with the English when you get to your final draft. (Note, however, that different universities have different rules about how much language editing help is allowed. Before you hire a language editor, check the regulations.)

The choice of which language to write in is not always obvious. If you write in English, you will have a better chance later of getting your work published in an international forum, and you will gain valuable experience writing in a language that is likely to dominate your academic writing in the future. On the other hand, if you write in your own language, you are likely to have a deeper connection to the language and the material, making it easier to develop your own voice. Regardless of what you decide, your early drafts can be filled with a combination of languages. This means that the thinking you do on paper can take place in the language that is most convenient. Rough drafts, after all, are meant to be for you. During the rewriting, when you start taking your audience into account, you can make more definitive decisions about your terminology, and in the final drafts you can worry about grammar and punctuation.

ⓘ LIFE HAPPENS

Things don't always go as planned. You may have developed a healthy writing routine, made good choices, kept up your motivation and made good progress in developing your voice, but sometimes larger events intervene. You or someone in your family can get seriously ill or injured; a fire might damage your home or your university; you can lose your source of income; or you might not be able to carry out fieldwork as planned. Big life events don't have to be tragic to be seriously disruptive: you can have a child, you can move house, or an opportunity might arise to participate in an exciting project that unfortunately is not related to your thesis. Whether the interruptions are good or bad, there are times when you need to reassess how you will continue with your work.

Academia is often seen as a calling, to which everything else in your life takes second place. But there are times when this cannot, or should not, be the case, even for the most dedicated students. What will make the difference in the long run is not the event itself, but rather how you manage it.

First, think through your priorities. What are the most important things in your life right now? Both in the short term and the long term? Maybe in the short term it is more important for you to recover completely from an injury so you can function better in the long term. Maybe in the long term you don't want to work in academia, so in the short term you just want to finish your thesis regardless of whether your fieldwork could not take place as planned. Being aware of your short- and long-term priorities can help you avoid feeling guilty no matter what you do (such as becoming a parent and feeling guilty about ignoring your thesis when you are with your child, and then feeling guilty about ignoring your child when you work on your thesis).

Second, think about what you can realistically manage under the circumstances. If your field notes were stolen along with your laptop, is it realistic to expect that you can recreate all your preliminary work? If you have a repetitive stress injury in your wrist or shoulder, how many hours a day can you realistically write, or even read? If you are planning to be a full-time caregiver for an aging parent or a young child, how much time and energy are you likely to have left over for anything else? If you are going to make a new plan about how to move forward, base this plan on what you are actually able to do, not what you wish you were able to do.

And third, let your supervisor and your university know what is going on. If you simply fail to deliver chapters as agreed, your supervisor cannot help you. But if you explain that you need to help your mother care for your terminally ill father, your supervisor might help you figure out how to ask for a leave of absence. If you tell her that all the transcripts from your fieldwork were lost, she might help you think through how to work around it. But there is no way she can help if she does not know what is happening.

Learning how to balance the rest of your life with your academic work and how to overcome unforeseen obstacles may be one of the most important lessons you can learn as a student. It is all too easy to think that hitting a snag – even a very large one – is a good reason to give up. This is particularly true if you have doubts about whether you belong in academia in the first place. If you are the first person in your family to pursue higher education and everyone around you is holding their breath waiting for you to fail, then hitting an obstacle or two may well provide the 'proof' to convince you to stop trying. But perhaps one of the reasons that students from academic families drop out less often than others is that they know that it can be a bumpy road and are better prepared for it. When it comes to higher education, finishing first is nowhere near as important as simply finishing – regardless of how long it takes.

ⓘ LETTING GO

Even if everything goes smoothly throughout the entire writing of your thesis, you still have to decide when it is time for other people to see what you have written. Letting go of something is difficult even for the most seasoned writers. For a student it can be close to impossible. 'Have I forgotten something?' you wonder. 'Surely there are more articles I should read, or more data I should gather. Maybe I should just read through it one more time.'

 EMMA

Writing the thesis was much harder than I expected, probably because I had very high expectations for how good it was supposed to be. I wanted it to be exceptional, which made it very difficult to get started – and almost impossible to submit. I wasn't really prepared for the amount of rewriting I had to do, and how difficult it was to judge whether what I had written was good or not. Finally my supervisor just made me send it in. Looking back, I see that that was the right thing to do!

Using writing as a tool to think includes letting it go so other people can respond to it. Long before you submit your final version, you should be sending your work to others for feedback. This means accepting that even though what you have written is not perfect (yet), hearing what other people have to say about it will help you make it better. The next chapter discusses how you can get valuable feedback (and other types of help) from both your supervisor and other students.

'It is the silence between the notes that makes the music; it is the space between the bars that cages the tiger.'

The space between writing sessions can make all the difference. When you write a little bit every day (or as close to every day as you can make it), you continue to think in between so it becomes a continuous process. But when you write only occasionally, with big gaps in between, you have to start over each time. The silence between the notes is the thinking you do after you put down your pen or close down the computer file you're working on. It is here that thoughts ripen and grow, ready to bloom the next time you sit down again to write. The tiger is you, the writer. If the gaps between the writing sessions are too wide, your thoughts get away from you and dissolve before you can trap them on paper, leaving you stuck at the starting point, unable to build on what you have done in the previous session.

Finding your path: Points for reflection

What kinds of writing practices work for you?
- Does location matter to you? How?
- Does the time of day matter? In what way?
- What 'rituals' do you have? What things do you do before you sit down to write?

What stops you from writing, and what can you do to change that?

What can you do to make sure you write regularly?
- How much time can you realistically set aside each day or week?
- What can you do to motivate yourself even if you don't feel inspired?
- How can you involve other people (e.g., writing groups or writing events)?

REFERENCES AND FURTHER READING

Boice, Robert (1990) *Professors as Writers: A Self-Help Guide to Productive Writing*. Stillwater, OK: New Forums Press. Grounded in both personal experience and research, Boice describes how academics (at all levels) can develop productive writing habits.

Elbow, Peter (1998) *Writing with Power: Techniques for Mastering the Writing Process*, 2nd edn. New York: Oxford University Press. A classic work on how to get words on paper that still resonates today. The chapters in section V are all about feedback.

Goldberg, Natalie (2005) *Writing Down the Bones: Freeing the Writer Within*, expanded edn. Boston, MA: Shambhala Publications. Aimed at fiction writers, Goldberg's book can also provide inspiration and ideas for academic writers, especially about how to find your own voice.

Kellogg, Ronald T. (1994) *The Psychology of Writing*. New York, NY: Oxford University Press. Kellogg provides an academic look at writing as a process and introduces the term 'binge writing'.

Murray, Rowena (2011) *How to Write a Thesis*, 3rd edn. Maidenhead: Open University Press. Targeted at those who are writing a doctoral dissertation, this book nevertheless provides excellent guidance on the overall process of writing at the Master's level as well.

Murray, Rowena (2013) *Writing for Academic Journals*, 3rd edn. Maidenhead: Open University Press. Murray describes 'binge' and 'snack' writing, and provides a number of useful ways to approach the writing process – whether you are writing a journal article or thesis.

Murray, Rowena and Moore, Sarah (2006) *The Handbook of Academic Writing: A Fresh Approach*. Maidenhead: Open University Press. This book demonstrates how the feelings associated with Impostor Syndrome exist at all levels of academia, and suggests strategies for coping with these feelings. Particularly useful are the discussions on writing groups, writing programmes and retreats.

Petre, Marian and Rugg, Gordon (2010) *The Unwritten Rules of PhD Research*, 2nd edn. Berkshire: Open University Press. Chapter 12 focuses specifically on the writing process.

Silvia, Paul J. (2007) *How to Write a Lot: A Practical Guide to Productive Academic Writing*. Washington, DC: American Psychological Association. After reading this, you will be left with no more excuses for not writing a little bit every day.

SUPERVISION AND GUIDANCE

Getting help along the way

....

a What you should (and should not) expect from your supervisor

b Juggling more than one supervisor

c Keeping track of agreements

d The elephant in the room: Power imbalances and poor supervision

e Where else can you get help?

f What to do with the help you get: Managing feedback

....

In fiction, the relationship between mentor and mentee is powerful and sacred: the wise and weathered sage knows just what to say and when to say it to help the hero on the journey to greatness. In real life, the relationship is more complicated – mainly because it involves real people and not archetypes, but also because the nature of supervision has changed. Increasingly, the apprentice model of supervision is being replaced by a New Public Management model. Under the apprentice model, professors take on only a few students at a time and train them as they see fit, for as long as they feel is necessary. The New Public Management approach means that supervisors have to take on more students and focus on getting them through the system as efficiently as possible – replacing their own judgement of the student's progress with key performance indicators.

On the upside, moving away from the apprentice model also means that students are no longer solely dependent on their supervisors for help. They are free to draw on other sources: student groups, classes on transferable skills, librarians, writing centres, and so on. In addition, the entire system is far more transparent than it used to be, and students today have a much better idea of what is expected of them – making them less vulnerable to the whims of their supervisor. It also means that you are increasingly responsible for your own learning, which means you will have to learn to identify both the things that you need help with and where you can get that help.

This chapter discusses what you should (and should not) expect from your supervisor, as well as the kinds of help you can get from others.

ⓐ WHAT YOU SHOULD (AND SHOULD NOT) EXPECT FROM YOUR SUPERVISOR

Few supervisors receive formal training in supervision, so they tend to base their approach on their own experiences. Most have deeply held beliefs about what works and what doesn't, and these beliefs can be quite different from those held by the person across the hall. Some supervisors see their main role as guiding you through the administrative formalities and technical aspects of research. Others believe that part of their mission is to teach you the core values of the discipline and academia. Some see their role as teaching you how to think critically, develop an academic argument, and carry out analysis, while others want to foster independence by leaving you to figure it out yourself. Some consider it a natural part of supervision to help you think about work-life balance, career planning, and stress management, while others want to focus strictly on academic matters (see Lee 2008; Petre and Rugg 2010: 46).

Different supervisors also have different strengths: some might know a lot about your topic, but little about your method, or vice versa. Some are very approachable, others more distant. And at the same time, different students have different needs. Some are confident about academic writing, but are struggling with a transition to a new discipline. Others might have a very good understanding of the literature but seem unable to apply it to their topic. So it can sometimes take a while for supervisor and student to find the right tone and figure out how to relate to one another.

 ROBERT ▬▬▬▬▬▬▬▬▬▬▬▬▬▬▬▬▬▬▬▬▬▬▬▬▬▬▬▬▬▬▬▬▬▬

Since I had been out of academia so long, I felt like a real outsider on campus – especially because I was only studying part time. The most important thing my supervisor did for me was to help me understand what was expected of me as a student writing a thesis. She got me organized with respect to deadlines and provided me with great examples of other Master's theses so I knew what kind of thing I was supposed to be writing.

Some universities have supervisors and students sign official contracts that spell out many of the formal expectations, but leave the informal expectations for you work out. Discussing these expectations, both formal and informal, with your supervisor can help prevent the tension that may arise when you each have different ideas about what the supervisory relationship should be about. Although it should be your supervisor's job to initiate this conversation, the chances are that you will probably have to bring this up yourself. Here are some things that should be clarified.

Meetings: Many institutions specify how often you should be meeting with your supervisor, and the form these meetings should take. But institutions (and individual supervisors) can differ greatly. Some expect a monthly meeting, while others prefer weekly. Likewise, some supervisors set aside 15 minutes to talk to their students; others will clear their afternoons. If you know what the common institutional practice is, you will have a better idea of both what to expect and what you can ask for. If the standard practice is 15-minute sessions once a week, but you think 15 minutes is too short, you might suggest meeting once a month for an hour – which is the same amount of time in total, just arranged a little differently. But if the expectation is 15 minutes once a month, asking for a full hour might be problematic.

Feedback on drafts: Although giving feedback on drafts is a core function of supervision, there is little agreement on what kind of feedback should be given, whether the feedback should be written or oral, how many rounds of feedback are expected, how polished a draft should be before it is submitted to the supervisor, and what a reasonable turn-around time is. Some supervisors roll up their sleeves, throw themselves wholeheartedly into your work, and correct every little misplaced comma they can find in the document itself; others are less interested in the specifics of language, prefer to make no comments in your manuscript whatsoever and would rather discuss their general thoughts about the content directly with you. Some are prepared to comment only on one version of each chapter and prefer a highly polished draft, while others want to shape the evolution of your thinking and prefer to see multiple rounds of each chapter. If you and your supervisor are operating with different expectations, considerable friction can result. If a supervisor is expecting to provide only one round of comments and the student sends an email saying 'Hi! I made some changes to my theory chapter based on our conversation. What do you think?' the supervisor might think the student was extraordinarily demanding (see textbox 'Putting yourself in your supervisor's shoes'). Likewise, some students expect that their supervisor should respond within 24 hours, whereas some supervisors think that a month is soon enough. Rather than being irritated at your supervisor for taking so long to get back to you, it is a good idea to ask at the very beginning, 'As a rule, when should I expect to hear back from you when I send you a draft?'

Putting yourself in your supervisor's shoes

When you talk with your supervisor, the focus is normally on you and your work. However, supervisors are usually juggling any number of tasks at the same time: several other students, their teaching obligations, and their own research. Chances are that shortly after you left your meeting, your supervisor was thinking of something other than your thesis. So when you send a file a few weeks later and say, 'Here's what we talked about. See attached!' and they open up a document with no obvious revisions in it, it will take them a very long time to figure out what is going on.

You can save your supervisor an extraordinary amount of time and energy by keeping this in mind. Instead of sending an email saying only 'New version attached!' try something like this: 'Dear Prof Oracle, In our meeting a couple of weeks ago, we talked about how my presentation of critical realism was both too detailed and yet failed to explain how this theoretical perspective would help me better understand how students learn. I have rewritten the chapter

(Continued)

(Continued)

with this in mind. I've shortened the presentation of the history of critical realism, and high-lighted the main concepts I want to use. I have also added a few examples to demonstrate the relevance of these concepts. Do you think the examples work? I've attached the new version with the changes tracked'.

In this letter you have not only reminded the good professor what you talked about, but also how you interpreted her comments. You then let her know what you were thinking during your revision, and the main changes that you made. You also ask a specific question to focus her attention on the aspect you feel most unsure about, and provide her with a marked-up copy of your chapter so she can see exactly what you did. Do be careful, however, that when you send a version with tracked changes that the changes showing are the most recent ones, not every single change you've ever made since the first draft.

Remember that supervisors are human. While it is their job to help you, it is not always obvious how best to do that. And while they are working on helping you, at the same time they are also working with other students, performing administrative duties, and doing their own research. The easier you can make their task by making it clear what you want them to look at and why, the more likely it is you will end up getting the help you need.

Finding literature: Supervisors vary greatly in how responsible they feel for setting you on the right course towards finding the literature you need for your research. Some believe that figuring it out yourself is part of the learning process. Others consider it part of their role as expert to provide you with the best sources. And still others fall somewhere in between: perhaps they will get you started with a few core readings, or point you in the direction of a relevant article, but they more or less let you get on with it.

Designing the research: The extent to which your supervisor is directly involved in the research design (including formulation of your research question) is mostly related to your geographical location, discipline, and methodological approach. In some areas of the world, it is very common for supervisors to be very involved in this process. The same is true for disciplines that favour quantitative methods, especially if your thesis is part of a larger project involving other people. If your thesis is part of an industry study, your research question might be set by the company that hired you. But for the most part, developing a good research question and research design is primarily your responsibility (see Chapter 2), and some friction can arise if you feel either that your supervisor is interfering or that you have been left to cope on your own before you are ready.

 AMINA

I worked really closely with my supervisor throughout the whole project because this was also part of his research. When I finished my thesis, he helped me turn it into an article. When I was working on my thesis, his feedback was mostly on the research. But when we co-authored together afterwards, I learned much more about writing.

ⓑ JUGGLING MORE THAN ONE SUPERVISOR

If you are planning a thesis that combines different areas of expertise, you may be assigned (or be allowed to request) two supervisors. If you are doing an interdisciplinary thesis, you might have one supervisor from each discipline. Even if you are within a single discipline, you might have one supervisor chosen for their expertise in method, while another is chosen for their expertise in your topic. Having two supervisors can double your chances of getting the help you need, but also double the number of awkward situations you may find yourself in if you are not entirely sure what is expected from you. More importantly, this may also lead to your getting conflicting advice. For example, one supervisor might tell you that you need more theory, or different theory, while the other tells you that you need to focus on your data and downplay your theory.

If you do get conflicting advice, there are a few things you can think about. First, who is in charge? If you have more than one supervisor, one will normally be designated your primary supervisor. In most cases, this person should have the last word. Second, if you are doing an interdisciplinary thesis and have supervisors from different departments, think about where you are based as a student. You are probably formally associated only with one department, and the supervisor from that department should probably be given more weight. Finally, keep in mind that ultimately *you* have to defend the choices you make, regardless of what your supervisors say. 'My supervisor told me to do that' is seldom, if ever, a good excuse for a poor choice. In the end, you might have to simply use your best judgment and follow the advice that you think best serves your thesis, regardless of who that advice comes from.

ⓒ KEEPING TRACK OF AGREEMENTS

Once you and your supervisor have clarified your general expectations, it is a good idea to write them down. It is also a good idea to summarize each of your meetings in writing, paying particular attention to the action points – that is, the things each of you will follow up on before the next meeting. Some departments even require you to do this. Summarizing your meetings serves two important functions: (1) it allows each person present to make sure they are in agreement about what was said and agreed on, since it is likely you are focusing on different things and you might have additional thoughts after the meeting is over; and (2) it provides a written record, so if your supervisor says, 'Didn't you say you would do X?' you can go back and say, 'I don't see that anywhere in the notes', or 'according to the notes of the last meeting, we agreed I would focus on Y'.

Having a written record is not a sign of distrust. It simply represents an acknowledgement that everyone has a lot on their minds. When you are meeting with your supervisor, it is very likely that at some point you will not be fully listening to what they say because you are still thinking about what they said 10 minutes earlier. If you are tasked with writing a summary of action points after the meeting, your supervisor should then have the opportunity to say, 'This looks good, but remember we also talked about the importance of double-checking the figures for 2014' – at which point you can pretend you remember this part of the discussion and quickly add it to your list of things you need to do before the next meeting. The sooner you write this summary after your meeting, the greater opportunity you will have to ask your supervisor to clarify if necessary, and to carry out the task before the next meeting. This will also reduce the chances of showing up at the next meeting unprepared.

This process is startlingly similar to the process you will go through when, as a professional, you work on large research projects, especially if they involve multiple researchers in different geographical areas. In project meetings, where participants report on progress, share findings, and discuss challenges, everyone has a slightly different focus, and if you do not take notes from the meeting and make them available to everyone, there is a good chance that each of the participants will walk away with a different understanding of what was talked about and agreed on. Unless everyone is brought back to the same page, it will not take long before the project will suffer considerable damage.

ⓓ THE ELEPHANT IN THE ROOM: POWER IMBALANCES AND POOR SUPERVISION

While most of the time relationships between students and supervisors work well, few relationships are sunshine and roses the entire time. Sometimes supervisors do not understand how they come across; they might be shocked to hear how their words and actions are interpreted. Many think they are treating their students almost as equals, but the students seldom see the relationship the same way. An innocent, well-meaning comment from a supervisor can be easily misinterpreted by a stressed, anxious student. It is not at all uncommon for students to project their insecurities onto their supervisors: if a student is worried that they are not making sufficient progress, a slightly raised eyebrow from the supervisor can quickly be interpreted as a judgement that insufficient progress has been made.

These unspoken power imbalances are a by-product of the way academia works, and they can become destructive. In some settings, supervisors fear that if a student files a complaint – justified or not – they could lose their jobs, so they may be overly cautious. But usually it is the student who is the most vulnerable: poor supervision (whether unwitting or intentional) can block a student's progress, undermine their confidence, and fail to give them the tools they need to become an independent researcher. If a student fears that complaining will result in reprisals, they will put up with almost anything for a very long time, even if the problem is a result of miscommunication. This is especially true for students who come from countries with more authoritarian traditions.

KEIKO

I was really intimidated by my supervisor at first. I wanted so much to make a good impression because he is so well known in our field, but I felt like I kept disappointing him. He left me very much on my own to figure out what I was doing, which made me think he did not think enough of me as a student to follow up by giving clear instructions. He told me later that he pushed me on purpose to think for myself, and that he was really pleased by my progress.

It is not always easy for either student or supervisor to see when a line has been crossed. Simple favours or innocent gestures can quickly lead to awkward situations. Most of us know that supervisors are not supposed to ask students to babysit their children, wash their cars, or do any other personal tasks. But what if the two of you are working late on a common project and suddenly you find yourself running downstairs to get coffee and snacks? Does it make a difference if the food is for both of you? If you are splitting the cost? What if the supervisor treats you to dinner one time? Does that set a precedent? Do you feel like you owe something in return? Are there situations in which you would feel less uncomfortable (or more uncomfortable) if the supervisor were a different gender?

Keeping mild discomfort from blowing up into an unworkable relationship might require you to speak frankly about how you are interpreting the signals your supervisor is sending you. For most students this feels so awkward that they would rather put up with an uncomfortable situation. But if you keep the conversation focused on how you would like your future interactions to be, rather than trying to dissect and analyse things that have already occurred, you might save both of you from feeling mortified. For example, rather than asking, 'Were you making a pass at me when you asked me to dinner last week?' you could say, 'I understand you were probably only trying to be nice, but I would feel more comfortable if we met only during office hours'. Likewise, instead of 'I'm tired of being asked to do all your slave work', you could say, 'I'm a bit confused about all of the tasks you have been assigning to me lately and I'm not sure how they all relate to my thesis. Could you be more clear about what you expect from me and what the purpose of these things are?'

Although thankfully very rare, there are unfortunately some situations where talking either is not enough or might even make things worse (see, e.g., Lunenburg and Irby 2008: 55). All the talking in the world will not help essentially poor chemistry, when for some reason you and your supervisor just cannot seem to understand each other. And if your main challenge with your supervisor is that they do not answer email or phone calls, and they might even have taken a leave of absence without informing you, a conversation is unlikely to help. But in some of the truly worst-case scenarios, talking might make the student even more vulnerable, especially if there is no third party present. Situations in which you should tread especially carefully include the following:

- **Suspected discrimination:** Even in academia we are not safe from social discrimination. If you feel that your supervisor is treating you differently because of your gender, race, ethnicity, nationality, age, disability, or sexuality, you will have to think carefully about how to proceed. While you may be able to address discrimination based on unconscious bias by saying something like 'I'm not sure if you are aware that I am the only student you have not yet included in the discussion group, but even though I am in a wheelchair I have no trouble making it to the classroom and would be happy to lead a session on my topic', this might not always work. Those who are not aware that they are discriminating might respond defensively if you address the issue directly. And those who are aware of their behaviour are unlikely to thank you for pointing it out.
- **Plagiarism or scientific misconduct:** Not all supervisors are as respectful of their students' intellectual property as they should be, and might help themselves to their students' findings and publish without giving credit. When this happens, the student might fear that if they claim plagiarism they won't be believed and they will then face reprisals from the professor. Likewise, if they suspect that their supervisor is engaging in scientific misconduct, perhaps by falsifying data that the student is depending on for their own study, the student will understandably be worried about the repercussions of reporting their suspicions. As with any situation where you need to protect your own work and reputation, regardless of what other action you take, make sure there is a paper trail that can establish ownership of your ideas and the origin of your data.
- **Harassment or bullying:** The inherent power imbalance between supervisor and student is seldom more obvious than when that power is abused. Unwanted sexual advances, particularly when accompanied by the implication that your success depends on your acceptance of these advances, is a clear abuse of power. Systematic belittling of you and your work is another abuse of power that simply cannot be allowed to continue.

The question you need to ask yourself in all three of these worst-case scenarios is whether you want to protect yourself and try to change supervisors as discreetly as you can, or whether you want to bring this destructive behaviour to light, which might help future students but hurt you. It is not always obvious what the best alternative is.

Regardless of whether you want to file an official complaint, you should certainly look into changing supervisors. Most, if not all, departments have systems in place for doing this. In some settings, this is done quite regularly with few questions asked. In other settings, such a change is seen as reflecting poorly on both the student and the supervisor. If you find yourself in a situation where changing supervisors is frowned upon but continuing is unthinkable, then you might want to consider involving a third party. If you can find someone – perhaps another professor or someone from support services – to confide in, they might be able to give you some good advice on how to proceed. And keep a record of every communication with your supervisor in the event that you need to argue your case.

ⓔ WHERE ELSE CAN YOU GET HELP?

Even if you get plenty of help from your supervisor, they should not be the only person you turn to. Support systems are not always obvious, and sometimes you have to build them yourself, but they are an essential supplement to supervision. The ability to look around your particular setting and see what kind of help is available will serve you well as you move on in academia. There are several different avenues of support.

Peer feedback: Asking a fellow student to read through and comment on your work can be extremely helpful, not least because being able to talk to someone who has read your work brings to life the conversational nature of academic writing (see textbox 'Peer feedback'). Likewise, reading through the work of other students not only sharpens your ability to think critically, but also gives you a better idea of what rough drafts look like. Instead of comparing your own rough draft to a published article that has gone through multiple revisions and several rounds of editing, you get a much better sense of what is 'normal' for a rough draft when you look at the work of other students.

....

Peer feedback

When peers give each other feedback, no one is 'the expert' and comments should not focus on 'fixing mistakes' and trying to edit each other's work. Instead, peer feedback – whether given individually or in a group context – involves asking good questions that help the author think through the big picture:

- What is the ongoing academic conversation?
- What is the puzzle or knowledge gap?
- What is the question the author is trying to answer?
- How will the author answer that question (method and sources)?
- What key ideas and concepts will the author use in their work (theory)?
- What claims are the author making?
- How does the author support these claims?

Use these questions to guide your reading, and make a list of things you want to ask the author about. For example, 'Your introduction focuses on gender in higher education, but your research question seems to be about writing practices among faculty. I'm not sure if I see the connection'. When you have finished reading and have jotted down some good questions, meet face to face in a relaxed setting and talk through the questions. You might even use the questions above as a kind of interview guide if the author has very little on paper.

If you find that you understand very little of what you are reading and are not sure where to start commenting, then you can probe a bit by asking questions that prompt the student to talk about their work:

(Continued)

(Continued)

- What attracted you to this topic in the first place?
- What is the most interesting thing you have found, or have read about, so far?
- What is the hardest thing for you to write about?
- Who will be interested in reading this, and why?

The point of peer feedback is to have a good conversation that helps you to think through your work, both during the conversation and afterwards.

....

Writing groups: In addition to, or instead of, getting individual feedback on your drafts from your peers, you can establish or join a group that meets regularly (every week, every month, or whatever suits the group members). Some groups circulate drafts and comment on each other's work (which again helps you get a feel for audience and the conversational nature of writing), while others just talk about the writing process. Groups that focus on the writing process tend to meet more frequently for shorter periods of time (usually about an hour), and give each person equal time to talk about their current challenges and writing goals for the next week. If the purpose of the group is to provide feedback on the writing, it can be organised in at least two different ways: one way is to base feedback on oral presentations, where drafts are not circulated beforehand and participants base their comments and questions on a 5- to 10-minute presentation of the paper given by the author. This works best for writing at an early stage and keeps the focus on the core argument. Another way to organize the group is to circulate written drafts a few days in advance, then each member can comment on the draft during the meeting. This works better for writing that is closer to completion, or when the author wants focus on the sentence or paragraph level rather than the central ideas. Still other groups combine the two formats: drafts are circulated ahead of time, and the author gives a short presentation. This gives those who did not have time to read the draft the opportunity to comment, while the others can compare the written draft to the oral presentation. Whatever format you choose, make sure the expectations are feasible and that all members of the group have the same understanding of what the aim of the group is and what level of commitment is expected.

Librarians: A librarian is not just someone who re-shelves the books you leave on the table in the library when you are finished thumbing through them. Librarians have extensive knowledge of how to track down obscure volumes, how to limit or widen electronic searches, what databases are available, and so on. Librarians and other library staff also offer courses or training in reference management software, search skills, and other invaluable tools you are likely to need, not only as a student, but also as an independent researcher.

Writing centres: Many universities have writing centres that offer various kinds of help to students and faculty. Although many of those who take advantage of the writing centre are non-native speakers seeking help with their language skills, writing centres do more than just help you with grammar. The writing centre staff can help you understand how to develop an argument, find your own voice, work with references, and just generally learn how to write academically. The writing centre may arrange courses, seminars, or one-on-one coaching.

SAMIR

At first I felt uncomfortable about asking for help with the writing because I consider English my first language. But UK English is quite different from Indian English, and the style of writing for business is very different from the kind of writing we did in engineering. The writing centre helped me get a better idea of what kind of writing style was expected from me.

Editors: You do not have to be a non-native speaker of English to benefit from language help. Trying to make sense of new writing norms in a specific discipline or country, or just needing a fresh set of eyes to look through your work, are both good reasons to have a language expert comment on your writing. If you do not have access to a writing centre, you may want to consider hiring an editor (see Chapter 13 on finishing touches). Editors come in all sorts: they can focus on language, structure, argument, or content. Universities have very different rules about what sort of editing help is acceptable, so before you contact an editor, find out what kind of help you are allowed to get.

Role models: One underappreciated form of help is role models – that is, other students who have successfully completed their degrees and can give you the benefit of their experience. Even if you are not personally acquainted with any former students, you have access to successful theses from your department. Track down and read through some of them, both those that are close to your topic and those that are not, to get inspiration.

❶ WHAT TO DO WITH THE HELP YOU GET: MANAGING FEEDBACK

As a Master's student, one of your biggest challenges is to make the transition from getting feedback in the form of grades that you can do little about to getting feedback that you have to actively process. This will require realizing that criticism of your writing is not criticism of you. It is natural to feel that they are one and the same because you have, after all, been pouring all your thoughts into that paper. But if you think of your work as a part of you, it becomes difficult to achieve the distance you need to benefit from the feedback you get and, ironically, to take ownership of what you write. Owning what you write means that you can separate yourself enough from your writing to entertain the possibility that the words you wrote may not express what you intended to write, and that listening to feedback will help you figure out how to express what you want to say more clearly. So instead of seeing criticism of your writing as a criticism of you (or perhaps even of your ideas), it is useful to think of it as a unique opportunity to glimpse what is missing from what actually made it to paper. The more you can see feedback this way, the easier it is to not only accept it, but to make good use of it.

EMMA

I had a really hard time not taking feedback on my writing personally. I think of myself as a good writer, and it was really hard to hear that not everything I was writing was working. But later I understood that even good writers don't always explain things very well the first time, especially because it takes some time to figure out what you really want to say.

Perhaps the best way to see this is to observe it in other people's work. Instead of comparing your work to finished, published pieces that have gone through multiple revisions and rounds of editing, get to know what rough drafts normally look like. Exchanging drafts with your peers can be particularly helpful. The early drafts of other students may not only make little sense, but also bear absolutely no resemblance to how eloquently they spoke about their topic only minutes ago. Once you realize this, it becomes easier to accept that the same may be true for you.

When you can accept that the true benefit of feedback is to help you recognize and correct the mismatch between what you are thinking and what you wrote, it also becomes easier to see how important it is to understand the positionality of the reader. Feedback is always subjective. Different people will see different things when they look at your work because they have different perspectives. A person who is an expert on your topic but not your method will give you very different feedback than one who is an expert on your method but not your topic. And even brilliant scholars have off days and sometimes give bad advice. Rather than slavishly and uncritically trying to treat all feedback you get as orders that you must follow ('My friend says this example is bad so I will delete it'), consider both the source and your options: 'My supervisor does not like this example, but she comes from a very different background and I can see how this example does not make sense to her. Besides, I think she read it a bit too fast. I will try explaining it a different way'.

Taking ownership of your work also means considering which battles are worth fighting. Let's imagine that you have switched disciplines or departments. In your previous department, it might have been perfectly acceptable to use 'I' and to explain how your positionality might have an impact on your research. But in your new department your supervisor is vehemently opposed to your use of 'I' and does not want to hear anything about your positionality, finding it irrelevant. Simply dropping the use of the first person pronoun is a grammatical issue, and one that is likely to cost you little to comply with. You might think that without 'I' your writing becomes less personal, more cumbersome, and drier, but this does not affect your key message. Insisting on using 'I', knowing full well that it will cause your audience to take your work less seriously, might not be wise. But even if you feel that letting go of 'I' is something you can accept, you might feel differently about the issue of positionality: if you are doing qualitative research on your own organization, it would be a serious omission not to address how your relationship with your participants might affect your findings. If your supervisor has only ever done quantitative research, he might not fully appreciate how important a discussion of positionality can be; it will be up to you to convince him.

If your supervisor suggests a course of action for your research that you feel uncomfortable with, then simply complying will not be the best course of action in the long run. If you follow advice without understanding why, or despite your conviction that your way was better, then you lose ownership of your work. There is a very good chance that your supervisor made that suggestion for a good reason, but unless you express your reservations, you may never understand why.

None of the help discussed in this chapter involves getting someone else to do the work for you, or even necessarily makes your job easier. Indeed, soliciting feedback sometimes makes things harder because you then have to figure out how to make use of the help you have been given. But interacting with others in this way helps you to build your own repertoire of skills and experience.

'When the student is ready, the teacher will appear.'

Academia can be a lonely place, but there is far more help around than you realize. In addition to your supervisor(s), peers, library staff, writing centres, and others can provide invaluable assistance. Getting help when you need it is not a sign that you are deficient in any way; it is a sign that you understand the nature of the challenge and are working hard to meet it. And no matter how much help you get, you are still the one who is responsible for your own work. Find out what your supervisor excels at, and take advantage of that expertise. But don't be afraid to look elsewhere to supplement it. In particular, don't discount your peers; it is not always expertise you need, but the feeling that you are not alone. Perhaps the greatest help they can provide is moral support: the assurance that whatever challenges you are facing, you'll be able to meet them.

Finding your path: Points for reflection

What do you expect from your supervisor?
* What kinds of things do you expect to get help with?
* What kinds of things do you expect to manage on your own?

What do you think your supervisor expects from you?
* What do you think an ideal student is from a supervisor's perspective?
* How can you find out what your supervisor expects?
* What are the departmental guidelines?

(Continued)

(Continued)

What other kinds of help are available to you?
- What services does your library offer?
- What kinds of support can you get from your peers?

REFERENCES AND FURTHER READING

Harwood, Nigel and Petrić, Bojana (2017) *Experiencing Master's Supervision: Perspectives of International Students and their Supervisors*. London: Routledge. Although not written as an advice book but rather as an academic study, this book provides useful insight into the relationship between students and supervisors at the Master's level.

Kamler, Barbara and Thomson, Pat (2014) *Helping Doctoral Students Write: Pedagogies for Supervision*. London: Routledge. This book gives a good idea of what supervision is like from the supervisor's perspective.

Lee, Anne (2008) 'How are doctoral students supervised? Concepts of doctoral research supervision', *Studies in Higher Education*, 33(3): 267–81. Based on interviews with supervisors, Lee categorizes how they see their own roles.

Lunenburg, Fred C. and Irby, Beverly J. (2008) *Writing a Successful Thesis or Dissertation: Tips and Strategies for Students in the Social and Behavioral Sciences*. Thousand Oaks, CA: Corwin Press. The book includes a short but useful section on how to be a desirable student.

Murray, Rowena and Moore, Sarah (2006) *The Handbook of Academic Writing: A Fresh Approach*. Maidenhead: Open University Press. Particularly useful in the context of getting help are the discussions on writing groups, writing programmes and retreats.

Paltridge, Brian and Starfield, Sue (2007) *Thesis and Dissertation Writing in a Second Language: A Handbook for Supervisors*. London: Routledge. This book provides a useful look at the challenges facing those writing in a second language from the supervisor's point of view.

Petre, Marian and Rugg, Gordon (2010) *The Unwritten Rules of PhD Research*, 2nd edn. Berkshire: Open University Press. In addition to discussing different models of supervision, this book contains a separate chapter focusing on various challenges related to supervision, relevant for graduates and postgraduates alike.

Wellington, Jerry (2010) *Making Supervision Work for You: A Student's Guide*. London: Sage. Aimed specifically at students, the book looks at how you can manage your relationship with your supervisor.

PART II
THE PRODUCT

STRUCTURE AND ARGUMENT

What's the logic of your story?

....

a The heart of your story: Core argument

   i The question you ask

   ii The answer you give

   iii The support you provide

b The logical flow of academic storytelling

   i Introduction

   ii Literature review

   iii Methodology and method

   iv Results and analysis

   v Discussion and conclusions

c Rules and conventions: Navigating expectations

....

Conducting research is a bit like digging for buried treasure: After searching for a likely place to look, you bring out your shiny new equipment (NVivo, SPSS, EndNote) and start to dig with enthusiasm. After a while, the digging gets harder. Your enthusiasm may wane. You hit roots or rocks or pipes, which make you rethink the wisdom of digging here in the first place. But you persist. And keep digging.

And digging.

Until finally you discover something: 'Eureka!'

This is usually the point where you start writing. The problem is that now you are up to your knees in mud, completely exhausted, and depending on how deep you have dug, very far away from everyone else. Finding the treasure is only half the job: now you have to climb out of your hole and manage to communicate to others what you have found.

This is what has been called 'the curse of knowledge': the more you know about something, the harder it is to explain to someone else because you are no longer able to imagine what it is like to not know what you know. You don't even know where to start explaining. If you ask someone at the beginning of their journey what they are writing about, they will happily explain at great length; if you ask them towards the end, they will just stare at you with tortured, glazed-over eyes and say, 'Stuff, lots of stuff, can't really explain … go away'.

The knowledge curse also makes it close to impossible to see the difference between what is in your head and what is on paper. You can look at something you've written that is hopelessly convoluted and still think, 'Yes, that is exactly what I wanted to say' because you already know what you want to say. Those words on the paper are not communicating an idea to you; they are simply reminding you of what you already know. Getting the words on paper to say exactly what you have in your head is a tremendous struggle. Writing in your native language, by the way, does not necessarily make this any easier. Native speakers may make fewer grammatical mistakes, but still they seldom end up saying what they think they are saying. They are just able to make no sense more fluently than non-native speakers.

To tell a story you need to know it well enough to tell it in a way that will reach the readers you want to reach. This chapter shows you how to do that. It describes the logic of academic argument and connects it to the basic elements of structure in a thesis. Chapters 8–12 take a more detailed look at these basic elements of structure and what you need to be thinking about when you write.

ⓐ THE HEART OF YOUR STORY: CORE ARGUMENT

The essence of all academic writing, and what should be the core of your thesis, is an academic argument – you ask a question and then answer it. Or, to put it more accurately: grounded in an ongoing academic discourse, you ask one or more pertinent questions, and then answer each question using reasons and evidence you have meticulously collected and analysed using critical thinking (see Figure 7.1).

Your core argument comprises the question you ask, the answer you give, and the support you provide to back up your answer. This core argument provides the narrative backbone for your entire thesis, and represents the highlights of the story you want to tell.

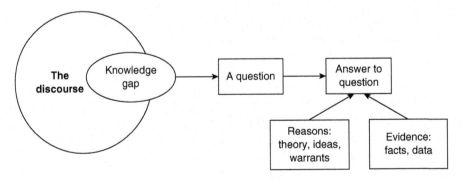

Figure 7.1 The big picture of academic writing: When you write academically, you ask a question based on a gap you have identified in the discourse, and then answer that question based on reasons and evidence you have compiled through your research.

94

ⓘ The question you ask

When you get to the writing of your thesis, as opposed to the planning of your research, it's time to take another hard look at your research question. The job of the research question in the written product is to tell the reader what you are trying to do. Because the research and writing processes often change your focus in unanticipated ways, it is very easy to end up with a question that reflects what you *thought* you would be doing when you first started your research rather than what you have actually done. Many students feel that they cannot change that original question because it was the question they got approved in their project proposal. But instead of thinking of your research question as a commitment you made to your supervisor at the beginning of your research journey, it helps to think about it as a promise that you are making to your reader now that you've reached the end of your journey – and are now ready to guide the reader on theirs. It is almost like a contract: 'If you read this thesis, I promise you I will answer this question'.

Because you are guiding the reader's journey, the question shapes the reader's expectations about what the reading journey will entail. If you ask a question about one thing, you should not be answering a question about another thing. The question you ask has to be intimately related to the answer you give. For example, if you ask a question about the impact of climate change on the tourist industry, that's what the reader will be expecting you to say something about. If you proceed to answer the question by claiming that national climate policy seldom takes into account the needs of local industries, your reader is likely to think, 'Well, that's all very interesting, but what has that got to do with the issue of how climate change affects the tourist industry?' If you rephrase the question to ask how the impact of climate change on local industries is reflected in national climate policies – with tourism as a particular case – your reader will be less confused.

The more your research has changed focus since the beginning, the more important it is to rethink the question. If you are using a fixed research design, the question you end up answering should be very similar to the one you started out asking; the logic of a deductive approach requires that you do most of your thinking about your question and your specific hypotheses very early in the process, probably before you get approval on your project. But if you are using a more flexible design, the question usually starts off as rather broad and then gets narrowed down and refocused as you continue to read the literature and analyse your material. The end result can be that the question you end up with bears only a passing resemblance to the one you started out with.

ⓘ The answer you give

Rephrasing the question in the final drafts of your thesis cannot be done without taking a hard look at what you are trying to argue – taking a step back from your work, asking yourself what claims you are trying to make, and what you are actually able to demonstrate through the analysis you have carried out. Ask yourself: What is it I'm really trying to say? Am I trying to say that the tourist industry is particularly vulnerable to climate change but has not done anything to prepare for long-term changes? Am I trying to say that it is the responsibility of the national government to instigate policies that would better enable the industry to adapt? If you cannot figure out what you are trying to say, your reader will find it impossible.

ROBERT

The focus of my thesis shifted quite a lot over the process of the writing and research, so by the time I got to my final draft I had to look at my argument all over again. When I first started my project, I thought I was going to write about why immigrant teenagers have a greater chance of relapse, but by the end I saw that I was really writing about the role of organized religion in helping immigrant teenagers overcome addiction.

Once you do figure out what you want to say, you can revisit your question again and ask yourself, 'Does this claim I want to make work as an answer to this question? Or is it the answer to a different question?' Although it might seem illogical from a research perspective to work backwards from your claim to your question, it makes perfect sense from a writing perspective. By the time you finish analysing your material and arrive at a claim you want to make, you have taken tremendous steps forward in your thinking from where you were when you originally asked your question. When you go back and rephrase your question, you are simply acknowledging this and adjusting the questions accordingly to shape your reader's expectations.

(iii) The support you provide

Because academic writing requires that you back up your claim with something more substantial than 'because I say so', you will have to provide some support for whatever claims you make, either through evidence (facts or data) or reasons (theory, ideas, concepts, or warrants), or a combination of the two (Booth et al. 2008; Toulmin 2003). The type of support you can provide is closely connected to the methods you have used. Empirically oriented research (both qualitative and quantitative) relies more heavily on evidence than research that is more theoretical or philosophical in nature, but nearly all forms of research need some combination of evidence and reasons to make sense. Even purely philosophical arguments draw from concrete examples to illustrate various points being made.

KEIKO

I wanted to say something about how teachers in Japan focus mainly on success in exams rather than helping students learn communication in the classroom, but I only looked at four informants so I couldn't generalize. Instead, I focused on describing in depth how these tensions were felt by the individual teachers and how their challenges and coping strategies could be seen in the classroom. I supported this by referring to both what was said in the interviews and focus groups, as well as what I observed in the video data.

What is important here is the connection between the claims you are making and what you are using to support these claims. For example, if you want to claim that women are more prone to perfectionism than men, but you have only collected data on women, the data you have will not be able to support your claim – no matter how much you think your claim makes intuitive sense. If you are working quantitatively, then the support for your claims will be found in the statistical analysis you carry out. If you are working qualitatively, you will find support for your claims in the interviews you conducted or the documents you have analysed. If you are working more theoretically or philosophically, then the support for your claims will lie in the logic you have used to build up your argument. No matter what your approach, the claim you make has to be tied directly to the research you have carried out.

ⓑ THE LOGICAL FLOW OF ACADEMIC STORYTELLING

The narrative logic that guides the presentation of your argument goes like this: you begin by introducing the reader to the conversation you want to participate in (see Figure 7.1). You give the reader enough background about this conversation that they understand not just what the conversation is about, but where the knowledge gaps are – that is, what is disputed or unknown (see textbox 'The vocabulary of argument'). When you have made it clear what the puzzle is – what is problematic and why this is important – readers are ready to hear where you come in. They want to understand what your research question is and the approach you will be taking to answer it. When they have a good idea what kind of research you are doing, they are then ready to hear what you have found, and what you think your findings mean. In other words, you draw a picture of a puzzle, ask a question that will help fill in some of the missing parts, and answer that question on the basis of what you have found in your study.

··

The vocabulary of argument

Different traditions of academic writing have developed slightly different vocabularies to describe the basic elements of an argument. Here are some of the terms you might encounter:

Knowledge gap: A knowledge gap describes what is not yet known about a given phenomenon. This includes what has been researched but is still in dispute because findings are unclear or inconsistent.

Problem statement: The problem statement is a sentence that identifies the problem you intend to address in your thesis. It sometimes functions as an overarching research question.

(Continued)

(Continued)

Purpose statement: While a problem statement identifies the problem you are trying to solve, the purpose statement identifies what your research aims to achieve. It states the overarching purpose of the research (Cresswell 2003: 88), which may be the same as the overarching research question, but may also be slightly different. For example, the question might focus on how those with English as an additional language approach learning in higher education, but the overarching purpose might be to improve their learning experience.

Research question: In some contexts, including this book, the research question represents the question you are attempting to answer in your thesis. In addition to one or more main questions, you might also have sub-questions that break down the main questions into smaller parts. In other contexts, the research question is specifically the operationalized version of the question(s) you are asking.

Hypothesis: If you are working deductively, with the intent of testing a particular theory, you might start with an overarching research question, but then develop a series of hypotheses, which are specific statements that will be tested in the thesis.

Thesis statement: The thesis statement can be seen as the main claim you are making. If you start with a research question, the thesis statement provides your answer to that question. If you are using hypotheses, the thesis statement would be your claim about the extent to which the theory was supported. The thesis statement usually contains a 'because' element that makes explicit the grounds on which the claim is based, for instance, 'Women produce fewer publications than men because academia is a gendered social practice where women dispro-portionately carry out activities that are not captured in productivity indicators'.

....

This basic narrative will, of course, have to be broken up into chapters, sections, and sub-sections. A Master's thesis is commonly broken up into the following five chapters:

- Introduction
- Literature review
- Methodology and methods
- Findings
- Conclusions

Some university departments have more specific expectations for how a thesis should be organized, based on the type of research normally carried out in that particular setting. A discipline or field of study that relies heavily on fieldwork carried out in different geographical locations might expect a thesis that is organized as follows:

- Introduction
- Literature review and theory
- Background on area of the world studied
- Methodology and methods
- Results and discussion
- Conclusion

If your department has rigid expectations for how you should organize your thesis into chapters, then it is probably a good idea to comply with them. But many departments have no such expectations, or they have guidelines that are presented as 'suggested' or 'recommended' rather than 'required'. If your department allows any degree of flexibility, then you need to think about how to organize your thesis on the basis of the research you have carried out and the story you want to tell.

Before you start from scratch and invent entirely new sections that no one is familiar with, it helps to take a closer look at the conventional sections to understand their deeper rhetorical functions.

(i) Introduction

The introduction sets the stage for the reader so they can figure out what you will be talking about, why it should be talked about, and how you fit into the discussion. This is where you describe your topic and explain why it is important. Sometimes you might ground this presentation in a 'real-world' context – such as 'University administrators are aware that they need to accommodate the needs of international students, but are not always aware of what these needs are'. Other times you might want to go directly to the academic discourse – such as 'The integration of international students in UK universities has generated a tremendous amount of research on challenges related to massification and internationalization'. And sometimes you might be able to provide all the necessary background in your introduction, but with some topics or methods it might be a good idea to have a separate chapter to explore the contextual setting of your study more deeply. The introduction should culminate in presenting your research question and showing the reader your strategy for organizing the rest of your dissertation. The way you can go about positioning yourself in the discourse is discussed in more detail in Chapter 8.

(ii) Literature review

The literature review explores more deeply the conversation you want to take part in, as well as the ideas you will be using to structure your thinking. You will be expected to discuss what has already been researched and how that existing research will shape what you are doing in your work. This applies not only to the topic of your thesis, but also to the theoretical ideas (concepts, mechanisms and normative assumptions) you will be using to help make sense of your material. When you publish your research in an academic journal, the literature review is often integrated into the introduction. But as a Master's student, part of what you need to demonstrate to your examiners is your understanding of the ongoing discourse, which means that part of your thesis must be explicitly dedicated to looking critically at the existing literature. Your examiners want to see not only that you understand that other research has been done, but that you can see both the contributions and the limitations of that research in the context of your study.

The same is true for theory: they want to see that you know not only what kind of relevant theory is out there, but also how it relates to the work you are doing. The question for you is whether it makes sense to address previous research and the theory you will be using in the same section of your thesis, or whether you should cover them in different sections. Sometimes it is enough to provide a list of definitions of key theoretical concepts in your introduction and use the literature review to focus on previous research. Other times it will make sense to distinguish between the research on your topic and the theory that you will be actively using in your research by having both a 'literature review' chapter and a 'theoretical framework' chapter. The literature review on your topic is discussed in more detail in Chapter 8, while your discussion of theory is the subject of Chapter 9.

 ROBERT

I ended up having separate literature review and theoretical framework chapters because they covered two very different discussions. The literature review covered the empirical literature on addiction, special challenges for immigrants, special challenges for teenagers, and the importance of social structures. The theoretical framework looked at the more abstract ideas of addiction being a social illness, the importance of belonging, and transnational identity.

ⓘⓘ Methodology and method

The methodology and method section tells the reader how you went about answering your question. What kinds of data did you gather? From what kinds of sources? How did you gather it? What was the underlying logic behind what you did and how you did it? This gives readers an indication of how you intend to back up the claim(s) you will be making because you explain what will constitute reasons and evidence in the context of your work. Some of this logic will be based on theoretical notions about the world, the things in it, and how we gain knowledge about those things. It might make more sense to discuss theoretical ideas about methodology in your method chapter than in the literature review. If you are doing non-empirical work – that is, if your thesis is more theoretical in nature – you will not have a method section in a traditional sense. Instead, the way you go about answering your question will be described either in your introduction or in a chapter called 'Analytical framework' or 'Theoretical framework' (see Chapter 9). The kinds of things that are normally talked about in a methodology and methods chapter are discussed in more detail in Chapter 10.

 EMMA

Because I didn't do an empirical study, I didn't have a traditional method section, but I had an analytical framework that described how I intended to go about interrogating the theoretical literature. My final structure looked something like this:

1   Introduction
    a   Crime statistics and gender differences
    b   Research question

2   Analytical framework
    a   The nature of gender
    b   Understanding gender, gender difference, and otherness

3   Gender as performativity
4   The masculinity of crime
5   Heteronormative discourse and the punishment for 'otherness'
6   Conclusion
    a   Main argument
    b   Implications for future research
    c   Implications for practice

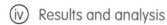 Results and analysis

A large portion of your thesis should be devoted to explaining what it is you found and what you think it means. What did your informants tell you? What were the results of your survey? What did you see when you examined the documents? How do you make sense of this? The results will provide the evidence for the claim(s) you are making. If you work quantitatively, you will probably present the results separately from the discussion, which is where you tell the reader what you think those results are telling you in relation to the question you are asking. Most qualitative and theoretical work, however, will combine the results and discussion sections. Chapter 11 discusses how you can present your results and analysis in more depth.

(v) Discussion and conclusions

Obviously you will want to end your thesis with some final remarks that wrap up everything you have been talking about and put your argument as concisely as possible. You may also want to explore the implications of your findings – perhaps for policy or practice, or for future research. One of the big questions you will face is what to discuss in your 'discussion' and what to leave for your conclusion. This will vary considerably from context to context. Chapter 12 looks at the discussion and conclusion in more detail.

You may need also to talk about other things that don't fit quite comfortably into sections called 'Introduction', 'Literature Review', 'Methods', 'Results', or 'Conclusion', or that seem to fit into more than one. Depending on the kind of research you are doing and the expectations of your department, you will probably need to address at least one of the following:

- **Ethics:** Social sciences study the world we live in and the people in it. It is very difficult to do research on people without somehow touching their lives. As a result, you will most likely be asked to reflect on how you thought through the ethics of your approach, and perhaps provide evidence of formal ethical approval. See Chapter 3 for a discussion of some of the things you should reflect on. Some students might discuss ethics in their introduction, others in their method sections. Still others might have an entire chapter devoted solely to this subject.

- **Reflection and reflexivity:** Some fields and approaches require you to become more personally involved in your research than others. Certainly, if you are carrying out insider research on your place of employment you will be asked to reflect on your positionality, both in the sense of your epistemological beliefs and in the sense of how the position you hold as a researcher might affect the kinds of responses you received from your informants. 'Reflection' means to think deeply about events and what they might mean, while 'reflexivity' means to think critically about your own role (see Bolton 2014). Even if you do not have such close contact with your informants, you might be asked to reflect on the impact your research has had on you as a researcher or a professional. Some students might discuss their positionality in the introduction, others in their method section, while some might devote a separate section to reflecting on how their role in the study might have influenced their access to participants, how their participants interacted with them, or how they interpreted their results.

 AMINA

I used the basic five-chapter model to structure my thesis, and it ended up looking like this:

1 Introduction: Access to maternal health in post-conflict zones
   a Why this is a problem
   b The case of the DRC and the South Kivu region
   c Overarching research question

2 Literature review and hypotheses
   a The role of poverty
   b The role of infrastructure
   c The role of insecurity related to conflict

3 Method
   a Variables
   b Description of questionnaire
      i Questions asked
      ii Informants
   c Coding procedures
   d Limitations
   e Ethics

4   Analysis and findings
    a   Descriptive statistics
    b   Regression analysis

5   Discussion and conclusion
    a   What the findings mean with respect to the research question
    b   Implications for future research
    c   Implications for practice

The actual way you tell your story, the way in which you decide to divide up these elements, depends very much on what makes your story special and what your audience is expecting to hear you talk about. You might find yourself having to compromise between telling your story exactly as you would like it to be told and telling it in a way that makes your listeners comfortable. For this reason, it is a good idea to do a little more research into what your audience will be expecting.

(c) RULES AND CONVENTIONS: NAVIGATING EXPECTATIONS

What your department will expect from you depends on where you are. All universities have particular rules related to format: page limits, how wide the margins should be, what sort of paper it should be printed on, the kind of binding you should use, and so on. These are usually quite rigid. If you submit your thesis as a pile of paper with a rubber band around it when you are required to get it bound at one of two local copy centres that carry a customized template for the cover, it may be rejected. There is zero point in fighting this kind of battle. Generally speaking, the more localized the rule, the less likely you can bend it. So it's in your best interest to follow rules that are particular to your specific department in your specific university.

Your most difficult challenge will probably be figuring out what these rules are. Because these rules are so ingrained in the specific department, it is easy for the staff to assume you should know what they are and where to find them: 'How could you not know that we require you to use 14-point Comic Sans typeface? We stated it very clearly on a slip of paper in the information pack you got when you first arrived at this university'. Sometimes it's not just the rules that are unclear; it's also not clear who you should ask for more information. This is when a network of peers can come in handy. It may well be the case that no one person knows everything, but within the group at least one person usually knows the answer to your question – or at least knows who you should ask.

You might find that some of the 'rules' aren't really rules at all, but rather conventions. Although the guidelines might describe in great detail how you should submit your paper copy, there might not actually be any rule against submitting something digitally as well (or even instead). Likewise, the five-chapter thesis structure might be recommended but not required. You shouldn't take for granted even what language you might be expected to write your thesis in (see Chapter 1), or what kind of voice you should be using.

Because conventions are rarely described explicitly, you have to learn them through observation. How do other people do things? And not just any other people – how have other people in your position done these things? Get hold of some highly regarded completed theses from your department. Look at as many as you can. If you look at just one, you might think of that one as a model you have to copy – which may be very constricting. The more examples you look at, the better sense you get of the range of possibilities. Even a glimpse at the way different candidates have handled their tables of contents will give you an idea of how similar or different each thesis is, and thus also an idea of how much freedom you have. Examining the work of other candidates can also be inspiring, even if they are writing on a completely different topic: 'Oh, look at the way she managed to integrate her discussion of theory into her methodology section. Maybe I should do that' or 'Hey, that's a smart way to present the findings. I wonder if that kind of structure would work for my findings as well?', or even 'This introduction seems way too long. I think I will divide mine up into more sections to make it easier on the reader'.

SAMIR

I couldn't decide whether I should present each village in a separate chapter, or whether I should discuss the main themes (the challenges and opportunities presented by Corporate Social Responsibility) in their own chapters (and combine the findings from the two cases). But seeing how other people organized their multi-site case studies gave me ideas about what would work best for me.

Learn about the rules and conventions as far ahead of time as possible so you can think through your options. There is a big difference between intentionally challenging a convention (or even breaking a rule) and being prepared to defend your choice, and doing so unintentionally because you didn't know better. There is no question that there is a certain risk associated with submitting a thesis that is technically not against the rules but defies convention – such as a multimodal or interdisciplinary thesis. You might be judged more harshly simply because the examiners are unfamiliar with the unconventional genre. If what matters most to you is to finish on time and move on with your life, then an unconventional choice might not be in your best interest. But if what matters to you most is to create something that is uniquely yours, something that represents what you have to say in the way you want to say it, then taking the extra time and effort required to do something unconventional might be worth the risk.

Chapters 8–12 in this Part describe in more detail the key rhetorical moves you need to make to tell your story: positioning yourself in the discourse, explaining how your ideas fit in with other people's ideas, explaining how you approached answering your question, explaining how you analysed what you found, and presenting your conclusions. The final structure you adopt should be tailored to your particular needs, but these rhetorical moves are essential regardless of how you finally end up organizing your work.

'Only the crystal-clear question yields a transparent answer.'

Your question and answer work together and form the backbone of your structure. If your question is unclear, it will be difficult to answer, and the structure of your argument will also be unclear. Although it makes intuitive sense to first have a question, then have an answer, and use those to develop the structure of your narrative, you will often find that in developing and structuring your narrative, your argument becomes clearer, and your question sharper – at least in your mind. Your work as a writer means revisiting that question and clarifying it yet again for the reader so your answer is as transparent as possible.

Finding your path: Points for reflection

What is your overarching argument?
- What is the topic you want to say something about?
- What is it you want to say about this topic?
- What kind of evidence or reasons will you use to back up this claim?

How will you support this argument through the structure of your thesis?
- Does your department have guidelines for how to organize your thesis? How rigid are they?
- If you have some flexibility, what kind of chapters do you think you need?
- How do each of these chapters play a role in supporting the argument you want to make?

REFERENCES AND FURTHER READING

Bolton, Gillie (2014) *Reflective Practice: Writing and Professional Development*, 4th edn. London: Sage. While not directly focused on research, Bolton explores various ways to think reflectively and reflexively about your own role. This should be particularly helpful for students who are new to thinking reflexively.

Booth, Wayne C., Colomb, Gregory G., and Williams, Joseph M. (2008) *The Craft of Research*, 3rd edn. Chicago, IL: University of Chicago Press. The book provides a good discussion about the difference between 'reasons' and 'evidence' and how to support a claim.

Cresswell, John W. (2003) *Research Design: Qualitative, Quantitative, and Mixed Methods Approaches*, 2nd edn. Thousand Oaks, CA: Sage. Cresswell's perspective shows how different approaches to inquiry lead to different types of argumentation.

Hennink, Monique, Hulter, Inge, and Bailey, Ajay (2011) *Qualitative Research Methods*. London: Sage. Chapter 11, 'Writing qualitative research', provides an excellent overview of how to present qualitative research, particularly emphasizing the circular nature of the thinking and writing process.

Robson, Colin (2011) *Real World Research*, 3rd edn. West Sussex: John Wiley and Sons. In Chapter 18, Robson discusses some of the differences between reporting on flexible design studies and fixed design studies.

Thody, Angela M. (2006) *Writing and Presenting Research*. London: Sage. This book provides an excellent demonstration of how to build arguments using different types of data derived from different kinds of research designs.

Toulmin, Stephen E. (2003) *The Uses of Argument*, updated edn. Cambridge: Cambridge University Press. Toulmin presents the classic philosophical reasoning behind how academic arguments are built up and supported through facts and evidence, on the one hand, and warrants and ideas on the other.

8

YOUR INTRODUCTION

How do you fit into the conversation?

a Making assumptions about your reader

b Providing background on the topic and setting

c Summing up the academic conversation: Literature review

d Who are you in this conversation?

e Dealing with hostile audiences

f Shifting from listener to speaker: Joining the conversation

Like any other conversation, academic conversation flows best if what you are saying builds on, or at least acknowledges, what others have been saying. This means you neither repeat what everyone else has said without adding anything yourself, nor do you ignore what everyone else has said and just plough ahead, oblivious to everyone else in the room. What you are trying to say gains meaning by placing your point in the context of a larger conversation. This is true regardless of whether you are writing a term paper, a thesis, a dissertation, or a journal article. For the reader, sometimes what you say may not seem interesting or meaningful at all unless you place it in contrast to what else has been said.

This means that for your examiners to really appreciate the point you are trying to make in your thesis, you need to orient them to how you understand the nature of the ongoing conversation. Although it is commonly believed that academic writing should get right to the point, for the reader getting 'right to the point' may feel like walking into the middle of someone else's conversation: it's hard to figure out what's going on, and even though you understand the words, you don't understand their significance. That only becomes clear when you understand the context. And in academic writing, context is very much about the ongoing academic discourse. Despite occasional evidence to the contrary, explaining what other people have said before you is not primarily about referencing the right people; it is about engaging with the other people in the conversation, whether you are agreeing with them, disagreeing with them, or doing some of both.

The purpose of your introduction is to engage your reader in the topic by giving them enough information about the context of your study that they are convinced that you have a relevant point to make. This is why the introduction – whether it is your Master's thesis or any other genre in academic writing – is so difficult to write. Before you can get to the familiar comfort zone of your own research, you have to reach out to the reader: based on your assumptions about what they know from before and what they might be sceptical of, you need to draw them a picture of the conversation in which your research is taking place and how your work fits into this conversation. Identifying the conversation and placing yourself within it are key rhetorical moves that take place in the introduction, but they may not take place *only* in the introduction. The purpose of this chapter is to discuss how you can accomplish these moves depending on what you need to say and what your audience needs to hear.

(a) MAKING ASSUMPTIONS ABOUT YOUR READER

Reaching out to your reader and tailoring what you write to what they need to know means making some important assumptions about who your audience is. The most important audience for your thesis is not your supervisor, but rather the examiners who will ultimately determine whether or not you have produced a piece of work that is satisfactory for the Master's level. The question for you to consider is who these examiners might be: What discipline(s) do they represent? How much are they likely to know about your topic and the ongoing conversation around it? What are they likely to accept easily, and what will you have to work harder to justify? In other words, how expert and how friendly are they likely to be?

A knowledgeable or expert audience is one that knows a lot about your topic, in contrast to a general audience who knows very little. A friendly audience is one that shares your assumptions about how the world works (what kinds of methods are valid, what theories are relevant, and what subject matter is worth talking about), whereas a hostile audience is sceptical about what you are doing, or how you are doing it. Remember that 'expert' and 'friendly' are relative to the actual topic of the conversation; if you change your focus, you will have to re-examine your assumptions about your audience.

Say you are writing about how the tourist industry in the Maldives will be able to adapt to the impacts of climate change. Maybe your audience knows a lot about the tourist industry in general, but little about adaptation to climate change. Or maybe it's the other way around: they know a lot about climate-change adaptation but little about the tourist industry. Maybe they know a lot about the Maldives; maybe they know almost nothing. Maybe they are sceptical about the whole idea of climate change, or maybe as quantitative researchers they think that your approach of 'hanging out' with a few local hotel owners to talk about their perceptions of their business was a flimsy excuse for getting academic credit for your vacation.

The better you know your audience, the easier it is to decide how much to explain each of these elements and what angle to take. It is always smartest to start with the area the audience knows best: if you are aiming primarily at climate researchers, talk about climate change first – and then bring in the tourist industry. If you are talking to experts in the tourist industry, then start with that. If you are, for example, based in a department that emphasizes geographical location, then maybe you should start by making clear you are grounding your discussion in a small island state in the Indian Ocean. The assumptions you make about your audience, how much they know and how friendly they are to your approach, can then help you tailor the way you present background on your topic and the ongoing discourse(s).

ⓑ PROVIDING BACKGROUND ON THE TOPIC AND SETTING

Even if you do have a pretty good idea of who your audience is and what they know, it's not always easy to know how much to explain about your study site (for example, the organization you studied or geographical location where you carried out your research), relevant past events, and so on. Say you are writing about innovations in local healthcare provision in Iceland, but you are submitting your thesis to a university in the UK; you can probably assume that your examiners know little about Iceland, but more about local healthcare provision – particularly in the UK. So you need to provide some background on Iceland, and the temptation to write everything you know about Iceland will be almost overwhelming. Resist. Think about what your readers *need* to know about Iceland in order to understand the points you will be making in your research. If a low population density and mountainous terrain make it difficult to provide localized healthcare, then the topography and geographical features of Iceland will be relevant information, although it might be unnecessary to speak in glowing terms about hot springs and northern lights. Will readers need to know about religion, governance, or currency? It seems unlikely, but if any of these things at some point enters into your argument, then you will have to explain it.

When you move on to explaining the specific healthcare system in Iceland, again you will have to restrain yourself from writing everything you know. Instead, think carefully about the questions you are asking about that healthcare system. You probably know everything, down to the size of the cotton swabs they use, but not all of this will be important. Is your question about challenges related to an aging population? Then you need to focus particularly on the healthcare needs of the elderly and the extent to which the current system is designed to accommodate those needs. Is your question about how healthcare providers incorporate alternative and natural medicine approaches? Then you need to focus on that. And regardless of your particular focus, you can use the UK as a point of reference if you can assume that your examiners share it. For example, you can say 'In contrast to doctors in the UK, who are expected to treat xx patients annually, doctors in Iceland see only yy, but these patients are spread over a larger geographical area'.

Once you decide what kind of background is relevant for your question and important for your audience to know, you can decide whether a few paragraphs in your introduction will be enough, or whether you need to present the context for your research in richer detail in a dedicated chapter, or whether you want to spread it around, presenting relevant informa-tion as you move closer to your findings – or maybe a combination of all three. There is no rule about this, but there might be some local conventions in your setting. Clearly it is important to provide some background at the outset. Readers need to know from the begin-ning why you have picked Iceland as a study site, and what makes it similar to or different from other cases they might be familiar with. Keep in mind, though, that it might be hard for your reader to remember or appreciate the significance of things that you briefly present in your introduction if they are not mentioned again until much later in the analysis. For example, if you mention in your introduction the difference in daylight hours between summer and winter, the reader might wonder, 'Why are you telling me this?' It only becomes relevant later when you talk about the incidence of seasonal depression. Rather than expect your reader to remember what you said about daylight hours 50 pages ago, you might want to bring it up again. And then you might ask yourself whether you need to have that information in two different places.

AMINA

My discipline is political science, not health sciences. Even though my question was about access to maternal healthcare, my focus was more on how conflict makes that difficult, not about the healthcare in itself. So I had to make sure I didn't over-explain the health dimensions, but instead focus on the issues related to conflict. I had to give some background as well about the conflict in the DRC, and particularly in the South Kivu region where I did my fieldwork. I decided to cover the background on the DRC conflict in the introduction, but I discussed the existing research that covers the impact of conflict more generally in a separate chapter that also developed the hypotheses.

It does not hurt to write a fairly detailed background section early on in your writing process – as long as you are willing to ruthlessly cut it down and move sections of it around later. An outside opinion about what information seems unnecessary and what seems miss-ing will be invaluable. Supervisors can certainly play this role at an early stage, but at some point they will become too familiar with your work. As you get closer to a final draft, it will be helpful to have a new person – perhaps a peer – read through the background section and let you know if it seems like either too much or too little.

ⓒ SUMMING UP THE ACADEMIC CONVERSATION: LITERATURE REVIEW

In addition to background on the topic, the introduction of your thesis is also likely to contain a review of the literature (or it may appear as a separate chapter immediately following the introduction – depending on how much you have to say, how well it integrates into the rest of the introduction, and the conventions of your department). Regardless of whether you put your literature review in the introduction or have it as a separate chapter, keep in mind that its function is to bring the reader up to speed on how the discourse on your topic has developed to show that the question you are asking is relevant. When you are writing a thesis, connecting your topic to an *academic* discourse is essential. If your topic has been discussed in the media, among policy makers, or in practice, a recap of this non-academic discussion can be included in the background. But what will make your work academic is the extent to which you are also able to link your discussion to an academic discourse. The literature review identifies for the reader exactly which academic conversation you want to be part of. The difference between background and the literature review is comparable to the difference between reporting the scores of a football game and providing expert commentary. While the background normally focuses on the relevant facts that are important for the reader to know, the literature review tells the reader how the topic is being discussed by an academic audience.

No matter what your organizational strategy, what you don't want to do is treat the literature review like a report on everything you read last summer – or a list of all the books you think your supervisor or examiners will be impressed by, or a presentation of all the required reading for the coursework. Nor should it be a printout of all the hits that came up when you entered your more or less relevant search terms. A literature review should be a critical look at what has already been done before in the fields that are relevant to your study, and it should be linked to the discipline in which you are based.

 SAMIR

Because I'm doing an industry-based study, I was thinking that my audience was the company that hired me and the conversation was basically about the feasibility of expanding services to remote villages. But then my supervisor reminded me that the thesis was supposed to speak to a larger academic discussion, so I framed it more generally as a dilemma about doing business in a post-colonial era, where, on one hand, the business concept has to be sound, but, on the other hand, the company does not want to be exploitative.

Showing the contours of the research frontier, and marking the lines between what we know and what we don't know, should set the stage for your research question, while communicating to the reader how you understand the field of inquiry. At the very least, the literature review is your way of bringing the reader up to speed on what has been happening in the academic discourse so that they will be able to understand your point. Remember that academic discourse is like a long, rambling conversation with a lot of people shouting all at once, but nevertheless with some sort of communication taking place and progress being made. But an academic conversation differs from a real-life conversation in two main ways: (1) the length of time between each contribution; and (2) the ability of people who are not talking directly to each other to take part in the same conversation.

In real life when one person says 'A', another person says 'B', and you say, 'Well, sometimes A and sometimes B', we are able to follow the conversation because we are right there watching the conversation develop. In an academic conversation, however, one person says 'A' and then, five years later, the second person says 'B', and then three years after that you start thinking, 'Hmm, sometimes A, sometimes B'. For us to understand your point, we need a recap, somewhat like the short voiceover at the beginning of your favourite TV series that says 'in previous episodes of *The Secret Life of Bob the Frog ...*', and then you are treated to very short snippets of key scenes that trigger your memory of episodes past: 'Oh, that's right. I forgot about that. That was last season, wasn't it? Whoa! What happened there? I don't think I saw that part, but it's clear that Bob had a serious falling out with Jennifer. And it looks like this episode might tell us what happened after JoJo escaped from prison'.

But it is not only the elapsed time that makes a recap necessary. In an academic discussion you weave together contributions from authors who may not even have been participating in the same discussion: the person saying 'A' might have been an anthropologist talking to other anthropologists, whereas the person saying 'B' might be a political scientist talking to other political scientists, but you find that these two threads of conversation have something to say to each other. In other words, you are reconstructing a conversation that never actually took place. It's like you are putting together snippets from several different TV series that nevertheless tell a coherent story.

By weaving together these conversational threads, your literature review gives readers a sense of what is already out there. But more than that, the literature review should also suggest what is NOT out there so we understand why what you are doing is important. In the words of Swales (1990), you create a research space for yourself by showing us the limitations of what has been done before. Here, it is useful to point out the distinction between criticizing and critical thinking. Criticizing means saying things like 'Smith was completely off base. He should have done his study in a completely different way'. Critical thinking (see also Chapter 2) means asking yourself, How do I know whether what Smith says is true or not? What kind of evidence has he presented? Is it sufficient? Can it be interpreted in another way? Is the claim equally true in a different context? How does his claim relate to the subject I'm writing about? Does it raise questions about claims other people have made? What has Smith contributed to this conversation that I can build on? (See Figure 8.1.)

Remember that no single work will be able to answer all questions. So your goal isn't necessarily to find fault with existing research, but rather to paint a picture of a larger puzzle where previous research has contributed some pieces, but other pieces are missing, leaving gaps in our knowledge. The most important thing here is to convey the sense of a conversation that is not yet finished: as readers, we need to understand what has been talked about so far, and why we need to continue talking. For example, say you are doing a study that looks at how autistic children learn a second language. Many of the studies you refer to are likely to focus either on second language acquisition in children, without considering the complication of autism, or on language acquisition for children with autism, without considering the issue of a second language. These are not failures on the part of the studies in question, because they were never intended to combine all of these aspects. The fact that

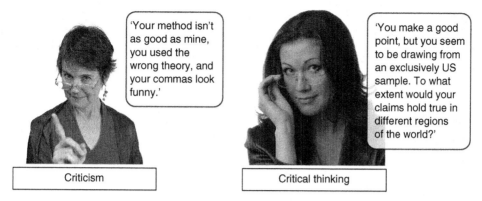

Figure 8.1 Criticizing vs critical thinking: When you are reviewing the literature, keep in mind that your job is to look critically at the literature rather than to criticize it. Finding a knowledge gap does not mean looking for mistakes, but rather exploring the questions raised by what others have done (or not done).

they shed light on only part of the picture does not make them irrelevant, it just means that you have to weave together their findings with findings that shed light on different parts of the picture. Thus you could well accept findings from the studies on second-language acquisition, but question the extent to which the same could be assumed for autistic children; likewise, you could accept the findings from studies on language acquisition for autistic children and question whether they would be true for acquiring a second language.

In thinking about the literature you will present in your review, it is helpful to remember that your examiners will be looking at the extent to which your thesis is solidly based in your discipline. This means that if you have done a lot of reading outside your discipline, you will have to make an effort to tie it to the discussion that takes place within the core literature in your discipline. Likewise, your examiners will want to see a convincing mixture of classics and recent research. There is no magic formula for the perfect balance in this respect: Each literature review is unique, and its sole purpose is to engage your particular audience with the academic context of your particular research. A different audience or a different research question will demand a different literature review.

The final version of your literature review might reflect only a fraction of what you have actually read, which can be very frustrating. As a student, you might want your supervisor and examiners to know just how much effort you've put in by showing them all the sources you have at least glanced at, but part of the challenge of writing a good literature review is being selective about the literature you discuss. A good literature review shows the development of ideas in the field, pinpoints areas of uncertainty, and draws our focus to points of contention. You can organize it in any number of ways: you can show a chronological development of an idea; you can point to different fault lines where the literature disagrees; you can pick apart the key elements of your research question and provide a summary of what is known about each one. No matter how you arrange your literature review, however, the important point is that when it is finished, the reader should be completely convinced that you are on to something and want to find out the answer to your question.

And unfortunately, it is difficult to know beforehand which literature will turn out to be the most relevant and which principle of organization the most meaningful. It is common to write the literature review towards the beginning of the research process, but as you continue your research you will also continue to read, and your research might take some unexpected twists and turns. This means that the literature review will have to change as well. Even if you have essentially stayed on the same path throughout the entire process, it might be a good idea to re-evaluate your literature review once you have completed a draft of your entire thesis to see whether it effectively sets the stage for the discussion of your own research.

d WHO ARE YOU IN THIS CONVERSATION?

The way you talk about the conversation you want to be a part of tells the reader a lot about who you are: your authority as an expert, who you align yourself with theoretically, and how you see the world methodologically. In rhetorical terms, you communicate your *ethos*. And depending on your context, your ethos – the authority you use to help persuade your reader of your expertise – can vary substantially. For example, if you are writing about social programmes that help individuals overcome drug addiction, you will have a different ethos if you present yourself as a former addict, or as a psychologist who has specialized in addiction, or as a social worker who has worked on the streets helping addicts, or as a student whose only exposure to addiction has been through reading about it.

 ROBERT

One of the hardest things for me to do in this thesis was to make it academic and at the same time relevant for social work in real life. One way I joined the two was by starting off the introduction by describing things I had observed in my position as a social worker, and then connecting some of these observations to the academic research. In this way I showed that I knew what I was talking about on both fronts.

In some settings, 'who you are' is considered an essential part of your research, and you will be expected to reflect on your positionality explicitly. This will be particularly important if you are a mature student who is returning after many years as a professional. The ways in which your professional knowledge and academic knowledge interact will undoubtedly shape your thinking and who you are in the conversation, and if you are in a setting that allows or encourages reflecting on this (such as the field of education), explicitly addressing your unique perspective can add considerable strength to your argument. In other settings, it might (unfortunately) be seen not only as irrelevant and distracting, but also as unscientific and unprofessional.

KEIKO

I decided to discuss my own positionality in the introduction of my thesis because it shaped the focus of my research. As someone who has gone through the Japanese education system and experienced how teachers emphasize test-taking when they teach English, rather than having students practice communication, I wanted to understand more why it was done this way. And in the interpretation of the data, my Japanese background also helped me understand the nuances in communication that an outsider might not have been able to pick up.

Explicitly addressing your positionality is not the only – or even most important – way you communicate who you are to your reader. An equally powerful, albeit far more subtle, way to demonstrate your ethos is through the vocabulary you choose and the way you reference others. The vocabulary you use shows where you feel you belong. Although common sense suggests that you avoid unnecessary jargon, the careful use of technical terms that cannot be easily replaced by everyday vocabulary tells the reader that you are comfortable with the language of your field, and thus that you belong there. This is not the same thing as arming your sentences with every difficult word you come across in your reading; there is a difference between being able to pick up a sword and wield it with grace, precision, and restraint, and just stabbing desperately at everything that comes your way. And note that the way you present these terms reveals how you position yourself relative to your readers. For example, if you use the terms 'habitus' and 'schemata', you make a connection between what you are talking about and what Bourdieu has said about the way people embody and reproduce social structures. If you use these terms correctly, you place yourself firmly within classical sociology. If you define them briefly (but elegantly), you not only imply that your readers are also familiar with the terms, but you also demonstrate your own knowledge (and perhaps also by clarifying how you interpret them if they tend to be used differently by others in the field). If you describe and discuss these terms at length, comparing and contrasting them to other terms, you imply that the audience might be unfamiliar with them, or that they are associated with some hostility. But be careful. If you use terms like these incorrectly (for example as awkward synonyms for 'habits' and 'schemes'), you demonstrate that you do *not* know what you are talking about, and that sociology is not where you belong. Moreover, even if you do define them correctly (and at length), but do not at the same time show how these terms connect to your research, then you demonstrate that you are uncomfortable with the terminology and are just trying to look like you know what you are doing.

Similarly, the way you reference other authors is more than a mechanical or technical process. More than any other activity, it illustrates the conversational aspect of academic writing, and the way you talk about the other authors in this conversation says a lot about you. Remember that the reader needs a summary of the ongoing discourse so they can figure out what is going on. But if this summary consists mostly of verbatim quotes from other authors, strung together with very little input from you, you communicate to the reader that you do not really understand the ongoing conversation very well. A big part of what you need to demonstrate in a Master's thesis is that you understand the significance of what you read, and that means explaining the content in your own words and putting the literature together in a way that tells a story. Consider this fictitious example:

Smith (2008: 14) argues that 'blue frogs are semi-mythical creatures, beloved for their symbolism of the absurd and impossible'. As Hansen et al. (1987: 3) point out, 'The okopipi, or blue poison arrow frog, is indigenous to the forests located in Sipaliwini savanna in the north of Brazil'. Jones (2005: 45) says, 'Worship of blue frogs reached its pinnacle during the growth of New Age mysticism'. Bordeaux (2011: 870) writes, 'By projecting meaning onto visage, we transform and trans-create meaning in the meaningless, emote and abstract the potential of our (un)becoming'.

In this passage, the author has left the cited passages in their original forms, correctly referenced, but with no effort to explain or connect them. Even though the quote from 'Hansen et al.' comes from a different field with a different vocabulary, the author neither interprets the meaning nor explains the significance. Similarly, the obscure quote from 'Bordeaux' is left untouched, suggesting that the author has no idea what it means, but thinks it sounds profound. In an Anglo-Saxon style of writing, such minimal paraphrasing suggests that you are uncomfortable with the material. (In a less individualistic style of writing, this might simply reflect that you do not feel that you can improve upon the words of the original authors and are showing respect for their craftsmanship.) Integrating references into your own writing and voice looks more like this:

Blue-frog worship appears to have gained popularity in conjunction with the growth of New Age mysticism (Jones 2005). In the context of this thesis, it is particularly noteworthy that the areas in which blue-frog worship arose in the 1980s have no blue frogs in nature (Hansen et al. 1987). This raises the question of whether the blue frog has a symbolic meaning that does not stem from animism. Both Smith (2008) and Bordeaux (2011) suggest that this might be the case, with Smith arguing that the symbolism is related to 'the absurd and impossible', and Bordeaux connecting the symbolism to ideas of personal growth embedded in New Age mysticism.

Here, the author is acting more like a skilled facilitator – summing up the contributions, clarifying their significance, and putting them into their proper context (that is, the thesis). The author is particularly careful to simplify outside voices such as 'Hansen et al.', who come from unfamiliar disciplines, and 'Bordeaux', who is located within the social sciences but from a non-Anglo-Saxon style of writing that is likely to confuse the reader who is not familiar with his work. Demonstrating a deep understanding of the essential ideas and where they come from (which you can show by describing in your own words central ideas from core readings and interpreting them in the light of your particular topic), as well as an awareness of where the conversation stands today (which you can demonstrate by convincingly referencing newer studies), communicate to the reader that you know what you are talking about. Once the reader is persuaded that you are indeed an authority on this particular subject, then they will be more likely to accept your arguments.

ⓔ DEALING WITH HOSTILE AUDIENCES

Positioning yourself in the discourse not only means showing the reader where you stand relative to the other voices in the conversation, but also taking into account where you stand relative to your reader when you know (or strongly suspect) that your reader will be hostile towards a fundamental part of your work – for example, if you are conducting a qualitative study in a field dominated by quantitative research, or you are using key theoretical ideas that challenge the mainstream research or come from a different field. You will be better able to persuade your audience that your ideas are worth listening to if you can also express your ideas in terms that they are familiar with. In other words, you need to be able to pick up and wield the verbal sword of your opponent. If you are a qualitative researcher facing a quantitative audience, for example, you can explain the justification for your work in terms your audience will understand:

Quantitative studies have contributed considerable knowledge about the demographic composition of recruits to the Church of Croak (Brown et al. 2007; Jones and Robertson 2008; Smith et al. 2010). However, little is yet understood about why these particular groups find the church appealing. While qualitative findings should be interpreted with caution and cannot necessarily be generalized, in-depth interviews with recent recruits might shed light on individual motives that can subsequently be tested more formally.

Here, the author has demonstrated awareness of the ongoing quantitative discourse by referencing a careful selection of quantitative studies and emphasizing their overall contribution, and then has anticipated the objections to qualitative research by a quantitative audience and addressed these objections in terms that a quantitative researcher can understand. Contrast with the following:

The only research that has been done so far on the Church of Croak has been quantitative, which has resulted only in so-called statistics, but no knowledge about personal motivations. Qualitative research is the only approach that allows the researcher to understand what new recruits are thinking and why the church appeals to them.

Here, the author has made no effort to meet the audience halfway, and her ethos is clearly that of someone who is both ignorant of and hostile to the existing quantitative research. She shows this both in the lack of references to the existing research and through obvious discomfort with the terminology of quantitative research.

 **EMMA**

> Although criminology in general is influenced heavily by insights from feminist and queer theory, the specific department that I'm in is more conservative and quantitatively oriented. I made sure to start the thesis by summarizing the insights from the quantitative literature and giving due credit for its contributions. But then I pointed out some internal contradictions and raised some questions that are impossible to answer using the more common approaches. This gave me room to discuss my alternative approach.

Writing in an interdisciplinary context means constantly having to tread a bit lightly. If you have read very broadly and incorporated ideas from different disciplines and theoretical traditions, you will have to introduce these ideas carefully – not only explaining why they are useful, but also why they are necessary and cannot be replaced by similar ideas within your own discipline. This is tricky because in the social sciences there are a lot of theories and concepts that say essentially the same thing but have been developed in different disciplinary contexts; if you pick a concept that is similar to, but not the same as, a concept normally used in your field, you will have to anticipate the reaction of the evaluators: 'Why did the student not use our favourite theory?' You will need to demonstrate not only its usefulness, but also its superiority to any other ideas that you might have been expected to draw from, otherwise your audience will think that you chose that 'foreign' idea simply because you did not realize that a similar one existed already, and thus that you do not truly ground your work in the discipline. (See Chapter 9 for more on writing your theoretical framework.)

🟦 SHIFTING FROM LISTENER TO SPEAKER: JOINING THE CONVERSATION

As you move from novice to expert, your general role in the conversation shifts from one of observer, who merely tries to get the answer right, to one of participant, who makes a point and argues for its validity. Writing a Master's thesis often marks this shift towards writing for an audience that does not sit with an answer key in hand but needs to be persuaded to see the value of your contribution. Before they can see the value of your contribution, they first need to be able to identify it. Your presentation of the background and ongoing academic discussion should culminate in a clear presentation of where you come in. As described in the previous chapter, you can use one or more rhetorical devices, including presenting a problem statement, a purpose statement, or a research question, to help you do this (see textbox on 'the vocabulary of argument' in Chapter 7).

All of these devices are similar in that they are based on your presentation of the ongoing conversation and signal to the reader what it is you will be doing to add to this conversation. Which one of these devices you use, and whether you use more than one of them, depends on the conventions of your discipline, department, or methodological orientation. For most fields in the social sciences, the research question will be the most important of these devices.

For the reader, the device you choose is less important than the degree to which it makes clear what you are trying to do in your thesis. I cannot emphasize enough how important it is to make this as explicit as possible. Because you are so familiar with your own research, you will probably think that it is very obvious what you are trying to do. It might even feel awkward to write a statement that sums up your purpose or specifically states what question you are trying to answer. But for the reader, this statement is essential: it establishes their expectations for what you will be talking about. Every word counts.

If you are presenting qualitative research, it matters very much which verb you use (see Figure 10.1): explore, identify, examine, and so on. They are all different activities, and thus they suggest you have taken different actions. Likewise, it matters how you describe the phenomenon you will be exploring, identifying, or examining. The more precise you are about what you intend to look at, the easier it will be for your reader to understand your objective. For quantitative research, you need to be precise about which variables you will be looking at (particularly your dependent variable), and what your variables are supposed to be testing.

Confusion or ambiguity about your purpose rarely works in your favour. If you are not conducting an obvious experiment, or some explicit research-oriented intervention (carrying out a survey, for example), the line between background and analysis can become very blurred indeed. Say you are doing a case study that looks at how a particular company implemented a policy on improving gender balance. The background on the company can very easily blur and merge into a section on various hiring policies, the situation of gender balance, and then suddenly we come to your conclusion without knowing exactly at what point you shifted from giving general background on the company to presenting the results of your case study. From the reader's perspective, the structure of your argument seems to be 'background, background, background, literature list'. Making your research question explicit, however, makes it easier to see what is simply there to provide context and what is the actual subject of the research.

If you are not explicit, your reader will unconsciously fill in the blanks: 'I'm talking about you-know-who doing you-know-what in the you-know-where'. You might think this is perfectly clear because in your head you can visualize who is doing what where, but I am quite sure that no two readers will fill in those blanks in exactly the same way. When your audience is operating under a misunderstanding, they are likely to blame you for failing to meet their expectations. Following the example above, say your purpose was to simply use the new policy on improving gender balance as a way to analyse how gender is perceived in the company, what aspects of gender balance are perceived as problematic or desirable, and how the formulation of the policy represents what is considered 'fixable'; if you haven't made this clear, the reader might well think, 'Why didn't you go into more detail about evaluating the policy? You should have looked more into the literature on policy evaluation'. If you are not explicit about what it is you intend to do in your dissertation, you might find yourself being criticized for not doing something you in fact never intended to do.

Positioning yourself in the discourse by introducing the conversation and how you fit into it makes it possible for the reader to understand the significance of your research. The more you can tailor this to the specific readers, the easier it will be for them to appreciate what you are doing. Background on the topic and a review of the academic literature provide important context. Another key aspect of this context is your theoretical perspective, which is the focus of the next chapter.

'You know the sound of two hands clapping; tell me, what is the sound of one hand?'

Some things just do not make sense in isolation – like one hand without another to clap against, or scholars who talk only to themselves. Conceptualizing your work as part of a larger conversation and positioning yourself within that conversation relative to other scholars and your readers gives your work purpose and identity. The background you provide, the vocabulary you use, and the way you refer to other scholars all help the reader understand where your work fits in the larger discourse. When you try to explain this conversation to your readers without thinking about who they are and what they need from you, you may explain some things too much, other things too little, and uncritically introduce ideas that they may be hostile to. This is less about engaging in conversation than it is about babbling into the void with your eyes closed. One hand needs the other to make a clapping sound; you need to visualize your reader and your conversation partners to give your work meaning.

Finding your path: Points for reflection

What is the ongoing academic conversation that your thesis is part of?
- What kind of knowledge gaps are there in the existing literature?
- How are you carving out a space for your own research?

What kind of assumptions can you make about your readers?
- How much do they need to know about your topic?
- What might they be sceptical about?
- What kind of terminology can you safely use? What will be unfamiliar?

How do you intend to communicate your ethos?
- How much do you need to say about who you are (as a professional, as a member of a particular community, in relation to the participants of your study)?
- How will you demonstrate where you fit into your discipline?
- How will you align yourself with (or distance yourself from) particular schools of thought?

REFERENCES AND FURTHER READING

Becker, Howard (1986) *Writing for Social Scientists: How to Start and Finish Your Thesis, Book, or Article*, 2nd revd edn. Chicago, IL: University of Chicago Press. Chapter 2, 'Persona and authority' touches on issues related to ethos, and Chapter 8, 'Terrorized by the literature' discusses what it is like trying to get a handle on all the literature in your thesis.

Graff, Gerald and Birkenstein, Cathy (2014) *They Say, I Say: The Moves that Matter in Academic Writing*. New York: W.W. Norton & Company. This book provides an excellent concrete demonstration of how you can position yourself in an academic discourse, giving tips on how to refer to other works as well as your own ideas.

Jesson, Jill K., Matheson, Lydia, and Lacey, Fiona M. (2011) *Doing Your Literature Review: Traditional and Systematic Techniques*. London: Sage. Chapter 6, 'Writing up your review' talks about different strategies for writing your literature review and how to avoid making it a simple descriptive list.

Kamler, Barbara and Thomson, Pat (2014) *Helping Doctoral Students Write: Pedagogies for Supervision*. London: Routledge. Chapters 3 and 4 talk about writing oneself into the thesis and writing the literature review. They use an excellent image of 'persuading an octopus into a jar' to explain how it feels to get a handle on the literature.

Lunenburg, Fred C. and Irby, Beverly J. (2008) *Writing a Successful Thesis or Dissertation: Tips and Strategies for Students in the Social and Behavioral Sciences*. Thousand Oaks, CA: Corwin Press. Chapter 7 covers writing the literature review, providing some good examples as models.

Ridley, Diana (2012) *The Literature Review: A Step-by-Step Guide for Students*, 2nd edn. London: Sage. In addition to explaining in detail what a literature review is, Ridley also explicitly covers how to be critical and how to foreground your voice.

Swales, John (1990) *Genre Analysis: English in Academic and Research Settings*. Cambridge: Cambridge University Press. In Chapter 7.4, 'Introductions', Swales presents his famous CARS model (Creating a Research Space) of how to demonstrate to the reader the importance of your research and how you fit into the discourse.

Sword, Helen (2012) *Stylish Academic Writing*. Cambridge, MA: Harvard University Press. Chapter 10 on 'Jargonitis' talks about how your use of vocabulary helps position you as a scholar – or not.

YOUR THEORETICAL AND CONCEPTUAL FRAMEWORK

What ideas are you using?

....

a (Re-)writing about theory: A beginner's guide

b What kinds of things might need explaining?

   i Assumptions about the world, how it works, and the role of the researcher

   ii Concepts: What things are

   iii Mechanisms: How things work

   iv Normative ideas: How things should be

c Modelling: Providing a big picture

d What about terms or ideas you coin yourself?

e How do you deal with a theory chapter if your whole thesis is a theoretical work?

....

When you are introducing your topic and the literature to your audience, you might legitimately wonder what you need to say about theory and where you should say it. While seemingly a simple question, the answer depends on how you understand theory and what role theory is playing in your thesis, which will probably get more confusing the more you think about it.

To help untangle things, it helps to keep in mind what the purpose of theory is. You can think of it as a kind of lens through which you view the world. By giving you a vocabulary for describing the world and how it works, theory functions much the same way as a pair of glasses; it allows you to see particular things in particular ways. No set of lenses is inherently better than another, until you take into account what you need them for. The lenses that are right for you are the ones that will help you find what you are looking for – whether it is far away, close up, or somewhere in the dark. Sometimes to find exactly what you need, you will need more than one pair. For example, if you are studying relationships between teachers and second-language students, you will need theory to help you understand both how students and teachers relate to one another and the challenges second-language students face in learning. You can think of your theoretical framework as the specific collection of conceptual lenses you put together for the particular purpose of answering your research question, because like any good pair of glasses, a theoretical framework has to be custom-made rather than bought off the rack at the supermarket.

Sometimes it is natural to present this framework in your introduction, or within the literature review if you decide to make that a separate chapter (see Chapter 8). But there are some good reasons why you might want to discuss theory separately, in its own chapter. The primary job of the literature review is to focus on what's out there, how much we already know, and what the ongoing discourse is focused on. The job of the theoretical or conceptual framework, on the other hand, is to answer the question 'Which ideas directly inform my study?' While these two discussions might be identical in some cases, in others they will be very different – particularly if you want to argue that the ongoing discourse could benefit from insights provided by a different theoretical perspective. When you write about theory in your thesis, you are essentially describing to the reader which glasses you put on for which purpose in your study. The purpose of this chapter is to help you think through how to accomplish this – how to decide, in other words, what should end up in the final version of your thesis.

ⓐ (RE-)WRITING ABOUT THEORY: A BEGINNER'S GUIDE

To the inexperienced eye, the final draft of a theoretical framework seldom reveals the enormous amount of thinking that went into creating it. A common novice mistake is thinking you can sit down one night with Wikipedia and knock out your theory chapter in one go, cross it off your 'to do' list, and never look at it again. But this theoretical framework has the crucially important function of linking your ideas in your thesis to ideas that others have described in their work. Just because the final draft of a theoretical framework need not be long, don't be fooled into thinking it will take a short time to write. Especially if you are using a flexible design, your discussion of theory is likely to evolve as your ideas evolve.

During the course of your research and the early drafts of your thesis, you will probably try different ideas on for size, which means a lot of writing through theory you don't really understand, and aren't quite sure whether and how it relates to your work. Because you don't really understand something until you've written about it, and because someone else's ideas about how the world works might have been generated from a context completely different from your own, sometimes it takes several drafts before you are able to really see how a particular idea fits into your own work. When you are combining ideas from different thinkers, different contexts, or different schools of thought, it will take longer – and more pages – before you understand how these ideas all work together. And sometimes theory that initially seemed useful may lead to a dead end, while other ideas and concepts may turn out to be more fruitful (even if you hadn't fully appreciated them in the beginning).

Because figuring out what ideas you are using is a very confusing process ('Am I a critical realist? But how is that different from structuration theory? Does it matter? What does this have to do with my research on classroom behaviour anyway?'), it helps to start by writing it all down just for your own sake: everything from your philosophical stance, to the concrete definitions you want to use. There is no question that this takes a lot of time and uses a lot of ink – and it almost inevitably involves staring at words so intensely that they lose all meaning, which is not a good place to be in if you are pressed for time to deliver a theory chapter.

 KEIKO

There is so much theory in this field! I was overwhelmed for a while. I had written almost 20 pages on Vygotsky's theory about language development when my supervisor just looked at me and asked me what the specific relevance of Vygotsky was for how the teachers in my study approached teaching English. In my final draft, my discussion of Vygotsky ended up being only a couple of paragraphs on how children learn languages by engaging in social experiences, which is why the teaching of English should necessarily contain more than just instruction in grammar and sentence structure. And then I discussed the main ideas of some other theorists who built on those ideas for the more specific context of teaching second languages. Deciding which theory was 'best' was difficult because, on one hand, Vygotsky was the most well-known, but the others were more relevant for my work.

As you begin to write for your reader instead of just for yourself, however, you will need to move beyond describing what the theory *is* and into describing what it is doing in your thesis. Once it is all on paper it will be easier to link your discussion of theory to your particular study, cutting out the parts that were written mainly for you and tailoring what's left to your particular audience. As with the literature review, the most important thing is that whatever theory you present is not divorced from your research. You should not be discussing a theory simply because you think everyone else will discuss it, because you want to show you were paying attention during the coursework, or because you need to talk about something and one theory is as good as the next. All the theoretical ideas you present should be evident in the rest of your thesis as well, particularly in the way you analyse and interpret your data. In other words, you need to explain what that particular set of glasses allows you to see in your study. How did the various ideas in this framework shape your question? How did they help you analyse your data and formulate your argument?

🅑 WHAT KINDS OF THINGS MIGHT NEED EXPLAINING?

As described in Chapter 2, there many different levels of theory: the assumptions you make about the world and the things in it (ontology), the assumptions you make about what constitutes knowledge and how such knowledge is acquired (epistemology), the ideas you have about how things work or what causes what (mechanisms), ideas about how things *should* work (normative assumptions), and notions about what things are (concepts). Methodology is also theory about how research should be carried out and what the role of the researcher should be. There is Big Theory that has a name of its own (such as organization theory, regime theory, neoliberalism, realism, developmental theory, game theory, and feminist theory); there are rich collections of ideas from particular thinkers (Foucault, Bourdieu, Goffman, and Butler, for example); there are generalized observations from empirical data that you find useful (such as Nygaard's observation that exaggerated perfectionism in writing can harm research productivity); and things in between.

What all these have in common is that someone has observed or thought about a phenomenon beyond the context of its particular setting and described it in words, perhaps even given it a name (such as 'social structures', 'habitus', or 'democracy'). Naming and describing something allows you not only to talk about it, but also (sometimes) to see it in the first place (much like the phenomenon of learning a new word and then suddenly seeing it pop up everywhere, even though it was there all along). Although some students are concerned about whether or not a particular idea has achieved the formal status of 'theory', perhaps the more relevant question is whether these ideas reflect what you are thinking and seeing, and whether they can give you a vocabulary that enables you to describe your research to your reader. If what you are talking about is an idea that is relevant beyond the immediate context in which it was first introduced, and that can in some way be used in your research, then it can be treated as theory. For example, imagine that someone has published a paper on the phenomenon of smart-phone-based networked consumer services and dubbed this phenomenon 'uberism', based on the taxi service 'Uber'. It is less important that 'uberism' is not a formal theory, and more important that you describe its salient features so that when you talk about how a new service in your case study community allows people to use their smart phones to come into contact with cyclists who can deliver takeaway food, your use of the term 'uberism' focuses attention on the network-based features of the service.

Below I discuss in more detail some of the types of theory you might want to present to your reader, and suggest how they might be linked to different aspects of your research.

(i) Assumptions about the world, how it works, and the role of the researcher

In your development as a scholar, you should be exposed to a number of different ideas about what society is, how it works, and what your role as a researcher is. How you become exposed to these ideas depends on your individual journey as a student. You might be forced to take a class in the philosophy of science and find the whole thing mind-numbingly boring until after class when you participate in a discussion about a concrete methodological approach and realize that it represents a completely different way of going about research than you are comfortable with, and you cannot put your finger on why until you remember some of the things you talked about in class. Perhaps the concepts of epistemology and ontology will seem senseless until you realize that the research you are reading seems to assume that the world consists of easily identifiable objects that can be measured and counted reliably, whereas you suspect that they are not easily categorized, impossible to measure, and difficult to gain knowledge about. Perhaps you feel that such discussions are irrelevant, until the department of geography where you are based claims that your research question is not 'geographical' enough, which makes you realize that geography sees things in terms of spatial relations and identity, and political science (where you have formed many of your ideas) sees things in terms of states and power.

In the social sciences, there is no consensus on what we can safely assume about society, the people in it, and how they relate to one another. What separates the disciplines from one another is often (more or less) different ideas about the assumptions we can make. We argue about what social structures are, what maintains them, what changes them, and the role of the individual. We disagree about what research on these questions is supposed to achieve, and how the researcher plays a role. For example, in studying inequalities between social groups, researchers have different ideas about whether it is more important to measure the actual differences in social capital between these groups (e.g., differences in income or representation in government), or perceptions about these differences. In other words, some are more interested in the 'truth' while others are more interested in people's perceptions of the truth. The way you think about these deeper questions will certainly have a profound effect on the way you approach your study. If you are more concerned about actual inequalities, you will attempt to gather data on income and political representation, for example. If you are more concerned about perceived inequalities, you will have to get at what it is that people believe – which then raises another set of questions. Can you ask people straight out and expect a truthful answer? If so, you could circulate a questionnaire or carry out short interviews. But if you think that these beliefs are at a more subconscious level, which means people might not know what they believe, or that they know what they believe but will not admit it to you, then you will have to use a different approach. Perhaps you need to observe them in a number of different settings and try to identify their perceptions based on a combination of what they say and what they do. And then you have to ask yourself another question: What should you do, as a researcher, if you see that there is a discrepancy between what people believe and what is more demonstrably true? Do you have a responsibility to simply report the viewpoint of your informants? Or is it more ethical to intervene?

As fascinating as these thoughts might be, and as important as they are to your intellectual development and maturity as a researcher, there is no reason to automatically include all of them in your thesis. The time to bring them out is when your department expects that you will discuss your theoretical positionality; when you make different assumptions than the majority of those in your department (for example, if you work primarily with quantitative researchers and need to justify an ethnographic approach); when your topic or approach appears to be only marginally relevant to your discipline and you need to make the connections more explicit (for example, if you are based in political science, are using theories from psychology, and need to address how individuals are connected with states); or when some of your basic assumptions have led directly to some of your specific methodological choices (for example, to include participant observation in addition to interviews).

ⅱ Concepts: What things are

Concepts describe or delimit various phenomena and can range from the abstract – 'power' or 'identity' – to the very concrete, such as 'tertiary education' or 'multimodality'. Defining key concepts helps ensure that the reader will understand the words you use in the same way as you do. For example, if you want to study juvenile criminal behaviour, you will want to be sure that your reader envisions the same age group you do when you say 'juvenile', and has in mind the same activities when you say 'criminal behaviour'.

Certainly when you are doing quantitative research you will need to define and operationalize your dependent and independent variables, but there might be other core concepts that are worth discussing as well – concepts that may be too abstract to measure directly but that nonetheless represent key ideas in your work. One of the main justifications for doing qualitative research is to explore concepts that are difficult to define or measure (such as 'belonging' or 'community'), which implies that you will need to be as precise as possible in the discussion of these concepts and where you fit into it.

 ROBERT ▬▬▬▬▬▬▬▬▬▬▬▬▬▬▬▬▬▬▬▬▬▬▬

When I first started this project, I was sceptical about needing any theory at all. But as I got deeper into my reading I realized that there were three main concepts I kept coming back to, even though in my head they don't really seem like formal theory: addiction as a social illness, not just physiological; social 'belonging'; and transnational identity. At one point, I read so much about 'identity' that I completely lost sense of what I was looking for: it seemed to mean everything and nothing at the same time. I finally narrowed it down to a core idea about how people define themselves, and I think it only took a couple of sentences to explain in the final version!

The concepts you use, and the way you describe them, position you in the discourse by linking your work to that of people who use the same terminology (see Chapter 8). For example, in peace and conflict studies, the concept of 'vertical inequality' means differences between individuals, while 'horizontal inequality' means differences between groups. The terms themselves are not intuitive, and anyone unfamiliar with the field is unlikely to guess what they mean. So if you are writing your thesis within the field of peace and conflict studies, you can probably use these concepts with some short definition and references to key works, and move right on to discussing how you will operationalize and measure them in your study. If you are working in the field of social psychology, however, these concepts might be unfamiliar, even though the idea of looking at differences and similarities between groups is common. If you have decided to use the terminology of horizontal or vertical inequalities – rather than group or individual inequalities – you might have to explain why.

If you are using a concept that is familiar within your field of study but the meaning or significance of which is disputed, you might need to specify how you will be defining or operationalizing it. For example, in the field of education the term 'literacy' is seldom taken at face value. In the non-academic world, 'literacy' usually means 'ability to read and write' and is seen as an absolute measure, whereas in education one might discuss literacy as a situation-specific ability; in other words, someone might be highly literate in some contexts but not in others. If you are doing a study on literacy in the field of education, it is precisely because that term is considered so complex that a lengthy discussion of your position on the concept will be expected.

Your theoretical framework at the very least should contain a discussion of the key concepts in your work that are analytically important (e.g., 'gender' if you are analysing gender differences), disputed (e.g., 'effectiveness'), or highly specialized (e.g., 'externalities').

(iii) Mechanisms: How things work

In addition to explaining to your reader how you define specific phenomena, you might also need to explain how you assume or propose that these phenomena come about, change, behave, or relate to one another. For example, you might describe learning not only as 'acquisition of knowledge', but also as a process, the mechanism by which knowledge is acquired.

Some of the mechanisms that inform your work come from (more or less contested) bodies of formal theory – such as structuration theory, game theory, organization theory, and social cognitive theory – and so on. Others come from less formal theory, such as one author's idea about what really led to the fall of the Berlin Wall. And there are many other kinds of theory in between. Some of the ideas you want to use about how things work will come from theorists or philosophers – such as Foucault, Butler, Bourdieu, Haraway, or Latour – who explain their ideas so abstractly that you may have to interpret and delimit them rather specifically for your thesis. Others will come from previous research on similar topics and not be closely linked to a specific person, such as the 'greed versus grievance' debate in political science about why individuals join rebel groups. It is less important whether the mechanisms that inform your work come from formal theory or theorists with big names, and more important that you explain exactly how you intend to use them.

 AMINA

I didn't really use any formal 'theory,' but I identified some mechanisms from what other studies have found and used them to develop the hypotheses I wanted to test. Based on my reading, I saw that some people argued that poverty was the main barrier because many pregnant women simply could not afford to either get to the hospital or follow the advice that was given to them by the midwife; others said it was infrastructure because even if people could afford to come to the hospital, bad roads, lack of access to transportation, and long distances simply made it too difficult or dangerous to travel; and there were some who thought that the insecurity related to conflict, including issues related to sexual violence, kept women from seeking help.

Some of the mechanisms you incorporate into your work might be at the level of an assumption: you simply take them for granted without directly engaging with the ideas themselves. You neither seek to test them, nor to use them explicitly in your analysis of your material. They simply make up part of the foundation of your world view. If your audience is likely to share that world view, then the assumptions may remain implicit – that is, given the particular setting of your research you might not have to explain that you assume that social structures change slowly or that states behave rationally. But you will have to make these assumptions explicit if you know they are contentious. For example, if you want to assume that people act in their own self-interest, but you know that many in your field disagree and point to explicit cases of altruism, you can acknowledge the altruism argument and still present a case for why you want to make the assumption of self-interest. But after that point, the idea of self-interest is unlikely to play an explicit role in your thesis.

The mechanisms that you must make explicit, however, are those that you engage with directly – either by using them to help you analyse your data, or by directly testing, challenging, or building on them. For example, you might take the ideas that (i) gender is 'performed' and (ii) because of 'stereotype threat' women will underperform in situations where a negative stereotype is present to explore how women perform in a particular workplace; you can interpret behaviours and statements in the light of these ideas. In your thesis you need to spell out exactly what mechanisms you intend to engage with, and explain how you are intending to engage with them. If they are going to help you analyse your data (interviews, focus groups, or participant observation), how will they do that? If you want to bring in the idea that gender is performed, how will you observe that it is being performed? And what is the value of bringing in this idea? What will it add to your analysis?

(iv) Normative ideas: How things should be

Some of the ideas that you work with do not represent notions of how things are, or how they work, but rather normative assessments of how things should be. For example, Rawls's idea of political liberalism informs discussions about the proper use of political power in democracy; he is not (just) describing what political power is, or how it works to bring about change, but when it is acceptable to use it. Many areas of research within the social sciences steer away from anything that can be considered normative because it might be seen as non-objective, and thus non-scientific. However, a good many disciplines critically examine such values as a way of looking more closely at the role of various social institutions and actors: What sort of value system are their actions consistent with? Given a specific notion of 'peace', 'justice' or 'fairness', how should a social institution behave?

To make this more complicated, sometimes normative ideas are disguised as simple concepts or mechanisms. The example of 'literacy' I used above, for example, could be seen as a concept with implicit normative assumptions: the way you define it reflects ideas about what *should* be taken into account when describing an individual's ability to use written and spoken language. Limiting your definition of 'literacy' to the ability to read and write, for example, suggests you value these skills above skills that involve numbers or images.

Whenever (explicit or implicit) norms and values are present in the ideas shaping your research, your most important job as a writer is to be transparent: the values that underlie your assessments need to be made explicit to your reader. Instead of saying 'this is an unjust social system', you will have to say things like 'given the ideas discussed above of what constitutes a just social system, I will demonstrate that this particular social system fails on many important points'.

SAMIR

I had to pull from two different areas of theory, both the traditional literature on strategies around corporate expansion and the Corporate Social Responsibility literature. They both have a lot of ideas about how things should be, not just how things are. So I put the key concepts up against one another, comparing and contrasting their implications. That later helped me structure my discussion of the specific case study sites.

These types of ideas in particular should be made explicit in your theoretical framework because they often play an important role in how you interpret your data. Moreover, because they cover such basic ideas about what is good or desirable in society, they often work best when you compare or contrast them with other ideas. For example, it is intuitively difficult to argue against the value of a just social system – until you are presented with a competing idea of what constitutes justice.

ⓒ MODELLING: PROVIDING A BIG PICTURE

Sometimes you might find it useful to draw a picture of how the ideas you want to work with are related to each other (see Figure 9.1). Drawing a model of some sort gives you an idea of how the various elements of your inquiry fit together. Sometimes this is much easier to see when it is visualized in a figure rather than described in words. By making decisions about what idea to put where, and how to visualize the links between them (arrows or lines, for example), you think through the relationships between the ideas. Drawing such a picture helps delineate more clearly which things you are foregrounding and looking at specifically, and which will be backgrounded and not investigated.

In any kind of modelling, there is always a trade-off between accuracy and parsimony. A very simple model that is easy to comprehend and test will not be able to capture much nuance. On the other hand, a model that is highly complex and detailed might be almost impossible to understand or work with. Making a model will force you to decide what it is

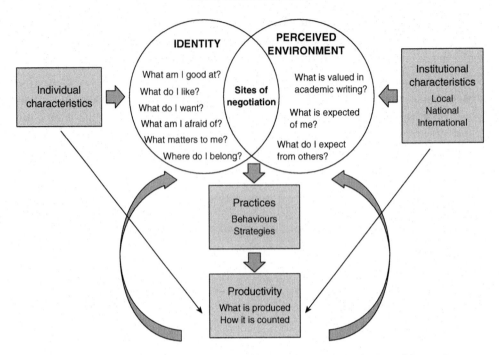

Figure 9.1 Visualizing your theoretical framework: In an early draft of my thesis, I drew a figure to sort out for myself how I saw the relationship between the various theoretical concepts (boxes and circles) and mechanisms (arrows) in my work. The figure later became central to an article I published on the basis of that work (Nygaard 2015).

you really want to be focusing on, and what you can safely relegate to the background. If your model or figure is well drawn, it will be easier for the reader to see what you are looking at, and not looking at. It can help communicate which ideas are important specifically for the context of your thesis. If it is not well drawn, your reader will see only a confusing pile of boxes and arrows (see Chapter 11). If you are in doubt, ask a colleague to read the model out loud – to look at the figure and tell you what they see. If they are able to say something like 'this shows me that you are looking at the relationship between indirect and direct causes of poverty', and that is indeed what you are doing, then the model is useful. But if your reader says, 'I'm not sure I even know where to start looking', then perhaps keep the model for yourself and work on explaining through words instead.

ⓓ WHAT ABOUT TERMS OR IDEAS YOU COIN YOURSELF?

Research, even at the Master's level, is not always limited to working with existing theory. Much of what we do as researchers is to generate new ideas, perhaps as propositions that others can test, or concepts that describe a phenomenon in a different way. It is a normal part of the research and writing process to have flashes of insight where you feel like you have touched on something new. And it is very important that you write down these insights, perhaps even giving them names. When you are sure you have adequately expressed what you are thinking, however, it is a good idea to double-check before you commit these ideas or terms to the final draft of your thesis. You do not want to find out that your brilliant newly coined expression has been around for years. At the very least, do a basic internet search for the terms you have come up with and other related terms. You might discover that your idea isn't as original as you thought – but this need not be a crisis. It is normal to internalize ideas through your reading; that is, you register the idea in some part of your brain but it doesn't immediately feel relevant. Then, a few months later, the idea resurfaces and feels like your own. If you do the double-checking instantly, then you might inadvertently kill off your thought process by saying to yourself, 'Oh, I guess that wasn't such an original idea. Never mind'. But if you write down 'your' idea first, and then double-check, you might discover that, yes, someone else said something similar, but your idea is somewhat different. Then, although you cannot claim to have 'invented' the idea, you can still refer to the original one and then build on it. Even if you don't build on it, you still have something you can refer to.

If, however, you cannot find that anyone has said something similar and you want to coin a new term or propose a new explanatory mechanism, think about the extent to which these innovations are the main purpose of your research. If they constitute a key part of your core argument, they will not be part of your theoretical framework because they will be presented in the main body of the paper. However, if they are smaller innovations, require little argument to support their presence, and are meant to be used as tools rather than be part of your conclusion, then they can be part of your theoretical framework. Say, for example, you would like to introduce the terms 'objective readiness' and 'subjective readiness' to reflect the extent to which a person formally qualifies for promotion, and the extent to which a person believes they are qualified and wishes to apply, respectively. These terms are relatively unproblematic and simply represent a shorthand for you as a researcher, and should be simple to integrate into your theoretical framework (or even introduction) as concepts that can help organize your discussion. In contrast, however, proposing a new concept like 'criminal addiction' to describe addiction to crime as being parallel to addiction to drugs would be a much bigger undertaking. You would first have to examine how 'addiction' is defined, whether or not it can apply to activities that do not involve the ingestion of a substance, and whether there is precedence (such as 'sex addiction'). It is unlikely that your audience will be satisfied with a short discussion, and proposing such a term will probably have to be integrated into your conclusion and argued for (see also Swedberg 2014 for an excellent discussion on theorizing).

ⓔ HOW DO YOU DEAL WITH A THEORY CHAPTER IF YOUR WHOLE THESIS IS A THEORETICAL WORK?

Normally, a theoretical or conceptual framework provides the reader with an explicit discussion of the ideas that will inform the main body of your work. If your work is primarily theoretical (whether or not you are coining new terms), then theory itself is the main body of your work and a theoretical framework in the traditional sense will be of little value. For example, if your research question compares how well regime theory and organization theory are able to capture the role of international organizations in the field of international negotiation, then the body of your thesis will look systematically at these theories. Rather than a 'theoretical framework', it might make more sense to have something that might best be called 'analytical framework': a section that would systematically go through on what basis you will be comparing the two theoretical traditions and why. This is a good example of how theory can start overlapping with method, and in the next chapter I will discuss how to go about explaining your method.

EMMA

My whole thesis was theoretical in nature, even though my research question was not about theory, and the goal of my research was not to say anything about feminist theory or queer theory as theories. But the body of the thesis was largely about the implications of these theories for understanding the situation of gendered criminal statistics. So I didn't have a traditional theoretical framework. In the analytical framework I described how I would use the theories, but then I had separate chapters for each theoretical tradition that focused on their core ideas and then explored their implications.

'All that we are is the result of all that we have thought.'

Who you are as a scholar, a researcher, is the result of all the thoughts you have had along the way. Some of these thoughts are inspired by things you have read. Others are inspired by things you have observed outside of academia. And still others arise as a result of the research you have conducted. It is not always easy even for you to separate these thoughts from one another, but for the reader it is still more difficult. One of the most important jobs you have as a writer is to organize these thoughts and put them into their proper context so the reader can see what ideas come from the ongoing discourses and how you position yourself in relation to these ideas.

Finding your path: Points for reflection

What are the concepts you are using in your thesis?
- What are the central terms you use to describe the things you are looking at in your study? (e.g., conflict, literacy, negotiation)
- Are there different ways of defining these terms? (e.g., does 'literacy' mean different things to different people?)

- How will you explain and define these terms for the purpose of your thesis? (e.g., simply define them without further ado, or explain the different ways of thinking about them)
- Where does it make sense to do this? (e.g., in the body of the text, in a glossary, etc.)

What kind of ideas are you incorporating in your thesis about how or why something happens or how things are related to one another?

- How are these mechanisms being used in your work? Are these ideas the basis for hypotheses, or do they help you figure out what to look for when you are analysing your data?

What kind of normative assumptions are you making?

- Are you using any explicit normative ideas about how things should be?
- What are the implicit normative assumptions behind the concepts and mechanisms you are using? (e.g., what does your definition of 'literacy' say about what skills are valued?)
- What are the implicit normative assumptions in the methodology you are using? (e.g., what kinds of 'truth' are valued, what kinds of interactions between researcher and participant are valued?)
- Is there consistency between the normative assumptions embodied by your methodology and those in your concepts and mechanisms?

REFERENCES AND FURTHER READING

Becker, Howard (1986) *Writing for Social Scientists: How to Start and Finish Your Thesis, Book, or Article*, 2nd revd edn. Chicago, IL: University of Chicago Press. Chapter 8 'Terrorized by the literature' does not differentiate between theoretical literature and the more empirical literature, but nevertheless covers how you can think through what theory (and the other literature) is doing in your thesis.

Lunenburg, Fred C. and Irby, Beverly J. (2008) *Writing a Successful Thesis or Dissertation: Tips and Strategies for Students in the Social and Behavioral Sciences*. Thousand Oaks, CA: Corwin Press. In their chapter on writing the introduction, the authors briefly touch on the theoretical framework, and provide an excellent example of modelling.

Nygaard, Lynn P. (2015) 'Publishing and perishing: An academic literacies framework for investigating research productivity', *Studies in Higher Education*, open access. This article contains a theoretical model that ties together concepts and mechanisms from different theoretical backgrounds and discourses.

Petre, Marian and Rugg, Gordon (2010) *The Unwritten Rules of PhD Research*, 2nd edn. Berkshire: Open University Press. In their chapter on 'Critical thinking' the authors have a brief but important section called 'What's theory got to do with it?' that looks at how theory helps structure critical thinking.

Roberts, Carol M. (2010) *The Dissertation Journey: A Practical and Comprehensive Guide to Planning, Writing, and Defending Your Dissertation*, 2nd edn. Thousand Oaks, CA: Corwin Press. Also using the metaphor of a lens, Roberts succinctly covers the function of a theoretical or conceptual framework in Chapter 11 'Writing the introduction'. She also provides some concrete examples.

Swedberg, Robert (ed.) (2014) *Theorizing in Social Science: The Context of Discovery*. Redwood City: Stanford Social Sciences. The first chapter of this book is called 'From theory to theorizing' and provides an excellent discussion on moving from thinking of theory in the context of justification to the context of discovery.

Wright, Colin (2006) 'Understanding the role of theory', in Alan Bond (ed.), *Your Master's Thesis: How to Plan, Draft, Write, and Revise*. Abergele: Studymates. This chapter succinctly covers elements of theory – explaining the difference between ontology, epistemology, methodology, assumptions, and concepts.

YOUR METHOD

What did you do to answer your question?

....

a Who are you in relation to your research? Objectivity and transparency

b How generalizable do you expect your findings to be? Describing the setting

c What kind of research is this? From big picture to detail

d What counts as data, and how did you get it? Sources, methodological tools, and sampling

e What did you do with your data once you got it?

f How do we know that what you say is true? Anticipating critical thinking

....

Many of us have grown up watching crime shows on television where the scientists enter a crime scene, instantly spot a potential clue amidst the normal mess, and pick up a tiny fibre, a powder of unknown origin, or a blob of goo. They then bag it, bring it back to the lab, and 'analyse' it by pressing a magic button and getting an answer – which usually involves a string of chemicals. Then, amazingly, someone on staff will immediately perceive the significance of what sounds like utter gibberish and say something like 'The only place in the world that has water with that particular composition of trace metal ions is Pazar Yeri in Turkey – which is exactly where the brother-in-law was vacationing last week!'

Would that it were so easy for the social scientist (or any other scientist who isn't a character on a TV show). But while the process for us is nowhere near as fast or unambiguous as it is on TV, there are some similarities: we enter a scene, collect data, look at it through a particular conceptual lens or subject it to a statistical procedure, state the significance of what we observe, and then solve the crime – I mean, answer the research question. The big difference is that the steps we take in our research are seldom as clear-cut as they are in fiction, and they need much more description than they do on TV.

At some point in your thesis you need to take your reader by the hand and explain in detail what you actually did and why. In Chapter 2, I looked at the kinds of things you need to think about when you are *planning* your method before you start your research; in this chapter, I focus on what you need to think about when you are *writing about* your method after the research is finished, which is not quite the same thing (not least because a lot may have happened between conception and implementation). Whether you call this a method chapter, an analytical framework, or something else, your readers need to understand the logic of how you went about answering your question in order to help them evaluate your claims. Qualitative, quantitative and non-empirical research all present different challenges when it comes to describing method. And yet, the overarching purpose of the method section is the same: regardless of your approach, you want to convince your readers – who in your case are your examiners – that what you have done constitutes a solid body of research within your chosen field. Part of the way you do that is to answer the questions they might ask before they have a chance to ask them.

(a) WHO ARE YOU IN RELATION TO YOUR RESEARCH? OBJECTIVITY AND TRANSPARENCY

To convince your reader that you have indeed carried out a solid piece of research, the key concepts that should be guiding your discussion of your method are objectivity and transparency. At the most basic level, objectivity simply means that you have based your claims on something other than your personal opinion, and transparency is showing the reader how you did that. But different methodological traditions understand objectivity and transparency in different ways (see also Chapter 2). Positivist approaches generally assume that objectivity (in the sense that your individual perspective had no discernible impact on your interpretation of your findings) is possible, desirable, and achieved by ensuring you have carefully considered issues of validity and reliability. Transparency can be partly achieved by giving the reader access to your raw data, in addition to carefully explaining the tests you subjected the data to. The ideal is for you to be able to explain your research well enough that someone else can carry it out in exactly the same way (which would allow them to replicate your findings). Because objectivity is both assumed and desired in positivist approaches, you as a researcher are unimportant: it is the actions that were taken and the data that was used that need explaining.

Interpretive and critical approaches are more sceptical about the degree to which objectivity in the traditional sense is possible, or even desirable. They are more likely to presuppose that regardless of what you do, you will somehow bring your personal perspective into your research with you, and the best way to make sure that your research nonetheless is valuable is to be as transparent as possible about your positionality: how you see the world and your relationship to both the participants in your study and the research itself. In other words, while the positivist researcher will assume that any other researcher will interpret the data in the same way because personal perspective is absent (or irrelevant), the interpretive or critical researcher will assume that other researchers may see different things in the same data because they bring different perspectives to bear. Your job as a researcher is to explain your perspective and connect your ideas as well as you can to the discourse you want to be part of. So instead of explaining everything well enough that another person can repeat your research and arrive at exactly the same findings, you need to explain it well enough so they understand not just what you did, but how you were thinking. For the critical and interpretivist researcher, the issue is not whether the data has been interpreted in the only possible correct manner, but whether the interpretation is justified given the theoretical framework. You need to paint such a clear picture of how you were thinking through your work that the reader can see it unfold. Providing the reader access to the original raw data, as is often possible with quantitative approaches, might not only be beside the point, but may also be unethical if your research is based on personal documents (such as diaries) or interviews with individuals who expect confidentiality. But if the reader understands exactly what you did and why you did it, they will be more likely to accept your interpretations, even if they cannot see your data in full.

One aspect of transparency that is particularly important for interpretive and critical approaches is the exploration of your own role in the research – which is often called 'reflexivity' (see also Chapter 7). In other words, you do not simply discuss how you see your research participants (as a result of your theoretical position and role in the research), but you also reflect on how they might see you – and what difference this might make. How do the research participants understand your role? How might that relationship have influenced what they said to you? Or how you interpreted what they said?

Being transparent about your method, regardless of your approach, requires that you discuss the setting and overall design of your study, what constitutes data in your study and how you gained access to it, how you analysed the data once you got it, and your thoughts about the extent to which the choices you made might have unduly shaped your findings – all of which are discussed below. The order in which you discuss these questions, and how much space you devote to each of them, will depend on your particular thesis.

ⓑ HOW GENERALIZABLE DO YOU EXPECT YOUR FINDINGS TO BE? DESCRIBING THE SETTING

One of the first questions a reader will have is 'Can I expect that what you are saying will be true in other contexts as well?' Whether you choose to discuss this in your introduction, in a dedicated chapter focusing on the background of your case or study site, or within your method section (perhaps under a discussion of limitations) depends on the kind of research you have done. In any case, the underlying question you need to answer is 'What makes my setting the same or different from other contexts in which the same research question is relevant?'

For example, if your research question asks how branch offices of international organizations are integrated into the area where they are carrying out their work, then presumably you want your research to have some relevance for all international organizations that have branch offices in different parts of the world. But most likely you are not able to look at all of those organizations. The question is whether the one(s) you are looking at have features that others share (which might make your findings more generalizable), or whether they stand out in some way by being different (which will make generalization harder).

 **SAMIR**

I thought it was important to look at at least two different case-study sites because I wanted to show that the opportunities and challenges for the company differed depending on local cultures. In my description of the two sites, I was careful to describe both the ways in which they were different from or similar to one another, and also ways in which they were different from other villages in India.

It is important to note that there is a geopolitical bias in research that tends to assume that Anglo settings (particularly the US and the UK) are central, and thus more immediately generalizable than settings considered more peripheral – African or Asian countries, even non-English-speaking countries in Europe. To compensate for this bias, you might have to argue more forcefully for the relevance and generalizability of your setting if it is 'peripheral', and connect features of your setting that might be unfamiliar to your readers with features of settings that are likely to be more familiar. For example:

Although Norway has a school system that covers 13 years, rather than the 12-year system in the United States, it shares some common features in that it is divided into three parts: primary school (grades 1–7), secondary school (grades 8–10), and tertiary school (grades 11–13), all of which involve a transition to a new school. This research focuses on challenges faced by schoolchildren in the transition from primary to secondary school. Because Norwegian children start school at age 6, they are about 13 years old during this transition, which is around the same age when many US children are starting middle school. I thus expect that the challenges associated with moving from a familiar environment to a new school will be similar.

ⓒ WHAT KIND OF RESEARCH IS THIS? FROM BIG PICTURE TO DETAIL

Overall research design and methodology is usually described as being primarily qualitative, quantitative, or mixed – although some prefer to describe it in terms of fixed versus flexible approaches (see Chapter 2 and Robson 2011). Research can also be non-empirical (sometimes described as theoretical), for example if you have carried out a philosophical analysis of certain ideas, or you are an economist and are using formulas to propose the likelihood of a certain outcome. Within these broad categories, however, you should be able to describe your approach in more specific terms: survey design, experimental, Grounded Theory, phenomenology, case study, ethnography, or something else altogether. The reason for trying to name what you have done is to help your reader more quickly understand what kind of research they are looking at. Each label you choose to put on your work creates a set of expectations in the reader, and a set of questions they will need to have answered. If you tell your reader you are doing quantitative work, the reader will expect you to say something general on the basis of a large number of data points – probably to test a hypothesis – and then the reader will want to know what these data points are and how you analysed them statistically. If you tell them you are doing qualitative work, the reader will expect that you are describing or exploring a phenomenon with more contextual information and are probably not testing a hypothesis.

ROBERT

In the early drafts of my thesis, I tried describing my method as a comparative case study, where the cases were individuals, but that didn't really seem like a good fit. I then tried to say I was using life-history narrative, but that wasn't quite right either. In the end, I just called it 'qualitative research with a flexible design' and put my energy into explaining how the first round of interviews was more exploratory, while the second was more focused because I became interested in the role of the religious community.

Labels will only take you so far, however. More important than giving your method a name is to explain *your* particular way of doing it. If you write that what you are doing is a case study, your reader will start wondering, 'A case of what? What makes this case special or typical? What will we learn by looking at this case in particular?' If you call it an 'ethnography', a 'quasi-experiment', or a 'correlation study', different sets of questions are raised – all dealing with how you translated the general category of that methodology to the specific setting of your research.

As you move from the big picture towards the more specific, look at how you described the intent of your research in your introduction. Examine the language of your research question, aims and objectives, or statement of purpose (see Figure 10.1). Look at your verbs. Verbs represent the actions you have taken, and each action needs clarification. For example, if you say you will 'test' something, then explain what you mean by 'test'. As with any other label you put on your work, the verbs you use will create a specific set of expectations in the reader. If you say you will 'explore' something, your readers will expect a very different type of thesis than if you say you will 'explain' something. If the verbs you have used in the presentation of your research aims do not accurately reflect what you have actually done, then re-think how you present your research aims.

Look at your nouns, which are supposed to represent phenomena you will be gathering data on and saying something about. For quantitative research, this means not only providing details about your dependent, independent, and control variables, but also discussing any of the secondary variables that are not specifically captured in your research question. Remember that the dependent variable is the thing you are trying to explain (such as voting behaviour), and the independent variables are things that you expect will

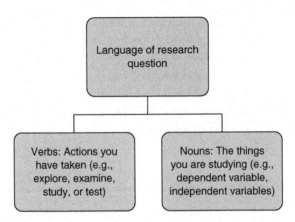

Figure 10.1 The language you use matters: In your research question (or whatever else you have used to tell the reader the purpose of your research) each word you use creates particular expectations in the reader. The methods section is where you can explain in more detail both the actions you have taken and the phenomena you are addressing.

explain variation in your dependent variable in a systematic way and you will therefore specifically test their effect (such as whether level of education or exposure to advertising makes a difference to whether an individual has a high or low probability of voting). Control variables (such as age or sex) are similar to independent variables in that they are expected to affect the dependent variable, but as you are not directly interested in testing them, you simply try to hold them constant so they do not interfere with your results. Although qualitative research as a rule does not use the vocabulary of 'dependent and independent variables', it is still important to let the reader know as specifically as you can the thing you are trying to say something about (for example, attitudes to violence, or behaviour while under a certain kind of pressure, or motivations for taking a particular action), and the things you are looking at that will help you say something about this thing (such as an individual's character traits, past history, or the social context). Regardless of what kind of research you are doing, clarity and consistency here are central. If your research question says that you are investigating 'adolescents' but later you seem to be talking about 'students', the reader will be confused. So choose the nouns in your research question with care, and make sure they represent what you have actually focused on in your research.

If you are doing non-empirical or theoretical research, you might find the whole discussion about research design and method somewhat foreign. Indeed, it is probably not natural for you to think of what you are doing as 'gathering data' as much as reading systematically. Still, it is no less important for you to deconstruct your question and your approach to answering it for the reader, because even if you are not gathering data in the traditional sense, you still need to provide evidence to back up your argument – even if that evidence is in the form of arguments from other authors. For example, if you are looking at the ethical dimensions of military interventions to protect civilians, it will matter very much whether you approach this from a perspective of pragmatics, international law, or religious doctrine, and you will need to spell out for us what perspective you are using – and why you have chosen it. The chapter you do this in will probably be called something like 'Conceptual Framework' or 'Analytical Framework' rather than 'Methods'. You might even integrate it into your introduction. It does not matter that much where you do this; what matters is that you do it.

Because this is a thesis, you will also have to make a case for why this was the best approach for the objectives of your study: in other words, you need to address 'fit for purpose'. How was this particular research design the best way to approach answering your question? The more self-evident your methodological choices were, given your particular context and the expectations of your department, the less you will have to explain. The more you have taken an alternative approach, the more you will have to explain. For example, if you are in an environment that values quasi-experimental approaches and you wish to take a more ethnographic approach, you may have to explain how a natural setting, while making it difficult to control environmental variables, will allow you to observe the particular interaction you are interested in without your participants' having to cope with the distraction of a non-familiar setting.

ⓓ WHAT COUNTS AS DATA, AND HOW DID YOU GET IT? SOURCES, METHODOLOGICAL TOOLS, AND SAMPLING

Research in the social sciences often involves saying something about people – but not always. Sometimes we are interested in organizations. Or states. Sometimes we are interested in events, or ideas. As a result, what counts as data can be everything from published information about people or institutions or events, to things people say in interviews with you, things you uncover in official documents, or things that appear in the media. Data can come from things you observe by watching people interact, or from what you read. Depending on what exactly your unit of analysis is (individuals, groups, social structures, events, ideas) and what you are trying to find out, almost anything (under the right circumstances) could be considered a relevant source of data. This is why it is important for you to explain to your reader exactly what you considered to be relevant data in your work, what the sources of that data were, and what you did to get it. To return to the crime-scene metaphor: the reader needs to know what counts as a clue and how you found it.

 KEIKO

I had to explain why I wanted to gather data using three different methods. I couldn't really call this 'mixed methods' because all the data was qualitative. But I explained that the initial classroom observation gave me ideas for things to ask about in the interviews, and based on the preliminary analysis of the interviews I put together questions to ask in the focus group. I explained that observation allowed me to focus on what my participants did, but the interviews let me talk about what they thought. The focus group let me go more specifically into how they viewed the institutional context.

Keep in mind that this is seldom as obvious as you think it is. If you are trying to say something about an event that happened in recent history, a violent protest for example, you could gather information about that event through official government documents, media reports, statements from witnesses – or some combination of these. Each source will tell you slightly different things, and each will raise different questions. Moreover, each methodological tradition has a number of associated methodological tools to help you get data, none of which are self-explanatory. These are issues related to planning your research (see Chapter 2).

When it comes to writing about your methods in your thesis, your task is to explain the connection between the overall research design, what you want data on, and what you did to get it. To continue with the above example, if you looked at official documents (such as police reports), you will have to explain what kind of information is included in those reports, what might be excluded, and how you were able to gain access to what are generally considered restricted documents. If you looked at media reports, we need to know what kinds of media (print? television? internet?), and what kind of reporting biases are to be expected (e.g., left-wing versus right-wing newspapers, moderated versus non-moderated chat groups, and so on). If you looked at databases, we would want to know what kinds of data were in there (what types of events? geographical regions? time periods?) and where they come from (direct fieldwork? crowdsourcing? harvested from secondary sources?). And if you interviewed individuals, you need to explain what kinds of individuals you interviewed (witnesses? officials?), and what you asked them.

A challenge that many of us face is that the phenomena we want to get data on do not lend themselves easily to measurement or observation. For example, it is hard to see attitudes, and even harder to measure them systematically. This is why you need to explain how you were able to operationalize the variables you were interested in – that is, how you were able to translate an abstract phenomenon into something observable and possibly measurable. Those doing quantitative research can often rely on instruments (such as personality tests) that other researchers have developed and validated. If you have used such an instrument, point to where it is described in the literature; if it is copyrighted, you will also need to demonstrate that you have permission to use it (see, e.g., Lunenburg and Irby 2008: 180–94). If you did not use a previously developed instrument, you will have to explain more generally how the data you gathered was able to tell you what you wanted to know.

 AMINA

I had to explain how I operationalized my variables in the questionnaire so I could show that I was getting the information I needed to answer my question. I explained what I meant by 'access to healthcare' and how the questionnaire captured various aspects of access, such as whether the pregnant women even knew where to go, whether they had access to transportation, how long it took to get there, and so on.

The reader will also wonder how much of the data you were able to get. The claims you can make on the basis of analysing 100 interviews are different than those you can make by analysing three interviews. Remember that 'more' does not always mean 'better'. It all depends on what you were trying to do in the first place. Analysing 100 interviews in depth will be virtually impossible, but you have a stronger basis for making comparisons on certain specific points and saying something that can be generalized. Saying something generalizable from three interviews will be difficult, but you can delve more deeply into the specific and nuanced layers of meaning in each interview, hopefully to root out some rich ideas that can be explored further in another context. And if the entire population of people you want to interview is only five, then analysing three interviews will have a different meaning than if the entire population is 1500. The important thing is to explain how your sample size will allow you to support the claims you want to make.

Similarly, we need to know how you got your sample. For example, did you aim for a random sample or a purposive sample? Or simply a sample of convenience? More important, how did that sampling strategy help you get the information you were looking for? If your question is about how people perceive an influx of refugees in their area, for example, you can explain that a broad random sample gave you better access to a range of attitudes than a small purposive sample would have. In contrast, if your goal is to explore how well refugees are able to integrate, you might explain that a purposive sample of refugees from one particular country who have been in the host country for 5–10 years gave you access to greater depth and nuance for that one group. The same would be true for documents. If you are examining media reports, for example, describe how the choices you made about limiting yourself to a particular period or a particular type of media helped you get access to what it is you want to say something about.

The decisions you made about sources and sampling determine what went into the foundation for the claims you make. Information from police reports might form the basis for very different claims than information from witness statements reported in the media. Data from a very large dataset that has been developed by other researchers but validated and made transparent to everyone allows you to build a different argument than data that you personally gathered through a small-scale questionnaire that cannot be made publicly available because it contains personal information. Even if you are doing theoretical work, for example, exploring the work of Michel Foucault and its relevance to massification in higher education, it will be important to let the reader know if you were working with just one particular Foucault text or his entire body of work, and whether you were reading in the original French or relied on a translation.

This might also be a good time for you to discuss the ethics of your research (see Chapter 3). Rather than simply saying 'I followed the ethical guidelines', identify dilemmas specific to your research and explain how you handled them. For example, if collecting written informed consent from your informants was difficult because you were conducting your research in a context where the informants would view signing documents with suspicion, then explain how you were able to make sure that your informants understood the nature of the research they participated in. Depending on the nature of your research and the setting you are in as a student, you might want to discuss ethics in your introduction, or even as a separate section in your thesis instead of in your methods section. If you have had no contact with human informants, or gathered no personal information about people, you might not even need to discuss ethics at all.

(e) WHAT DID YOU DO WITH YOUR DATA ONCE YOU GOT IT?

While many students are diligent about describing how they collected their data, fewer are equally diligent about describing what they did with it. Unlike TV detectives, you don't have any magic buttons to press that will just transform your data into something useful. There is no such thing as a generic 'analysis'. For example, even the decision to analyse documents raises the question of whether you are planning to look at content (what was said) or the discourse (how it was said). Very specific choices have to be made about what to do with the data. The question before the reader in your methods section is what you actually did to analyse your data, and whether the choices you made were the logical ones to make based on the question you are trying to answer and the data you have access to. So rather than just saying that you 'analysed the data', you need to tell the readers as much as you can about the choices you made and why you made them.

Depending on your methodological choices, the process you went through to analyse your data may have involved prescribed steps that have a name. For example, Grounded Theory has a strict sequence of coding, memoing, and integrating theories. Likewise, binomial regression has a clear progression of activities. But not all methods have a clear recipe for how to go about analysing data. This means that you are on your own, and instead of being able to give the steps of your analysis a specific name (e.g., 'constant comparison'), you have to be as transparent as possible about what you did and why, perhaps even connecting your choices to whatever similar precedents you can find in the literature.

What you do not want to do is simply fall back on naming the software you used without further explanation: 'I used SPSS', or 'I used NVivo'. While this is important information, not least because different software packages allow you to analyse data in different ways, in itself this is only marginally more helpful than saying 'I used Microsoft Word'. Software only does what you tell it to do, and the reader is more interested in what you told it to do. If you carried out quantitative research, what the reader needs to know is what kind of statistical tests you ran, and why. Even given the same data, the different statistical tests you might perform (or, sometimes, the different statistical software packages you can use) will yield different results. The same is true for qualitative research. It is not enough to say 'I coded the interviews in NVivo and several themes emerged'. It is not NVivo that does the coding – it is you. There is no dedicated function in NVivo – or any other software package – that decides what to code for. You decide what the codes will be and put them in there yourself based on what you are looking for. The more you can explain how you went about your coding, and what you based your decisions on, the more accurately your examiners can evaluate your research.

It is not always easy to describe this process because it feels intuitive: 'Well, a lot of people said the same thing so I called it a theme'. But you have to remember that the things that were said in the interview, or the things that were written about in documents you collected, came about because you asked certain questions or gathered particular documents and were looking for certain things. It is important to articulate this. Instead of saying 'In the interviews with those leaving the organization, five themes emerged', you might want to say something like the following:

In the semi-structured, in-depth interviews with those who left the organization, we talked both about specific precipitating events that caused them to take the final step to leave as well as the entire process, from having first doubts to taking action. In the analysis, I looked for both descriptions of feelings and concrete events, coding both for emotions and type of event. Ten of the codes were a priori, and 15 were added in the course of the analysis. While each person's experience was unique and the precipitating events were all different, their emotional processes seemed similar, and I was able to group the feelings into five main stages.

🕑 HOW DO WE KNOW THAT WHAT YOU SAY IS TRUE? ANTICIPATING CRITICAL THINKING

As described in Chapter 2, the reader will be looking at your claims and asking, 'How do I know whether this is true?' This means they will look critically at each of your findings, both to ask whether the findings are valid in themselves, and then later to ask whether these findings support the claim you are making. When you present your methodological or analytical approach, you can describe your reasoning regarding how you have ensured the quality of your findings and claims.

If you are doing quantitative research, you can double-check the robustness of your findings by doing a series of checks: using slightly different parameters for one or more of your variables to see how much it changes the results. For example, if you have defined 'armed conflict' as having 25 or more battle-related deaths in the course of a year and you find that the number of armed conflicts has decreased over time, what happens if you define armed conflict as having 50 battle deaths in the course of a year? If the answer is the same, then your findings are relatively robust. If the trend changes, then your definition of armed conflict might be too sensitive. Describing all of the checks that you did to ensure that your findings can tolerate close examination is an essential part of your methods section.

Qualitative research has a different kind of logic, and thus different kinds of checks are relevant. Triangulation means that you gather data from different sources or using different techniques in order to make sure that your findings are not simply an artefact of your particular source or method. For example, you can combine in-depth interviews with a brief questionnaire. Member-checking entails allowing your participants to review their interview transcripts or review a draft of your manuscript to be sure that you have represented their views fairly. Spending a prolonged period of time in the field can help avoid both your perceptions being coloured by your own context and the participants reacting to your presence (see Cresswell 2003: 196). Whatever you did to help you ensure that your findings are sound needs to be explained.

Even if you did not undertake any particular actions during your research to ensure the quality of your data, the way you present the data can help convince the reader that you interpreted your results fairly. For example, presenting data that went against your overall findings can help you present a more nuanced account. The more of these techniques you can use, and the better you are able to describe them to your readers, the better you will be able to stand up to their critical perspective.

Finally, you will have to include a frank discussion of your limitations. No method is perfect to begin with, and things seldom go exactly as planned. And even if everything went according to plan and you have done all the checks you can think of, your work will still have some natural limitations. It is frighteningly easy to spend an entire chapter discussing the possible limitations of any study, but this would not necessarily be useful. Focus on the limitations that might have affected your findings. For example, were there any threats to *internal* validity – like a response rate that was so low you didn't get a big enough sample size, or you ended up with one sub-group over-represented or under-represented? Were there any threats to *external* validity, making it difficult for you to apply your findings to other situations? It might be that even though you sent out 2000 email questionnaires, only 1200 were returned and 200 of those were incomplete. If the missing and incomplete ones were random, this might not be a problem. But if you were intending to get responses from all undergraduate students and discovered that the missing and incomplete responses were disproportionately from students in the natural sciences, you might have to think about how that might affect your results. If your research question was about the use of public transportation, the skewed response rate might not be that problematic. But if your question is about study habits, then unless you can assume that students in the natural sciences study the same way as students in the humanities, the observations on which you will base your findings might not be solid.

The more thoughtfully you can answer the questions your reader might have about what you actually did to secure the data that went into developing your claims, the more your examiners will be convinced that you are able to think critically and act like an independent researcher.

'To know and not do is not yet to know.'

Knowing something as an academic is different than knowing something as a regular person. While things you know outside of academia might be based on things you have done, or read, or thought about, these things are seldom subjected to the same level of critical examination as the things you know as an academic. Academic knowledge is purposeful, and based on something you have done intentionally to gain or test that knowledge. You might even start from something you 'know' already – that organization hierarchies are complex, that unemployment can cause depression, or that moving from one country to another can be difficult – but as a scholar, you have to subject this knowledge to a level of scrutiny that is seldom found outside of academia. So for your readers, knowing what you know is not enough; they need to know what you have done. Your method section describes the activities you have undertaken to gain that knowledge.

 Finding your path: Points for reflection

What does your reader need to know about your methodology?
- What labels will you use (e.g., 'case study', 'correlation study', 'ethnography')?
- How have you adapted that general methodological approach to the particulars of your study?

What does objectivity mean to you, and how do you express this to the reader?
- In your particular context, how will your readers expect you to explore your own role in the research (write reflexively)?

Look at the language in your research question
- How do you describe what you did (verbs)?
- How do you describe what you look at (nouns)?
- Does this reflect what you actually did?

How will you describe what counts as data and how you got it?

What do you need to tell the reader about how you processed your data?

What limitations to your method are important for your readers to know?

REFERENCES AND FURTHER READING

Bui, Yvonne N. (2009) *How to Write a Master's Thesis*. London: Sage. If you are doing an empirical thesis, particularly if it has a fixed design and uses quantitative data, Bui's detailed explanation of how to write a methods chapter should prove useful.

Cresswell, John W. (2003) *Research Design: Qualitative, Quantitative, and Mixed Methods Approaches*, 2nd edn. Thousand Oaks, CA: Sage. Cresswell's primary focus is on designing and carrying out (empirical) research, but the issues he covers are also important for explaining your methods to a reader.

Hennink, Monique, Hulter, Inge, and Bailey, Ajay (2011) *Qualitative Research Methods*. London: Sage. Chapter 11 'Writing qualitative research' goes right to the heart of the key challenges related to describing your qualitative research approaches to a reader.

Lunenburg, Fred C. and Irby, Beverly J. (2008) *Writing a Successful Thesis or Dissertation: Tips and Strategies for Students in the Social and Behavioral Sciences*. Thousand Oaks, CA: Corwin Press. Especially relevant for quantitative research and fixed designs, the book is particularly strong on issues related to method. Chapter 8 focuses specifically on writing the methods chapter.

Petre, Marian and Rugg, Gordon (2010) *The Unwritten Rules of PhD Research*, 2nd edn. Berkshire: Open University Press. Petre and Rugg are two of the few authors who even acknowledge the existence of non-empirical research (Chapter 7). Their chapter on critical thinking (Chapter 9) should be very useful for those who are attempting a theoretical thesis and are struggling with how to present their approach.

Roberts, Carol M. (2010) *The Dissertation Journey: A Practical and Comprehensive Guide to Planning, Writing, and Defending Your Dissertation*, 2nd edn. Thousand Oaks, CA: Corwin Press. Chapter 12 covers both selecting and describing your methodology, and includes a discussion about how to justify your choice of approach. Roberts provides some good concrete examples.

Robson, Colin (2011) *Real World Research*, 3rd edn. West Sussex: John Wiley and Sons. While focused more on designing and carrying out research, rather than on describing your methods to a reader, Robson directs your attention to the kinds of things you need to think about. Compared to similar books, he is strong on flexible designs and qualitative methods.

YOUR RESULTS AND ANALYSIS

What are you building your argument on?

....

a What kind of argument are you trying to make?

b Genre conventions of your methodological approach

c Presenting quantitative data analysis

d Presenting qualitative data analysis

e Presenting a non-empirical (or theoretical) analysis

f Presenting your data visually

....

You've given your reader a summary of the conversation so far, and you've given them insight into how you approached the subject both theoretically and methodologically. Now you need to tell them what you found. It can be helpful to think of presenting your findings as presenting evidence in front of a jury: the rules of the court are that you cannot base an argument on something that has not been called into evidence. The same is true in academic writing: you cannot base your claim on something that you cannot show your reader. When you present your findings, what you are doing is lining up the evidence you can use to make your argument for the jury.

The way you put this evidence together to tell the story you want to tell will depend heavily on the kind of context you are in, the audience you want to reach, and what you want to achieve. Keep in mind, however, that in almost every conceivable thesis-related circumstance, surprise witnesses and sudden confessions work less well than they do in fictional courtroom dramas. In a novel, stunning your reader with unexpected twists and turns might keep them turning the pages, but in a thesis it is more likely to make your readers think that you are making things up as you go along. 'I didn't see THAT coming!' is not the reaction you generally want from your reader when you write a thesis. So whatever storytelling strategy you pick, make sure that you let the reader know what you are doing. Warn them in advance how you intend to organize the presentation of your findings.

It might be useful here to think about the difference between analysing and interpreting your findings: you can think of analysing as pulling things apart and examining them in detail, and interpreting as putting them back together to see what they mean (Robson 2011: 418). In fixed designs you would normally do this in two different chapters of your thesis (perhaps one called 'results' and one called 'discussion'), whereas in flexible designs you will probably do both of these things in the same section (although this might be divided into different theme-related chapters). All of this ripping apart and putting back together is bound to be messier than you expect, and you can count on rewriting this section several times. Even if you have used a fixed design, you might find extra depth and nuance, perhaps even unexpected contradiction, as you move from the comfort of tables to the messiness of putting your story into words.

As you are smoothing out your story so that it makes sense to your readers, remember that your readers are tasked with being critical. Like a jury, they will be actively looking for signs that you have been trustworthy and diligent in your approach and that the claims you make are warranted. Unlike a jury, however, they will expect you to do the work of considering all sides of the argument. If they sense that you have been cherry picking – that is, that you are only presenting the findings that support your argument while studiously ignoring all the evidence that might weaken it – they will simply look harder for things to challenge. So rather than thinking of yourself as a lone attorney standing up to obtain justice for your misunderstood defendant, think of yourself as prosecuting attorney, defence attorney, and judge all rolled up in one. Your readers need to feel that they have been guided fairly through all sides of your case.

Below, I discuss the things you should be thinking about as you lay the foundation of your argument by presenting your results and analysis. Regardless of what kind of research you have done or what kind of thesis you are writing, what you are trying to do here is to systematically present the evidence that backs up the claims you want to make. There are different ways of doing this depending on your particular context and audience. Here I discuss some key concerns related to whether you have used a fixed design to test hypotheses or a flexible design to generate hypotheses, what storytelling genre is associated with your methodological approach, whether you are using qualitative or quantitative methods, and how you can present your findings visually.

ⓐ WHAT KIND OF ARGUMENT ARE YOU TRYING TO MAKE?

What constitutes sufficient support for your argument depends on what kind of argument you are trying to make. Fixed research designs usually aim to test hypotheses; that is, based on an existing theory, they develop hypotheses that they can test by systematically gathering and examining data. The argument is deductive in nature. Flexible designs, on the other hand, usually aim to generate hypotheses; that is, based on the data they gathered, they develop a proposition, or set of propositions. The argument is inductive in nature. The logic of your overall research design thus affects the logic of how you organize the presentation of your research. There are at least three different ways in which fixed and flexible designs present analysis differently.

Perhaps the main difference is whether you analyse your findings in one place and interpret them in another, or whether you weave analysis and interpretation together. If you have used a fixed design, where you determined beforehand exactly what hypotheses you would be testing, what variables would be involved, and what kind of tests you would perform, then you most likely will want to separate the presentation of your results from the discussion – in other words, to separate the analysis from the interpretation. You will generally want to organize your analysis section around a presentation of each hypothesis, systematically presenting the descriptive statistics, then the statistical tests, and then in a separate chapter discussing what these results mean in the light of your overarching research questions or hypotheses (see Chapter 12).

If you have used a flexible design, where you were guided by a general research question in exploring a topic that took shape over the course of the research, the presentation of your findings will be quite different. You will most likely present the analysis and interpretation of your findings in the same section (or sections) of your thesis. (See the section below on presenting qualitative analysis.)

A second difference between fixed and flexible designs is the amount of intellectual drift you can expect – that is, how much you can expect your argument to change over the course of the research and writing process. Fixed designs allow little intellectual drift. A lot of the creative intellectual work is done beforehand in developing the research design, while the research focuses on carrying it out and faithfully describing the findings. Flexible designs are by their nature less defined and more exploratory, and much of the analytical thinking – and thus the research – happens when you examine your data more closely in the writing phase. As you write (and rewrite) your analysis, you may well find that you end up making a different argument than you thought you would when you started writing. It might not be completely different, but it might have a higher degree of precision or a slightly different emphasis than you expected. The more you revise and polish these thoughts, the more you run the risk of asking one question in your introduction and answering a different one in your analysis. This may necessitate a change in the research question (usually by making it more precise). Your ability to change the research question in response to the development of your analysis is one of the key advantages of a flexible design, but it does require that you pay extra close attention to the connection between your research question, your data, and your analysis as you write and revise (see Chapter 7).

 KEIKO

I was unsure about the best way to organize the presentation of my results because I wasn't testing specific hypotheses. In the first draft, I wrote up the analysis of the video observations, then the analysis of the interviews, and finally the analysis of the focus group. Like this:

(Continued)

(Continued)

a   Analysis of interviews
   i Description of own teaching experience
   ii Stated strategies

b   Analysis of video observations
   i Content and language of teaching session
   ii Interaction with students (focus on grammar vs communication)

c   Analysis of focus group
   i Group understanding of explicit teaching goals
   ii Group understanding of implicit teaching goals.

But my supervisor pointed out that doing it that way did not help me answer my research question, which explored how teachers try to teach communication. So I tried organizing this section by looking at each person separately, and examining how each of the methods told me something different about that person. Doing it that way meant that I focused less on activities (such as 'correcting a student's grammar') and more on the tensions between things they said, things they did, and how they understood their goals.

A third difference between fixed and flexible designs has to do with how you communicate your positionality as a researcher to the reader – that is, to what extent you write reflexively in your analysis. In fixed, hypothesis-testing approaches, you are usually as absent as you can be. In fact, many of the tests you will want to present are designed to ensure that your analysis was not a result of any individual biases you might have, and referring to yourself as 'I' is unusual (if not outright discouraged). In flexible approaches, you as an individual are more likely to be much more present in the analysis, and using 'I' is much more common. Rather than showing the reader tests that prove you are impervious to bias, you will probably have a greater focus on being transparent about your reasoning and reflecting on how your positionality might have a bearing on what you think you are seeing in your data. Even if you include a separate section on positionality in your method section or introduction, you still need to consider the extent to which or whether you will also write reflexively in your analysis. Also note that the extent to which reflexivity is expected of you is as much a matter of local convention as it is a matter of what kind of research you have carried out; ask your supervisor about the expectations in your department.

ⓑ GENRE CONVENTIONS OF YOUR METHODOLOGICAL APPROACH

In addition to the constraints and opportunities provided by your sort of design, the way you tell your story will depend on the general conventions of your methodology. As I argued in Chapter 10, the labels you use to describe your methodology – case study, experiment, ethnography, survey, and so on – create expectations in the reader for how you will present and discuss what you have found. You do not present a case study the same way you present an ethnography or a phenomenological study; you do not present a correlational study the same way you would present an experiment. Each methodological approach carries with it conventions for storytelling, organization, and format. Find examples of the methodology you are using and take note of how they present their analysis. If all the examples you find follow exactly the same pattern, this should tell you that the expectations are quite rigid, and if you deviate from this format you should have good reason and communicate that reason clearly to the reader. If every example you find does it differently, then you have a high degree of flexibility; this does not excuse you from having to explain your choices to the reader, however, and the examples you look at can give you good ideas about how to do this.

Having a clear idea about what the general conventions are for the overarching methodological approach you are using can help keep you on track when you wish to integrate different methods in your analysis, or present different kinds of data (see textbox on multimodality). For example, if you are doing an ethnography and you present some quantitative data to illustrate some aspects of the setting, you do not want your reader to forget that this is in the context of an ethnographic study, not a correlational study: you do not want to be evaluated on the wrong set of criteria. In the next sections, I describe different strategies for presenting qualitative, quantitative, and theoretical analyses.

....

Multimodality

If you have worked with video and audio recordings as data, you might have to think creatively about the best way to present your findings. Fortunately, in many contexts you are no longer limited to what you can put on paper. If your institution allows, you might be able to present audio and video findings through hyperlinks to a website, for example. However, keep in mind that, for various reasons, it probably is not a good idea to rely completely on a net-based presentation. While allowing your reader to hear what you heard and see what you saw might make more of an impact than words alone, the words should probably be there as well in a (partial) transcription and description.

....

ⓒ PRESENTING QUANTITATIVE DATA ANALYSIS

Quantitative analysis generally aims to say something general based on a large number of observations. Your confidence about what you have found depends largely on how many observations you have, the extent to which you are accurately measuring what you want to measure and testing what you want to test, the degree to which the things you have observed are generalizable to other contexts, and how accurately you are able to interpret your results. This means that the reader will be curious about all of these things.

The number of observations you have – as well as the possibility of generalizing beyond those observations – is a direct result of the way you designed your research to get your data and the number of responses you are actually able to work with. In your method section, you should have already told the reader the strategy you used to obtain your observations: whether you used a pre-existing dataset (that you perhaps augmented with your own data) or built one up on your own. You should also have already said something about what kind of sampling decisions you made, and how you approached your informants or acquired documents. Now you can present what you ended up with: the size of the dataset, the response rate on the questionnaire, and missing observations.

AMINA

In the analysis section, I first gave some general descriptive statistics about my data: what the data from the larger study covered, the total number of women in the study, and some background on income levels and proximity to the hospital. After I finished the description of my data, I organized the rest of the section around the three main sets of hypotheses on poverty, infrastructure, and insecurity, examining what the data said about each of these hypotheses. Mostly I focused on simple tables and bivariate analyses, but I also decided to run a regression on the access to various maternal health services (such as pre-natal check-ups and giving birth at the hospital) to test the impact of the various determinants. I explained why I used a logit regression based on the way I coded the dependent variable.

Because all of your findings are based on the initial set of observations you were able to get, you need to explain these observations in as much detail as you can before you go about addressing each of your hypotheses. You might want to do this in the form of a table or figure that shows how many observations (n) fell into the various categories you were interested in (see the section below on visual representation of analysis). For example, if you are looking at the difference in grades between male and female university students and wondering whether the difference can be partly explained by the year of study and income of parents, you could provide a table that shows how many women and men were in your study, and how many fell into each category of parental income you looked at.

As you move on to presenting the findings for each hypothesis, think carefully about what kind of information will be important for the reader to know. Quantitative methods offer many different ways to look at and test your data. Not all will be equally useful for every purpose. A good place to begin is the descriptive statistics for each variable: measures of central tendency (such as mean, median, and mode) and measures of variability (such as range, deviation, or variance). Basically this means saying something about what the typical observation is, and how typical it is. In many cases the descriptive statistics might be sufficient – particularly if the quantitative analysis plays only a small role in your overall methodology – for example, if you are presenting the results of a small questionnaire conducted within a larger qualitative case study.

But be careful about misleading levels of precision. Much of what we observe in social science is somewhat imprecise, and yet it tends to result in a very precise number. For example, say you are studying leadership styles by observing meetings and counting the number of times people interrupt each other or demonstrate other strategies of dominance or power; deciding beforehand what constitutes a demonstration of power is difficult enough, but it might be even more difficult in practice. Did that person interrupt someone else on purpose, or just clear his throat for a natural reason? You will certainly have to make some judgement calls. And then when you add them up and describe your data as a whole, you will end up wanting to say something like 'During the average meeting, men displayed 14.83 power demonstrations compared to only 8.37 by women'. Here, the numbers after the decimal point suggest a level of precision that is simply not possible to achieve.

Your next concern is to decide whether you want to go beyond descriptive statistics and perform additional statistical tests, such as a regression. This is a good time to review – for both you and the reader – the criteria for performing such a test, and what exactly that particular test will be able to tell you, and not tell you. For example, if you want to run a linear regression, remind the reader that the purpose of this kind of regression is to measure the correlation between the dependent variable and some independent variables, as long as the data can satisfy a number of assumptions (e.g., a representative sample and the independent variables are not strongly related to one another, and so on). If your data do not satisfy the basic assumptions or criteria for running regressions, then a regression would be inappropriate; if you want to perform a regression anyway, then you will have to come up with a pretty convincing argument of why it would be a good idea and what it would be able to tell you.

Sometimes you might be tempted to perform additional tests that weren't planned when you designed your research (for example, you might want to look at how the independent variables are related to one another). If this is the case, then after you have finished going systematically through the results for each of your hypotheses you can then explain why you wanted to perform those tests and give their results.

End the presentation of your results in a summary that synthesizes your findings in a way that you might not have been able to do when discussing one variable at a time. This will give you a chance to point out contradictions and anomalies and prepare your reader for the next step: talking about what your findings mean. Most hypothesis-testing designs will discuss the significance of the procedures or tests in a subsequent section or chapter called 'Discussion'. There, you can talk about how the results of tests you performed support or fail to support your hypothesis, and what this means for the fundamental theory or your overarching research question.

ⓓ PRESENTING QUALITATIVE DATA ANALYSIS

There is no one clear, obvious way to analyse and present qualitative data. It is mostly about thinking clearly, using common sense, listening to what the data are telling you, and not saying anything more about that data than you can justify on the basis of what you find. Clear thinking and sensitivity to your data require being aware of your own tendencies to over- or underreact to what you see or hear, your desire to tell the story you thought you would be able to tell before you started your research, and how what you are seeing or hearing is shaped by what you were able to get access to. The way you analyse your data will also be more or less unique to your overall research design, methodology, research question, and the kind of material you are looking at. Qualitative data is normally associated with flexible, hypothesis-generating designs, but it is also possible to use qualitative data to test hypotheses – for example, if you use quasi-statistical approaches such as content analysis to look at the relative frequencies of words, phrases, or concepts. Remembering your purpose for gathering this data in the first place will help you think through the best way for you to present what you have found.

 ROBERT

I decided to present the results in three different chapters, each based on a major theme that arose in the analysis: how the religious organization acted as a tie to the country of origin, how being welcomed despite a 'moral' weakness helped these teenagers feel like they belonged somewhere and made it easier to cope with the pressures of getting clean, and finally how being turned away led to feelings of isolation. It would have been possible, I suppose, to put all of the results in the same chapter. But this kind of organization allowed me to go into more depth for each theme – to really dig into what my informants were telling me, to explore the nuances, and to connect what they were saying to what was in the literature.

One of the biggest challenges of analysing qualitative data is simply getting the sheer amount of it into manageable chunks, which is kind of like trying to wrestle a pack of lions into dog cages. Many researchers do this by coding their data, and then arranging the coded data into meaningful categories called themes (thematic analysis). Because the world generally does not organize itself into obvious categories for your convenience, you will have to make decisions about how to construct these themes and what it is you want to say about them – whether you want to focus on similarities and differences, or relationships or connections between them. In the presentation of your findings, you can organize your discussion around the main themes you want to draw attention to, based on the story you want to tell.

Alternatively, if you have used a multiple case-study approach where the cases are people or organizations, you might want to organize your presentation around each case – and possibly around themes within each case. Presenting on a case basis will give you greater opportunity to provide 'thick description', which is important in ethnographic approaches, but will make it far more difficult to anonymize your participants or cases. The more detail you add, even if you use fictitious names, the easier it might be for a reader to figure out the person or organization from the clues you leave in the narrative.

SAMIR

I decided to discuss each case separately, which allowed me to go into detail for each village. Using the concept of Corporate Social Responsibility (CSR) from the theory chapter to structure my analysis, I said things like, 'Village A has a high degree of corruption, as exhibited by both the experiences from previous companies and the lack of legal frameworks' and, 'Village B has little experience with multinationals; while there are few legal frameworks in place, there is also little corruption'.

The way you organize the presentation of your findings should thus be a deliberate move on your part to draw attention to where you want it: should it be on individual people, cases, chronology, themes, or something else? Looking back at your research question to remind yourself what you want to be saying something about should help in this respect. If, for example, your question is about how individual people cope with issues of work-life balance, then structuring your presentation around individual narratives will allow you to go into detail about the unique strategies of each person. But if your question is more about what kinds of obstacles people face, then organizing your analysis based on the themes that came up in the interviews will allow you to explore the obstacles themselves more fully, rather than the people who talked about them.

It is natural to combine the presentation of qualitative analysis with some interpretation of what you have found. But be careful to indicate the difference between what you found and what you think it means. For example, there is a big difference between saying 'An implicit gender bias was evident in the interactions among the leader team', and saying 'In my observations of the leader team, the men seemed to treat suggestions made by women less seriously than those made by other men, which suggests an implicit gender bias'. There is a fine line between giving your data extra depth by connecting what you see with what has been talked about in the existing literature and simply drawing unfounded conclusions based on insufficient evidence. As with interpreting quantitative results, the way to stay on the right side of this line is to stay close to your data. If you cannot find visible support for your claims in your data, then you simply cannot make those claims. But sometimes that visible support is hard to see unless you look at it through a particular theoretical lens. Perhaps you have what you consider to be a very 'telling' quote from one of your partici-pants, but to anyone else the quote might look perfectly ordinary. This is where interpretation comes in: you need to explain why the quote is 'telling'. What does your theoretical perspective allow you to see? How can you show this to the reader? It may take pages (sometimes many pages) to properly interpret one short passage of text, a short clip from a video or audio recording, or a quote from an informant.

Remember that inductive logic does not require you to argue that the themes you present were the only themes to emerge, and that all data is somehow included in these themes. Rather, inductive logic requires you to show how your data links to the theme and to explain – usually with reference to your theoretical framework (unless you are carrying out a strict version of Grounded Theory) – how and why this theme is significant or meaningful with respect to your research question. You do not need to say that this is the only way to look at it, but you do need to make an argument for why this is a valid way of looking at it, and be as transparent as possible about why you think so. This is not the same thing as trying to establish its statistical significance. It is not at all uncommon to have more data than you can do justice to (particularly if you are drawing on hundreds of hours of interviews or months of participant observation), so thinking carefully about your overall objective can help you decide what to focus on and what you can safely leave out – without jeopardizing the integrity of your research.

(e) PRESENTING A NON-EMPIRICAL (OR THEORETICAL) ANALYSIS

A non-empirical (or theoretical) thesis – one that aims to contribute an idea based on an exploration of other ideas – does not approach analysis in the same way as an empirical one, mainly because the claims you are making draw primarily from reasons rather than evidence (see Chapter 7). This means that you have a different relationship to 'data' than those doing empirical work. For both qualitative and quantitative research, writing your analysis requires you to demonstrate that you are listening closely to what your data are telling you. In theoretical work, however, your argument is based on ideas and logic. Perhaps you are deconstructing a concept, challenging the assumptions behind another person's theory about how things happen, or examining the implications of some normative assumptions. You may draw from facts and data – sometimes even data you have gathered yourself – to illustrate the point you are trying to make. But the point needs to be valid even in the absence of data. The logic alone is what carries the argument.

For example, say you want to critically examine the notion of liberal peacebuilding by looking at its ethical justification in the scholarly literature and examples of how it is practised. Even though you might be looking at some real-life examples of how liberal peacebuilding is practised, your main argument will focus on clarifying and evaluating the different positions on the notion of liberal peacebuilding. The concrete examples you draw on can be 'cherry-picked' in the sense that you do not have the same duty to 'stay close to your data'. Your analysis is based on how you deconstruct ideas and present this to your reader. The examples you provide are simply that: examples.

EMMA

The main thing I was trying to do in my analysis was to dig into: (i) what it means to understand gender as something you perform instead of something biological; (ii) how the categories describing crime and how the social understanding of what is 'criminal' reify masculinity and heteronormativity; and (iii) how the combination of these ideas means that women are simply not considered threatening, almost regardless of their actions – but once it is acknowledged that they have acted outside gendered heteronormative roles, they are treated more harshly than men. I used crime statistics to illustrate what I was saying, but they were statistics someone else collected. My main challenge was to explain how these ideas connect, and what these connections mean.

PRESENTING YOUR DATA VISUALLY

You can use more than words to present your evidence and reasons: a visual representation can help your reader understand what you are trying to say in ways that explanation solely through text cannot. Normally we speak of tables and figures, but figures can include anything that is not a table, including illustrations, photographs, line-drawings, flow charts, pie charts, bar graphs, histograms, scatter plots, and so on. There are very many excellent books and sources you can use to help you with the technicalities of drawing tables and figures (see, e.g., Few 2012; Yau 2011), but in the context of this book there are three specific things worth thinking about.

What does the table or figure communicate that is not evident from the text alone? If you decide to add a table or figure, you should do so for a good reason. In other words, that table or figure should be doing something that text alone cannot do. Tables and figures can exist for many different purposes: when you present quantitative data, the data in the table are usually more detailed than the results you discuss in the text. So you can argue that the table shows the reader all of the numbers, while the text only discusses those that are most important. But when you use a table to present qualitative data, the purpose is often the opposite: the table can summarize the relatively lengthy presentation you have given in the text and boil it down to some few key words or phrases to make it easier for the reader to compare one perspective with another.

Figures generally depict relationships between one thing and another – changes over time, networks, how one thing affects another, and so on. With quantitative data, a scatterplot will show something different than a histogram, so think carefully about the message you want to communicate. For example, are you more interested in showing means (or averages), or showing exactly how the data are distributed around those means? When you communicate an idea through a figure – for example, the relationship between overlapping bodies of theory – the choices you make about how you illustrate these relationships matter (see Figure 9.1 in Chapter 9). The clearer you are about the purpose of that table or figure, the more likely that table or figure will function as you want it to.

KEIKO

I really wanted to be able to include video clips in my discussion of the results, but my department currently does not allow multimodal submissions. Instead, I captured some still pictures that illustrated some of the points I wanted to discuss in the analysis. I also saved some segments where I had pixelated both the faces of the teachers and the children in the classroom and provided a link to the files. I included this as an appendix.

How do you know that your reader will understand what they are supposed to from this table or figure? Tables and figures can be confusing to the reader. Because you already know what they are trying to communicate, you are a poor judge of whether or not they work. Ask someone unfamiliar with your work to try to read them out loud – that is, to look at the table or figure and say out loud what they see. With tables, it is very easy to inadvertently include too little information, making it difficult for a reader to be sure about what a given number is supposed to mean. You can hear this if you ask your friend to pick a random row or cell from the table and read it out loud: 'This shows that in 2014, the number of incarcerated prisoners in country x was y'. With figures, sometimes elements are not differentiated clearly enough, the typeface is too small to read, or the labels are confusing. Models in particular can be problematic because they are often drawn to help you sort out your own thinking, but end up being too complex for a reader to understand. When you have a dense network of boxes, arrows, and circles, sometimes the reader does not even know where to start looking. Again, you may not realize this unless you ask someone to take a look at your model and tell you what they see and you watch them panic: 'This looks like, wait a minute, let's see, uh, that is to say, I can see that these things are connected, but there is a wavy line here that I don't quite understand the meaning of …'. If this is the case, then your model is worse than useless: it takes up a lot of space and ends up confusing the reader – especially if you made that model early on in your research without updating it as your thinking changed. If your figure is effective, the reader will say with confidence, 'This shows how local and national factors overlap, and when there is conflict between the two, this is resolved through the judgement of the individual'.

Is there a better way to show the relationships I want to portray? It might be conventional to display data in a certain way (such as a regression table), but that does not mean that that is the best way to do it. Fortunately, it is becoming more common to think

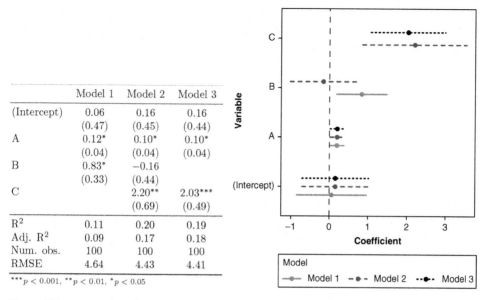

	Model 1	Model 2	Model 3
(Intercept)	0.06	0.16	0.16
	(0.47)	(0.45)	(0.44)
A	0.12*	0.10*	0.10*
	(0.04)	(0.04)	(0.04)
B	0.83*	−0.16	
	(0.33)	(0.44)	
C		2.20**	2.03***
		(0.69)	(0.49)
R^2	0.11	0.20	0.19
Adj. R^2	0.09	0.17	0.18
Num. obs.	100	100	100
RMSE	4.64	4.43	4.41

$^{***}p < 0.001$, $^{**}p < 0.01$, $^{*}p < 0.05$

Figure 11.1 **Presenting data in different ways:** The table on the left shows data presented in table form, while the figure on the right demonstrates how the same data can be visualized differently.

beyond the traditional table (which is more or less a printout of the results from the software package) and instead use visualizations such as the scatterplot (see Figure 11.1). You might not want to replace your traditional tables, but you can certainly think about augmenting your presentation by alternative ways to visualize your results. See, e.g., Few (2012) and Yau (2011) for some good ideas about how to do this.

The key point to remember here is that each of the findings you include in your analysis – whether presented in the form of statistics, organized into themes, or depicted through tables and figures – should help you in some way to answer your research question. These findings constitute the support you draw on when you construct your main claims, which is what we will look at in the next chapter.

'The foolish reject what they see, not what they think. The wise reject what they think, not what they see.'

Presenting your analysis means staying close to the data and showing the reader what you see, regardless of whether or not it was what you thought you would see when you started. Whether you are using a flexible or fixed design – or working qualitatively, quantitatively, or theoretically – the reader has to be able to see how your findings relate to both the method that you used and the claims that you are making. The reader has to be convinced that you are not simply picking the results that conform to a preconceived idea you had before you

(Continued)

(Continued)

started, but that by following the path you set out for yourself through your method, you are truly reporting what those data are telling you, and that these data are forming the basis of your claims. If you are working theoretically, you will have to be no less rigorous: you have to see all the logical steps you are making in your argument, and show them to the reader so they can see them as well.

 Finding your path: Points for reflection

What is the logic of your story, and what role is played by your data?
- Are your data expected to test a hypothesis? Or do they provide a point of departure for generating a hypothesis?
- What is the conventional way to present findings within your methodological tradition?

Given the logic of your story, what is the best way for you to organize your results?
- Do you have a set of hypotheses or variables that could structure the presentation of your findings?
- Do you have a set of themes or cases that you wish to highlight?

What kind of visualizations (tables, figures, images, etc.) can you provide to help illustrate your findings?

REFERENCES AND FURTHER READING

Booth, Wayne C., Colomb, Gregory G., and Williams, Joseph M. (2008) *The Craft of Research*, 3rd edn. Chicago, IL: University of Chicago Press. Chapter 13 covers things to think about when presenting your data, and Chapter 15 succinctly covers important considerations for presenting information graphically.

Bui, Yvonne N. (2009) *How to Write a Master's Thesis*. London: Sage. Bui presents a highly detailed, but also somewhat prescriptive framework for approaching data analysis that is mostly focused on presenting quantitative data.

Cresswell, John W. (2003) *Research Design: Qualitative, Quantitative, and Mixed Methods Approaches*, 2nd edn. Thousand Oaks, CA: Sage. Cresswell provides a useful step-by-step guide to analysing both qualitative and quantitative data.

Few, Stephen (2012) *Show Me the Numbers: Designing Tables and Graphs to Enlighten.* Burlingame, CA: Analytics Press. Particularly helpful for presenting quantitative data, the book looks at both the purpose of tables and graphs, as well as design issues.

Hennink, Monique, Hulter, Inge, and Bailey, Ajay (2011) *Qualitative Research Methods*. London: Sage. Chapter 11, 'Writing qualitative research' looks at how to present your qualitative analysis.

Lunenburg, Fred C. and Irby, Beverly J. (2008) *Writing a Successful Thesis or Dissertation: Tips and Strategies for Students in the Social and Behavioral Sciences*. Thousand Oaks, CA: Corwin Press. Chapter 9 looks specifically at presenting results, focusing mainly on presenting quantitative data.

Roberts, Carol M. (2010) *The Dissertation Journey: A Practical and Comprehensive Guide to Planning, Writing, and Defending Your Dissertation*, 2nd edn. Thousand Oaks, CA: Corwin Press. Chapter 14 briefly covers analysing and presenting results for both qualitative and quantitative data.

Robson, Colin (2011) *Real World Research*, 3rd edn. West Sussex: John Wiley and Sons. Robson's pragmatic approach to analysing and interpreting data is refreshingly useful, particularly if you are using a flexible design.

Thody, Angela M. (2006) *Writing and Presenting Research*. London: Sage. Chapters 8–10 look at how to write about quantified data, qualitative data, and narrative data, respectively.

Yau, Nathan (2011) *Visualize This: The FlowingData Guide to Design, Visualization, and Statistics*. Indianapolis, IL: Wiley Publishing. Written on the basis of concrete examples, the book challenges you to consider different ways to think about presenting data.

12

YOUR DISCUSSION AND CONCLUSION

So, what does all this mean?

....

a Summarizing your study

b The purpose of a discussion

   i Discussing quantitative data analysis

   ii Discussing qualitative data analysis

c Implications for existing theory

d Implications for practice or policy

e Recommendations for future research

f Concluding

....

You've now meticulously presented all of your evidence before the jury: Exhibit A, a gas station receipt! Exhibit B, a shattered wine glass! Exhibit C, a blood-stained carpet! Surely, your argument must be obvious to them now, right? Unfortunately, facts very seldom speak for themselves. The significance of each piece of evidence might be obvious to you because you have been working so closely and so intensely with your material for a long period of time. But that does not mean the reader will immediately grasp the importance of each thing you want to show them. And if, in your enthusiasm to make your case, you just pummel them relentlessly with numbers, quotes from informants, facts or ideas, without taking them step-by-step through your thinking, you will not persuade them so much as overwhelm them. Even the most compelling facts have an astoundingly poor ability to make an argument in themselves: it is the way you put them together and explain their significance that creates a compelling argument.

The 'Discussion' part of your thesis is typically where you take that step back and tell the reader what your results mean, and how they fit into the larger discourse. This is often the heart of the thesis, where the substance and significance of your argument is developed in full, where you explicitly construct your claims. The 'Conclusion' is where you wrap up your story by making your argument as concisely as possible. And somewhere in here you should be stretching out and thinking about the implications of your work for theory, practice, or future research. Be aware that there are enormous variations in local conventions regarding where you write about what. In the standard five-chapter thesis, it is normal to combine the discussion and conclusion in a single chapter. But there is still little agreement about what that chapter should actually contain (see Figure 12.1). Moreover, not everyone writes a standard five-chapter thesis. For some, it will be natural to merge their discussion with their results section; others may place their results, discussion, and conclusion in three different chapters. Your decision about where to discuss your findings and what should go in your concluding chapter should be guided both by your particular research and the particular conventions of your methodology and university setting. Below I talk about some of the main things that your reader will be expecting you to cover in the last chapter(s) of your thesis.

Lunenburg and Irby (2008: 225)	Bui (2009: 191)	Roberts (2010: 178)	Petre and Rugg (2010: 156)

• Introduction
• Summary of the study
• Discussion of the findings
• Implications for practice
• Recommendations for future research
• Conclusions
	• Introduction
	• Discussion
	• Limitations
	• Recommendations for future research
	• Conclusion
		• Introduction
		• Summary of the study
		  o Overview of the problem
		  o Purpose statement and research questions
		  o Review of the methodology
		  o Major findings
		• Findings related to the literature
		• Surprises
		• Conclusions
		
		  o Implications for action
		  o Recommendations for further research
		
		• Concluding remarks
			• Summary of results (may be compared explicitly against objectives stated in the introduction)
			• Discussion about how the results generalize
			• Discussion of limitations (phrased positively)
			• Statement of contribution to knowledge
			• Future work (phrased strongly and positively)
			• Speculation (in moderation)

Figure 12.1 **Multiple paths to concluding your argument:** While it is common advice to say that the discussion and conclusion is where you switch from presenting your findings to developing an argument about what they mean, there is little agreement on how exactly to do it. This table compares how four different books on thesis writing, all of which assume the discussion and conclusion are combined, recommend you organize your final chapter.

ⓐ SUMMARIZING YOUR STUDY

The final chapter of your thesis should start with a summary of the study. If you are combining your discussion and conclusion, that means providing a summary before you start discussing. If you have already discussed your findings when you presented your results, or if you decided to put your discussion in a separate chapter, then the summary appears after your discussion as the first part of your conclusion.

Summarizing your work is good for both you and the reader because at this point you might feel like you have run out of stuff to say. You might feel like you have looked at your findings upside down and sideways, and turned them inside out to explore their significance. You are probably also well and truly sick of this whole thing and are distracting yourself with visions of weekends without writing. But before you exit this conversation, you need to take one more deep breath and bring you and your reader back full circle.

When you introduced your thesis, you started by setting up a conversation and marking your place in it: you reviewed the existing literature and indicated where your voice was relative to the others. You pointed out knowledge gaps, made a space for the relevance of your work, and asked a question (or set of questions) that promised to add something to this conversation. After that, you dug deep. In your method section you laid your tools out for your reader, explained the purpose of each one, and got to work. You meticulously showed the reader what you found, and discussed the significance of each nugget you uncovered.

But now it is time to revisit that original puzzle which motivated your research in the first place, the one you've probably forgotten about by now. Use a couple of pages to sum up your study. Remind the reader (and perhaps yourself) of what that conversation was about, and the questions you asked or hypotheses you tested. Say briefly how you went about answering those questions or testing those hypotheses, including which theoretical perspectives and methods you used.

If you have already discussed your results, then summarize both the results and discussion. Focus on presenting your core argument as cleanly as possible: what claims are you making and how do your results support those claims? If you have not yet discussed your results, then it might make more sense for you to summarize your results one at a time as you discuss them. Below, I look at some things to think about in your discussion regardless of what kind of research design you have used, before considering quantitative and qualitative analysis separately.

 EMMA

My discussion was developed over three chapters, so I used the last chapter to go back to my research question and present my argument more concisely. Summarizing my argument actually forced me to rethink it because it didn't seem to come together as neatly as I thought it would. I had to go back to my analysis and look more carefully at each step of the argument, and I saw that I was missing a few crucial transitions – that I jumped from one idea to the next without explaining the connection. So, in a way I used writing the summary to see my analysis more clearly.

ⓑ THE PURPOSE OF A DISCUSSION

The main purpose of the discussion is to answer the 'so what?' question for the reader and spell out for them exactly what you are adding to the conversation. In your results and analysis, you meticulously stayed close to your data and told the reader what you found. Now you need to step back and talk about what it means. To return to the metaphor of the courtroom, this is like asking the expert witness – who has just described in painstaking detail how he ran the gloop from a carpet stain through a mass spectrometer and was able to determine the chemical composition of that gloop – to explain what he means in words the rest of us will understand; the expert then takes a deep breath and says 'It appears that somebody spilled silver polish on the carpet no less than two hours before the sample was taken'. So, when you get to your discussion section, imagine a lawyer telling you to explain to the jury exactly what your results are showing us – and not showing us. There are two main things you need to cover in this respect.

First, go back to your research question(s) or hypotheses. How do your findings shed light on your question? If you have used hypotheses, to what extent do your findings support your hypotheses? This is the part of your thesis where you develop your main argument in full (see Chapter 7). By closely examining the data and thinking through what it means, you formulate one or more claims that respond to the question(s) you asked in the beginning. Each question you asked and each hypothesis you tested must be reflected in these claims, but you can make an overarching argument that cuts across the various questions and hypotheses. This is where you put into words your contribution to the conversation.

 ROBERT ▬▬▬▬▬▬▬▬▬▬▬▬▬▬▬▬▬▬

I did a lot of discussing in the presentation of my results, certainly with respect to connecting the interview results to other studies on addiction and immigrant youth. But I wanted to get at the larger issues of belonging and the role of organized religion. I decided I could develop those ideas more deeply in a separate discussion chapter.

Second, you put your argument into a larger context by returning to the literature you presented in your literature review. Your question was motivated by some knowledge gaps in the literature. Think now about how your argument addresses these gaps – how it builds on, challenges, or supports the other literature in this conversation. You can think of this part of your discussion as being a kind of mirror opposite to your literature review: the literature review foregrounds the literature and your research plays a supporting role; in your discussion, your research is foregrounded and the literature plays a supporting role. Just be careful to avoid introducing entirely new strands of literature (see textbox on 'Bringing new literature into your discussion').

Bringing new literature into your discussion

Many students wonder whether or not it is acceptable to bring new literature (that is, literature you have not yet mentioned) into the discussion or conclusion. Depending on your particular setting there might be some strong (negative) feelings about this. In general, it is to be avoided, but there are some nuances here depending on the research design you have used. If you have used a deductive approach, introducing new literature in either the discussion or the conclusion is seldom accepted. In particular, bringing in a brand new *theory* that you have not yet introduced to the reader will feel like springing a surprise witness on the jury at the last second, and few readers will appreciate this. (If the new theory seems so important that you are tempted to bring it in anyway, then it is a good idea to go back to your literature review or theoretical framework and introduce it there.)

However, referring to as-yet-unmentioned empirical studies that relate to your findings might be something different; if you have foreshadowed a certain body of literature in your literature review, you can bring specific studies into the discussion that might not have been mentioned in particular. For example, if you are doing research on organizational mergers, relevant theory about mergers must have been mentioned in your literature review, but while discussing a particular finding you could bring up an example of a particular study that was not mentioned specifically: 'This is similar to what Albright (2012) found in her examination of organizational mergers in Ireland following the financial crisis'. If you have used an inductive approach, especially if you are modelling your design on Grounded Theory, then introducing new literature into your discussion is much more acceptable – maybe even expected. The conclusion, however, is never a good place to introduce new literature of any kind.

No matter what kind of research design you have used, the main focus of your discussion should be reflecting on your overall argument and putting it back into the context of the ongoing academic conversation. But there are some differences in how you do this for qualitative and quantitative research.

ⓘ Discussing quantitative data analysis

It is very tempting to let numbers speak for themselves. But running a pile of numbers through a program like SPSS or Stata and then pasting the result in table form into the text just shows that you know how to enter data into a computer and tell it to do something. Discussing your results shows your reader that you understand what this table is telling you, or not telling you.

The way you organize this discussion is up to you. You can structure your discussion around each hypothesis, each variable, or your research questions. To make it easier for you to write and less confusing for the reader, however, it is probably wise to organize the discussion in the same way as you organized the presentation of your results. That is, if you presented your results by going through each hypothesis one at a time, then present your discussion the same way – except now you will focus on explaining to the reader the extent to which your hypotheses seem to be supported, and what this means for your overarching research question. Likewise, if you presented your results one variable at a time, you can structure your discussion similarly, perhaps stressing the extent to which your results reveal relationships between these variables. What is important here is that you stay close to your data and evaluate your results in light of the purpose of the study. That is, you need to answer the question 'How does what I found help me answer the questions I was asking?' As exciting as it is to think about what your findings might mean, do exercise some caution when interpreting your results. For example, you might do well to remind both yourself and the reader that correlation is not causation.

 AMINA

I combined my discussion and conclusion in one chapter where I tried to make sense of my analysis. I had expected security issues to play a bigger role, but poverty and infrastructure seemed to be more important and interrelated. For example, even when physically getting to a hospital was not an insurmountable problem, the ability to follow through on the advice, for example, to eat a more balanced diet, was highly restricted by poverty. In my section on relevance for practice, I pointed out that some programmes funded by NGOs have started sending midwives to rural areas to follow up with survivors of conflict-related violence, so these women have a slightly better chance of getting follow-up.

Negative findings – that is to say, when you seem to find no relationship whatsoever between the variables you so meticulously tested – are the nightmare of the quantitative researcher, suggesting that all the work you did was for nothing. True, it is extremely disappointing to go through all the work of setting up an experiment or a correlational study and seemingly find nothing to report, to admit that your findings do not help you at all in answering the question you wanted to ask. However, 'nothing' is in the eye of the beholder, and the way you address this apparent lack of result can make all the difference. It is important here to remember the effect that the bias against negative findings has on research and science as an endeavour. If researchers publish only positive findings, then other researchers may keep trying those things that *don't* work because nobody has dared to report that they've already tried that. The law of statistical probability suggests that even if there isn't really a relationship between two concepts, if you test them often enough, then five out of a hundred times there will appear to be a relationship anyway. Imagine then you are interested in that topic, and your research leads you to those five studies in which there appears to be a relationship, and you find no other studies suggesting a lack of a relationship because no one wants to publish negative findings. Quite naturally, you will base your theoretical point of departure on the existence of a relationship, and statistically speaking you are likely to be proven wrong. So, if you find 'nothing', give this 'nothing' at least as much attention in your discussion as anything else, particularly when discussing implications for theory, practice, and policy, or future research (see below).

It is also natural here to discuss your limitations. When it comes to explaining why things did not turn out as expected – whether you found the opposite of what you expected or nothing at all – you can explore at least three different reasons for this: sampling, instrumentation, or research design (Lunenburg and Irby 2008: 230). Was there something about the sample you were able to get that might have skewed your results? Maybe you were trying to get a random sample of the population but you stood in a shopping centre in the middle of the day when most people are at work, so you ended up with a disproportionate number of retired or unemployed people. Did the instrumentation work as intended? There could be something wrong with the instrument itself, or perhaps the way you used it. Perhaps you used a personality test developed in Europe and even though you had it translated into Spanish, it did not seem to work as intended among your participants in Latin America; this leads you to wonder whether it had an implicit cultural bias that distorted your findings. Or maybe there was something wrong with your entire research design. At this point you need to again think through the questions about validity in Chapter 2: did the research design allow you to get the kind of information you needed to answer your questions?

(ii) Discussing qualitative data analysis

When you work with qualitative data, it is likely that to a considerable degree you will discuss your results as you present them (see Chapter 11). The question is, then, what do you discuss in your discussion if you have already interpreted your results? Remember that the purpose of a discussion section is to take a step back and look at your work from a broader perspective. This means you cannot bring in any new results at this point: the idea is to talk more about the results you have already mentioned. So even if you have already interpreted and discussed the significance of various results presented in your analysis, you might want to have a separate discussion where you look at the results as a whole.

 KEIKO

Because I decided to organize the presentation of my results as 'cases', where each teacher represented an individual case, I made sure that my discussion allowed me to talk about the more general themes that were raised across the individual cases. I compared and contrasted the teachers' approaches, and connected what they said to the literature I used in my literature review.

Because most qualitative research is associated with an inductive, hypothesis-generating design, this would be where you develop your hypotheses, propositions, or theory. The interpretation you have already done in your analysis was probably connected to specific themes, cases, or examples. But now it is time to think about how you can construct theory, hypotheses, or propositions on the basis of those findings. Your job is not to test your theory in your thesis, but rather to argue for its plausibility. This means not only demonstrating that the claims you make are connected to your data, but also expressing these claims in the form of theoretical propositions that are possible to test, or at least useful as a basis from which to derive testable hypotheses. If you present a theoretical idea that can't even be challenged (perhaps because it is a self-fulfilling prophecy or simply a personal opinion), then your argument will not be considered strong enough. There is a big difference between saying 'The evidence from those leaving the blue-frog cult suggests that the decision to leave is precipitated by a traumatic personal crisis', and saying 'People who leave cults have finally understood something'. The first proposes a mechanism that is both testable and connected to the data; the second is a vague opinion that is difficult to test.

SAMIR

The aim of this study, from Company X's point of view, was for me to come up with some concrete recommendations, so I separated my discussion and conclusion into two sections. In the discussion, I developed a proposition about how Corporate Social Responsibility could be used to redefine the notion of 'success' and guide investment policy. I made sure to draw from both the concepts of 'success' I defined in the theory chapter, and my findings from the analysis, to provide substance for this argument – as well as to make it more concrete and possible to test in other settings. In the conclusion I had a specific section on recommendations that was based on the argument I developed in the discussion. I could not just say 'Do this' or 'don't do this' without being able to explain why.

In thinking through the claims you are making, you will also need to think through the natural limitations of your study and how safe it might be to generalize from your findings. Do you want to propose something that is only true for a given situation? Or do you think you can develop more generalized theory that can apply to a variety of situations? As a point of departure, if you are working qualitatively, the relatively small size of your sample is likely to limit how much you can generalize beyond the setting in which you are carrying out your research. On the other hand, the greater richness of detail generally allows more thorough exploration.

When you are considering your level of generalizability, think about the thing you are actually trying to say something about: the topic of your thesis (as described in Chapter 7). Let's say you are studying leadership styles at one particular secondary school in California. You need to decide whether you are ultimately trying to say something about leadership styles only in that school, or whether you want to say something about leadership styles in general, where this case is just one example of a phenomenon that might be generally true in secondary schools throughout California, or schools at all levels in the United States, or schools anywhere in the world that encompass the 15–18 age group. The further you move beyond your case, the more difficult it will be to support the claims you want to make, and the more important the argument you make about generalizability will be.

If you are looking closely at leadership styles in one particular context and you want to generalize beyond that context, you will need to discuss how you think that particular context affects your findings. For example, if you want to generalize about leadership styles in all contexts, you would have to present a convincing argument that the leadership styles you observed were directly related to the age group of the students and not related to culture – and this might be a difficult claim to support even if you can rely heavily on literature from other studies.

Below, I present some other things you might want to address in the final chapter(s) of your thesis, regardless of what kind of data you have worked with.

C IMPLICATIONS FOR EXISTING THEORY

As suggested above, when you are discussing the results of your study, you need to consider how your study relates to the findings from other literature. If you have primarily talked about your work in relation to other empirical studies, you might want to examine separately how your study supports or challenges existing theory in your field.

If you are deliberately setting out to test theory, then clearly you need to talk about the extent to which your findings show support for that theory or not. If your findings do not show support for the theory, then you might want to speculate about why (beyond your discussion of the limitations of your findings). This part of the discussion allows you to think critically about what *could* explain what you found. For example, say you had expected to find that women and men exhibited different leadership styles, that men were more authoritarian and women more likely to seek consensus because the theory that you are using proposes that leadership styles are gendered; your lack of evidence for these differences might be a result of limitations related to your particular study (which you have probably already discussed), but perhaps something is wrong with the theory itself: perhaps the general theory does not properly take into account how gender roles vary from setting to setting. You might suggest that perhaps in your particular setting it is more common for women to be authoritarian in all aspects of social life, and that is why you also saw authoritarian leadership styles among women in your study. So you could propose that an important addition to the theory would be to avoid essentialism and look to the context of the larger society. This is an important step beyond just thinking about the extent to which your hypotheses were supported.

Remember that right now you are simply discussing the implications your findings might have for theory, and speculating on how this might be developed. Unless you are working with a theoretical research question, it is not the aim of your thesis to end up saying something about theory. If the purpose of your study was to, for example, observe a particular setting and interpret your findings through the lens of a particular theory, you are still ultimately trying to say something about that particular setting – the theory is just helping you do this. For example, in a study on gender-based interactions within a leadership team you might use theory on implicit gender bias to help you interpret the interactions you observed. The purpose is to say something about those interactions, not about the theory on implicit gender bias. If you *also* observed something that would have implications for the theory on implicit gender bias, then make sure your discussion of the theory is not mixed up in the discussion about the interactions: here, a separate section entitled 'implications for theory' might help you mentally keep these separate.

Similarly, if the purpose of your thesis *is* to generate theory, then having a section called 'implications for theory' might be a bad idea simply because it will give the impression that you are bracketing that discussion when in fact it is the whole point of your thesis. Instead, you might want an entire chapter called something like 'Developing a new framework for investigating leadership styles', and then, drawing on your findings (and the discussion about your findings), you could develop an argument for one or more theoretical propositions.

(d) IMPLICATIONS FOR PRACTICE OR POLICY

Although the main purpose of a thesis is to contribute to an *academic* discourse, it is not unlikely that some of your findings will have relevance for the 'real world', not least because social sciences are grounded in the real-world interaction between human beings and society. For example, perhaps you have been doing an ethnographic exploration of the lifeworlds of immigrants. While your main findings are relevant for an academic discourse about how refugees conceptualize 'home' and 'belonging', some of the things you find might have very direct implications for practice (e.g., how refugees are processed and treated in shelters), or policy (e.g., how the government regulates placement of refugees). In fact, some graduate programmes are specifically intended to be relevant for practice, and thus the thesis would be considered incomplete if it did *not* include a discussion of what your findings mean for your role as a practitioner or for related policy.

 ROBERT

Because this research was based on problems I've met in my practice as a social worker, I wanted to make sure that my thesis ended up being useful for people in the field – not just gathering dust on some library shelf. So I spent some time thinking about how what I learned would change the way I worked with teenagers battling addiction, and I wrote a separate section on 'Implications for practice' that explicitly talked about what my findings mean for people in the field. For me personally, it was one of the most satisfying sections to write because it gave my research real meaning.

Thinking through the real-world implications of your work is always a good idea, and may be of genuine value to you in future grant-writing endeavours. However, if you are in a programme that does not automatically expect you to discuss the real-world implications of your work, and indeed, the topic of your study does not lend itself to such a discussion, then you need not feel obligated to 'invent' a discussion that is not called for. Keep in mind, though, that if you cannot see any real-world implications of your work at all, this might signal a future challenge for you in securing funding for further research.

(e) RECOMMENDATIONS FOR FUTURE RESEARCH

One question you are likely to be asked if you go through an oral defence of your thesis is 'What would you have done differently if you could do this again?' Instead of panicking and answering 'I would have taken that job at my dad's accounting firm and skipped the whole thing', you can address the question 'What would the natural next step be if I were to continue exploring this topic?' in the final chapter of your thesis. This might help you focus on the positive steps you have taken rather than all the hundreds of real and imagined 'mistakes' you might have made.

In considering what the next step might be, be as concrete as you can and stay close to your data. Rather than just saying a vague 'Of course, more research needs to be done', try to be explicit about what kind of research and why. For example, you might say:

The qualitative interviews in this study painted a picture of the complex decision-making processes undertaken by healthcare professionals when they are evaluating patients in their initial interviews. Based on these findings, a next step would be to evaluate to what extent the outcome of these interviews (particularly with respect to whether out-patient treatment is recommended) is based more on an evaluation of the patient or the treatment preferences of the healthcare worker.

(f) CONCLUDING

As you are wrapping up, remember that the most important job of this last chapter is to present your argument as concisely as possible, to draw attention to your contribution to the discourse in as few sentences as you can. If you haven't already formulated a clear core argument, this is the time to do it. Ask yourself the following key questions: What is the thing you are trying to say something about? What are you saying about that thing? And on what basis can you make that claim? You might find this very difficult to do, but it will help both you and the reader understand what this whole thesis was about.

Make sure you end on a strong note. To again return to the courtroom metaphor, you are now the attorney making the final plea to the jury before they go out and deliberate. This is your last chance to make an impression, and, fortunately, the final paragraph of anything you write is the one with the strongest rhetorical power – the one with the greatest potential to leave an impression on your reader. So for goodness sake, do not squander this opportunity and end with something like 'unfortunately, however, the response rate was low'. Ending with a focus on the limitations of your study more or less tells the reader 'Umm, never mind. Just forget what I said about those findings and the whole study. It doesn't matter anyway'. By all means talk about your limitations in your discussion, or perhaps even in your method chapter – just not in your conclusion. Instead, think about the 'so what' of your work as a whole. Why is what you have done meaningful? There are wide variations in regional conventions about how bold you need to be about this, but in any case you don't want the reader coming to the end and not even understanding what it was you were trying to add to the conversation.

Writing your concluding chapter(s), particularly writing your summary, might give you some additional thoughts about the original conversation you introduced your reader to. You might also have some ideas about a better way to phrase your research question. That's fairly normal because by the time you write your conclusion, you have come much further in your research than you were when you wrote your introduction and literature review. This means you probably need to go back to that introduction and tweak it so it works with the conclusion. You don't want to invite the reader to one conversation and then take part in another. If you start off bringing the reader into a conversation about the impact of rising healthcare costs on hospital management and end up talking about the inability of hospital management to grasp the key challenges that nursing staff face in their daily routines, then the reader will be lost. Instead, if you find that you have narrowed your focus to nursing staff, then go back to your introduction and bring the reader into the conversation about nursing staff. Think of your introduction and conclusion as a complementary set of bookends: one starts the conversation, the other wraps it up. And it is only when you have wrapped up the conversation that you understand what it was truly about.

'The only Zen you find on the tops of mountains is the Zen you bring up there.'

It will be tempting to make a grand conclusion – to say something deeply interesting. But keep in mind that the conclusions you make have to be based on the analysis you have performed, which is again based on the method you have used. Depending on the kind of research you have carried out and the type of thesis you are writing you might integrate your discussion into the analysis, or integrate your discussion in the conclusion, or make them three entirely different sections. Just know that each step follows from the next, and that your discussion is one level of abstraction higher than the presentation of your analysis, and that your conclusion is one level of abstraction higher than your discussion, but they are all firmly based on the previous step. Everything you need for your conclusion must be found in what you have brought with you along the way.

Finding your path: Points for reflection

What are the important points for you to cover in the summary of your thesis?

Where and how will you present the overarching claims you wish to make in your thesis?
- How will you connect these claims to the evidence you have provided through your findings?
- What other support (e.g., theory, reasons) do you provide?
- How do these claims help you answer your research question(s)?

How will you connect your claims to the ongoing conversation you introduced your reader to at the beginning of your thesis?

- Are there implications for existing theory?
- Are there implications for practice or policy?
- Do you have suggestions for future research that might build on what you have found?

What is the main thing you want your reader to remember when they finish reading your thesis? How do you want to end your story?

REFERENCES AND FURTHER READING

Bui, Yvonne N. (2009) *How to Write a Master's Thesis*. London: Sage. Bui's discussion of how to write the discussion and conclusion is highly detailed, which is useful for those writing exactly the kind of quantitative thesis she assumes as a point of departure, but may seem constraining for those writing a different type of thesis.

Lunenburg, Fred C. and Irby, Beverly J. (2008) *Writing a Successful Thesis or Dissertation: Tips and Strategies for Students in the Social and Behavioral Sciences*. Thousand Oaks, CA: Corwin Press. This book provides a detailed discussion of how to write your discussion and conclusion, and is especially relevant for those using quantitative methods.

Petre, Marian and Rugg, Gordon (2010) *The Unwritten Rules of PhD Research*, 2nd edn. Berkshire: Open University Press. The book does not go into detail about what to cover in the various chapters of your thesis, but it presents the basic points, and more importantly, the overall logic.

Roberts, Carol M. (2010) *The Dissertation Journey: A Practical and Comprehensive Guide to Planning, Writing, and Defending Your Dissertation*, 2nd edn. Thousand Oaks, CA: Corwin Press. Chapter 15 briefly discusses what to cover in the final chapter of your thesis. The author usefully draws attention to discussing the surprises in your research.

Thody, Angela M. (2006) *Writing and Presenting Research*. London: Sage. This book provides an excellent demonstration of how to build arguments using different types of data derived from different kinds of research designs.

THE FINISHING TOUCHES

Polishing and submitting your work

....

a Editing for clarity

b Editing for language and grammar

c Editing for style

d Referencing

e Formatting and handing it in

....

We all wish we could live in a world where appearances don't matter, where other people wouldn't judge us by the clothes we wear – or the typos we make. Unfortunately, that is not the world we live in. Details matter. Many evaluators start by looking first at your references to see not only what you have been citing, but also to see how well you are able to understand how academic referencing works. They will not simply look past a sloppily thrown together literature list or pages that are liberally peppered with spelling errors. In fact, some people even seem to get a perverse joy out of hunting down other people's misuse of the semi-colon or inconsistent use of UK style conventions and holding them up as proof of the writer's profound inadequacy. So when you think you are done with your thesis, take a day off. Feel good about yourself. Take a walk in the park, have dinner with some friends. But the next day, roll up your sleeves and get to work again because now it's time to take care of the finishing touches.

If you can get help with this, all the better; because you know your work so well, your eyes will not let you see your own typos. The same helpful feature of your brain that lets you read quickly by recognizing words as long as the first and last letter are correct also makes it very difficult for you to spot errors – especially if they are your own and your brain is already antic-ipating what *should* be on that page. Universities vary with regard to their policies on hiring editors or providing help through writing centres. In some places – especially where second-language writing is common – it is expected that you will have your work copyedited (or what some people call 'proofread') before submitting it, and you might even be given a budget to help pay for it. In other places, getting editorial assistance is viewed as almost cheating, the assumption being that every syllable you write has to be yours and yours alone. In my view, there is nothing ethically wrong with getting someone to help you with copyediting and proofreading (see textbox on 'Bringing in outside editorial help'). As long as the substance is all yours, having someone else point out that you have repeated the word 'that' too many times here, or you are missing a verb there, will not threaten your ownership of your work.

But most of the revising and editing that needs to happen will be done by you. The purpose of this chapter is to review the things you need to look at when you are putting the finishing touches on your work (see Figure 13.1), regardless of whether you are getting help or not: editing for clarity, editing for language, editing for style, referencing, and formatting.

....

Bringing in outside editorial help

If you are able to get professional (or even amateur) outside help, keep in mind what an editor can and cannot do for you. Editors are good with language, but bad at mind reading. They will not be able to solve all your writing problems for you, and certainly won't be able to just 'fill in the blanks' of a half-written text. What they can do is act as a separate set of eyes when you can no longer trust your own.

If you are a non-native speaker of English, simply finding someone with English as a first language is no guarantee that they will be able to provide the help you need. However, if your department has strict rules against professional assistance, then having a native speaker read through your work is better than nothing. But be aware that there are many varieties of English (for example, US vs UK), and make sure that you and your proofreader are operating within the same variety. More important, remember that you will likely be using some specialized terminology from your field, which (although it may be in English) will be unfamiliar to your proofreader. The more inexperienced the proofreader, the more likely they will change everything that appears wrong to them without checking whether it might be correct in your field. So, if you are using a non-professional, be prepared to have to double-check their work to make sure they did not change what you meant to say.

Professional copyeditors should know better. They should be able to understand the differences between varieties of English and work around technical terminology. They should also be able to help you conform to whichever style guide you need to conform to. But they still cannot do your writing for you. They can only work with what is there. The changes they make in your writing are based on what they think you are trying to say. If they are wrong, the changes they make will not improve your work, but may actually make it worse, because instead of improving clarity, they inadvertently change the meaning. This happens because the meaning wasn't entirely clear to begin with, and the editor had to make a guess. If the editor suggested something that you suspect might have changed your intended meaning, don't just accept the change because the editor is 'the expert'. But going back to your original wording can be just as bad as accepting a change you don't feel comfortable with. If you go back to your original wording, the reader might be as confused as your editor was. Instead, look at what the editor did and ask yourself, 'What made the editor think that this is what I meant?' Often what needs changing is something that you said (or did not say) much earlier; confusion on page 35 might have been caused by something you wrote (or failed to write) on page 3. And while an editor can point this out, you probably have to be the one to fix it. In other words, getting editorial help does not relieve you of responsibility; the thesis is your work, and you are responsible for every word in it.

....

Clarity	Language	Style
• Summaries • Signposting • Parallel structure	• Grammar • Word choice • Voice	• Following guidelines • Referencing • Foreign terms

Figure 13.1   The finishing touches before submitting: Before you hand in your thesis, take some time to polish the rough edges. Edit for clarity, language, and style.

ⓐ EDITING FOR CLARITY

Editing for clarity is one of the hardest tasks for you to accomplish on your own. Because you already know what you are trying to say, it is difficult to achieve enough distance from your text to make sure you have said it in a way that others can understand. But what you can do is go through and check your signposting – have you signalled to your reader how you are organizing your writing and what you plan to do in the next section? In a long and difficult document like a thesis, you almost cannot do this too often. At the very least, at the beginning of each chapter you state the purpose and general structure of that chapter, and at the end of each chapter you summarize the main points. Within each chapter you can also give your reader a heads up about what's coming: 'Below, I describe three main reasons for this phenomenon'.

 ROBERT

What I had to work on most in the end was the signposting to make it clearer what I was going to talk about in each section and how that connects to the rest of the thesis. It seemed a little awkward at first because I thought it was really obvious what each section was doing, but when my wife read through it she showed me how some of the transitions were more abrupt than they seemed in my head, and how it could be confusing for someone else. It really helped to have someone else read through it. Even though English is my first language, I still managed to write quite a few things that must have made sense to me at the time, but even I couldn't understand them when my wife pointed them out.

It is a good idea to look specifically at signposting when you are otherwise 'finished' with the writing phase and the structure of the thesis is firmly in place. Because the thesis is likely to take some unexpected turns in the writing – as your thinking matures over time, and you find additional layers of nuance that you may not have anticipated in the first draft – the final organization may not be what you originally thought it would be. As a result, you might have a lot of statements like 'The main purpose of this section is to …' and 'in the previous section I argued …' that are no longer accurate. Looking specifically at what you are doing in each section and how you are signalling this to the reader can also give you a fresh perspective on your work – and perhaps even inspire you to make a few changes in your introduction or conclusion.

The title of your thesis and the headings you use to mark off chapters and sub-chapters are the ultimate signposts. The title and headings announce to the reader what your thesis and each chapter and section are about. It is quite common to think of a title early in the process, and jot down some chapter headings in the first draft, and then never look at them again. Even if you edited the text that follows multiple times, you might not have re-examined the titles and headings. While you are focusing on the general signposting throughout the thesis, this is an excellent time to do this. Do your title and headings convey the main ideas to the reader? Although many writers like to think of clever titles (with perhaps a play on words, or some intriguing metaphor), the main purpose of the title – especially for the thesis – is to communicate to the reader what the thesis will be about.

A second thing you can do to improve clarity is to use parallel constructions as much as possible: When you have headings, lists, or key sentences that you want to draw your reader's attention to, then use a parallel grammatical structure in each part. Here is an example of a list whose items aren't parallel:

Main reasons for leaving the organization:
- To get a better job
- Low pay
- They complained about having difficult co-workers

The three items include an infinitive phrase, a noun, and a complete sentence. Try using the same structure for each item, like this:

Main reasons for leaving the organization:
- Better options elsewhere
- Low pay
- Difficult co-workers

Likewise, if you have described the outcome of a statistical test in a particular way, you might want to use that sentence structure elsewhere in your thesis to describe the outcome of that same statistical test for different variables. Using parallel sentence structure helps draw your reader's attention to the connection between them.

And finally, make sure you have expressed the most important things in the same way throughout your thesis. For example, be careful about rewording your research questions. You are likely to repeat your research question(s) several times throughout the thesis, and you might be greatly tempted to rephrase the question(s) to add variety, to fit better into the context of the paragraph you are writing, or simply because you haven't figured out the best way to express it so you are trying out several options. But beware: there is a fine line between saying the same thing in different ways and actually saying different things. When it comes to such important things as your research question(s), the purpose of your study, and your main conclusions, you do not want to introduce any unnecessary confusion (see Chapter 10's discussion about the nouns and verbs in your research question).

ⓑ EDITING FOR LANGUAGE AND GRAMMAR

Even if you are writing in your native language, you need to read your thesis through once with a focus on language and grammar. Regardless of how well you know and understand grammar, when you are expending tremendous mental energy thinking about the content of your work, your fingers will occasionally take on a life of their own and type 'their' instead of 'there', or you'll change your mind about a particular word and forget to delete the old word (or you accidentally delete the word next to it). The point is that even if your language skills are impeccable, you need to edit your work. If you are writing in a second language and are a little unsure about the finer points of that language's grammar, that need will be even greater.

AMINA

Polishing the final draft took a bit longer than I expected. I had someone read through specifically to look at my English. I actually used a fellow student because he understood my research and how we write in my field. He managed to find quite a few typos, spelling errors, and grammar mistakes, and I learned a lot about English by looking at his corrections.

As I mentioned above, this kind of editing is difficult for you to do yourself because you won't see the typos, and the nonsense created by the collateral damage in a revising accident will still make sense to you because you know what you were trying to say. If bringing in outside editorial help is not an option for you, then try changing the appearance of the text by adding columns (or reducing the margins significantly), changing the font or the font size, and increasing the line spacing. The more different the text looks, the easier it is to see mistakes (you can restore the original formatting afterwards). You can also try reading it out loud. It might drastically reduce the number of places you can sit and work, but reading out loud forces you to pronounce every word, which makes it harder to overlook mistakes.

When it comes to language, things aren't always clearly right or wrong according to some unambiguous book of rules. Managing foreign terms, for example, requires more common sense than rules (see textbox 'Using foreign terminology'). Sometimes the choice of wording that is best for you will have more to do with voice, with the way you want to express yourself: how formal your voice is, how you use active verbs or passive verbs, how you refer to yourself as a writer, how you weave in references to other writers, how you vary the length of your sentences, and so on. Pay close attention to what you consider to be good writing, and what is considered good writing in the context that you are in (see, e.g. Sword 2012). Some traditions (such as the more positivist methodologies) value writing that appears objective, where the writer's individual voice does not stand out – while others (such as anthropology) demand a writing style that is more expressive and allows more room for individual observations. Even within a single methodological approach, the style you are expected to use might vary depending on where you are located geographically (see Chapter 1).

Using foreign terminology

If your case site is in a country with a different language than the one you are writing in or you are drawing from material written in different languages, you may have to decide how to manage foreign terminology. The easiest way for the reader is, of course, if you translate it. For example, if you are interviewing your participants in Polish, and looking at government documents written in Polish, and writing in English, you can simply translate the quotes you choose to put in, making sure you specify somewhere that 'All quotes from the original Polish are the author's translation'. (Unless a translation has been published somewhere that you can refer to, you still need to say that it is the 'author's translation' even if you have used professional translation help because you remain responsible for the content).

Sometimes, however, the language you are writing in simply can't express what you want it to and you will have to decide what to do. Your biggest concern should be what would best help you communicate with your reader. Say you are doing research in a different country on bullying in classrooms, and one of the derogatory terms used by the students translates to 'son of a hamster'. The English translation will simply not carry the sense of derision that the original *blichek* does. So rather than undermining your point about the seriousness of the bullying by quoting your informant as saying 'Every time they walk past my desk they whisper "son of a hamster"', which might simply make your reader giggle, you could say, 'Every time they walk past my desk they whisper "*blichek*"'; then add some explanatory text, perhaps in a footnote, such as '*Blichek* is a particularly obscene word in Gewortsch, and rarely used. It calls into question the legitimacy of one's birth, which in Gewortika is the gravest of insults'.

Be careful not to impede readability by including too many foreign terms. Translate as many as you can, but when the translation impedes rather than aids communication, then you can retain the foreign term. Just make sure you put all foreign words in italics and explain them on first use. You might even consider making a glossary if you have several of these terms and they are used throughout your thesis.

Regardless of what kind of voice you adopt, you might feel that sometimes there is a trade-off between clarity and elegance. In other words, the more of an effort you make to make things crystal clear for your reader, the less interesting your writing seems to become. However, these qualities need not be mutually exclusive. Even if you are using parallel sentence structure quite deliberately to improve clarity and make it easier for your reader to see connections between different parts of your thesis, you can follow up these more rigidly constructed sentences with others that are different. If you want to add freshness to your work, vary your verbs and sentence length, but avoid varying your nouns (see Chapter 10). If you have decided that the thing you are discussing is, for example, a 'hypothesis', in subsequent paragraphs do not call this same thing a 'thesis', 'proposition', 'notion', or 'idea' just to liven things up. The reader will think you are talking about five different things and be looking in vain for the other four.

If you are worried about becoming boring, remember what clarity and elegance have in common: specificity and concreteness. Both a thick description and a more parsimonious description of a study site come alive when the details you add are as concrete as possible and create a distinct picture in the reader's mind: 'The study site is an office setting where 65 employees work selling insurance from cubicles that contain only a computer, a chair identical to everyone else's chair, and no personal effects'. The quantitative study might stop there, whereas the ethnography might continue: 'Even the tallest employees cannot see over the thin walls that separate them from the others, but they can all hear the constant clacking of fingers on keyboards and the indistinct murmurs of people having phone conversations that they don't want others to hear'. What makes writing both unclear and decidedly inelegant is vague abstraction, such as too much passive voice or what we might dub 'block-style running string stacked nounification', that is, long strings of nouns and the occasional adjective with no verbs or prepositions to let us take a breath.

ⓒ EDITING FOR STYLE

As I suggested above, a lot of editing involves looking at things that are not directly related to mistakes in grammar but rather to the choices you make about the words you use and the way you use them. In a writing and editing context, 'style' can refer both to your voice in general (including degrees of formality), but also more specifically to the guidelines you follow that cover formatting, punctuation, capitalization, how you express dates or units, and so on. In the social sciences, the three main style guides are as follows:

- APA: Developed by the American Psychological Association, APA style is perhaps the most common style within the social sciences. See www.apastyle.org. *The Publication Manual of the American Psychological Association* is the complete description of the style.
- Chicago: *The Chicago Manual of Style* (often abbreviated to CMS) is a highly detailed style manual that is useful for most subject areas. See www.chicagomanualofstyle.org. *A Manual for Writers of Term Papers, Theses, and Dissertations*, which describes more general guidelines for these academic works within the conventions of the Chicago style, is also available.
- MLA: Mostly used in the humanities and liberal arts, the Modern Language Association (MLA) style is fully described in the *MLA Handbook for Writers of Research Papers*. See www.mlaformat.org

Often the department you are based in will have its own guidelines based on one of the above, but adapted to suit the needs of the department – not least because these major style guides are American, and institutions based outside the US might want to modify some of the guidelines to better suit non-US English and non-American paper formats. If your department does have its own guidelines, anything that is specified in those local guidelines will overrule the more comprehensive style guide, which can sometimes be confusing. They might seem to be telling you, 'We follow APA style, except we want you to do your references slightly differently, do your headings in this particular way, follow UK conventions for punctuation, and use this special format for your running headers' – which might make you legitimately wonder what part of APA style is left for you to follow.

d REFERENCING

Perhaps the most important question of style is how you handle your citations. Nowhere is the situated nature of academic writing more evident than in referencing traditions – what is normal and expected in one setting might be wrong and frowned upon in another. If your department has a set of local guidelines that is a variation on one of the major style guides, you can almost guarantee that one of the changes will be in how you are expected to format your references.

 EMMA

I think I went through the manuscript a thousand times. In the end, I just couldn't see the typos anymore. When I looked at it again before my defence, I was mortified to see that there were still a few left! I decided not to use reference managing software because I just did not want to experiment with new software in the middle of writing my thesis, but I did end up spending a lot of time at the end with a highlighter marking the in-text references and crossing them off in the reference list at the end. I was so sure I had been careful when writing, but there were three references in the thesis that were not listed in the reference list, and one that was in the reference list but not in the thesis. And I was surprised at how inconsistent I had been about the style I used for writing the references. It is the kind of thing I guess you don't really see unless you are looking for it.

As a general piece of advice, take the act of referencing seriously, even if the formatting rules you are being asked to follow might be best described as 'whimsical'. There is simply no point in getting annoyed by referencing guidelines; throughout the rest of your academic career, you will be getting your work published in any number of different channels, and it is likely that they will all do it slightly differently. This is perhaps the best argument for using referencing software (see textbox on 'Using referencing software'). So rather than expend a lot of energy memorizing the formatting rules of one particular style only to be frustrated by a journal that essentially tells you in its instructions to authors 'We use APA style, except we modified the reference style almost beyond recognition', it is perhaps more prudent to be aware that there are many different ways to format references, both in your text and in the reference list, and get used to asking the right questions, including the following:

- **Do I need a separate reference list, or should I use footnotes or endnotes?** In the social sciences, author-date styles are the most common – which means that in the text you refer to a reference using the author and the date, and at the end you have a full list of references in alphabetical order. Some settings, however, may allow you to use a footnote style (all references in footnotes or endnotes) or a numbered style (using numbers in the text to refer to a specific reference in a numbered list at the end of your thesis).
- **Do I need the full first name of the authors, or just their first initial?** If you use referencing software, get in the habit of entering the entire first name of the author into your database. When you select your desired style, the software will write a full name or initial as required. But it cannot add a full name if you have only entered in the initial. Believe me, you have better uses of your time on the night before you submit your thesis than madly Googling the first names of authors.
- **Where do I put the date of the publication?** In the reference list, MLA style puts the date after the publisher, without parentheses; APA puts the date after the author's name in parentheses; and local variations may require a combination (e.g., date after the author's name but no parentheses). If you are using referencing software, you can make this change with a touch of a button. If you are doing it manually, you should probably take a few deep breaths and settle in for a tedious hour or two.
- **What kind of capitalization is expected in titles?** Some styles want you to capitalize all the main words in a title (which is what we call 'upstyle' or 'title case'), while others capitalize only the first word (also known as 'downstyle' or 'sentence case'). Some use a combination: Book titles and names of journals in upstyle, and titles of journal articles and book chapters in downstyle. Toggling back and forth between upstyle and downstyle is, unfortunately, not something your reference software can do for you. So if you are using reference software, try to enter the references into your database in exactly the same way, and in the way that is used by most of the styles you are likely to be using. This means that at least your references will be consistent, which makes them easier to adjust later. (Do not be confused by the way the title appears in the original source: the way it should appear in your reference list is dictated by the referencing style you are using, not by how it appears in the original.)
- **How do I deal with non-standard references?** Chances are you will have some references that are not books, book chapters, or journal articles. Typical non-typical references include websites, blogs, personal communication, memos, reports, and unpublished manuscripts. Some of the more advanced reference software systems have enough fine-grained categories that you can just enter in the information and let the software take care of the formatting for you. If you are not using referencing software, this is when a more detailed style guide can be invaluable. If what you are looking for does not appear in the style guide, common sense and ethics need to take over.

Using referencing software

There are few activities less edifying than spending an entire day going through your references and changing them from one style to another – removing parentheses around dates, changing first names to first initials, and so on. For this reason alone, investing in referencing management software can be worth it. Most of these programs, however, offer far more than simply automatic formatting of your reference list. They ensure that all the references in your text appear in the literature list, and that all the entries in the literature list appear in your text. They maintain a library of your references that you can use for everything you write, and many allow you to archive pdf files linked to the entries (which can save you from frantically thumbing through your papers muttering 'I'm sure I had a copy of that article somewhere'). Many of them are well integrated into word processing software, so all you need to do is to type in the last name of the first author, select the appropriate reference, and the reference is both correctly formatted in the text and added in full to an automatically generated reference list at the end.

But there are also big differences between these reference management programs – not least when it comes to price. Some are better at storing a pdf version of the source, and some even allow you to mark up that pdf version. They differ in how they import references automatically, and how easy it is to work from different computers and still have access to your reference library. And while the newer and less well known programs might have appealing functionality, they cannot usually automatically import custom styles from places that have their own house style (individual journals, presses, and some universities).

One way to find the best program to suit your needs is to find out what the others around you are using or what is recommended by your department. Sometimes the objective quality of the program is less important than the convenience of using a program that is recognized by others around you. If your department recommends a particular program, they might also have a formula for their 'house style' ready made for you to import and start using. If others around you are using the same program you are, you have a better chance both of having someone to ask if you have questions and of having a platform for sharing references of mutual interest. Finally, when you are thinking beyond your thesis, if you would like to co-author with any of your colleagues, using the same referencing software will make working on the same document infinitely easier.

Common sense and ethics are perhaps the most important tools you can fall back on when it comes to referencing. They should help you remember that ultimately referencing is about being as honest and transparent as possible about where your ideas, inspiration, and sometimes words come from. This is not always as easy as it sounds – partly because it is not always easy to know (or remember) where you got an idea from, and partly because not all references fit nicely into the obvious categories (i.e., books, book chapters, or journal articles). But when it comes to being transparent, just ask yourself: with the information I have provided, would it be possible for the reader to track down and find this source?

One tricky area can be sources that are not in the language of the rest of your dissertation. Sometimes there will be an official translation: the works of Bourdieu, for example, have been translated into English, which makes it possible for you to check the English translation for the wording of quotes you might wish to include and have an English source in your literature list. If there is no official translation available, or you wish to refer to the original language material, then in your reference list use the title in the original language, and then provide a translation in square brackets afterwards, like this:

Nygaard, Lynn P. (2015) *Mitt liv som en amerikaner i Norge* [My life as an American in Norway].

This tells the reader that the document you are referring to is in Norwegian, but it gives them an idea of what it is about. If you provide only the translated title, it gives the impression that the source is in English, which will be very frustrating for them if they try to find it.

If the document in question is unpublished, it will be difficult at best for a reader to find it. There are different ways of tackling this. For example, if it is an essay you wrote as an undergraduate, you could put it online and make a link to it. But if it is something that you did not author yourself, or something that is not in written form (such as a record of a conversation), the best that you can do is to provide as much information as possible: 'Notes from guest lecture by Prof. Leroy Brown on "Gang violence in urban areas", Department of Human Geography, 3 February 2014, University of Iowa'. Because this citation refers to something that readers cannot track down themselves, it probably shouldn't appear in your reference list, but rather in a footnote or endnote.

 KEIKO

In my thesis I referred to a lot of Japanese policy documents that were not available in English, and some of the terms they used were not translatable because they referred to things that are specific to the Japanese school system. In my reference list, I listed all of these documents in one place, separate from the rest of the references. I translated each title as best I could (as well as using standard English terms for the government offices). As an appendix I made a glossary of all the terms that were difficult to translate.

A final consideration is whether or not you need to add page numbers in your in-text references. The guidelines can be ambiguous, suggesting that page numbers are required with direct quotes, but not otherwise. This raises the question of whether, or when, you should add page numbers, even if you have not quoted directly. Ultimately it comes down to how specific the information is. If you write 'Brown (2012) argues that blue frogs are a myth', and the document you have referred to is a journal article (perhaps entitled 'Blue frogs are a myth'), then a page number is hardly necessary – both because the document is short, but also because you are summing up his overall argument. But what if the document is an

800-page book on everything Brown has been thinking about for the last decade and blue frogs were only mentioned in one paragraph? By not providing the page number, you have made it quite difficult – if not practically impossible – for the reader to track down that reference (see, e.g., Rekdal 2014).

The lesson here is that even the best guidelines cannot cover every conceivable situation, and you need to be able to exercise some judgement. In academic writing, references are not just decorations: they show the reader how you are engaging with your conversation partners (which is one of the key things you are supposed to be learning as a Master's student). The details can make subtle differences. For example, the decision to write 'Smith and Jones (2002) argue' or 'Smith and Jones (2002) argues' is not simply a question of grammar or style: the first refers to Smith and Jones the people; the second refers to the 2002 article. Sometimes it makes sense to refer to authors; sometimes it makes sense to refer to their particular works. It is not just about the referencing conventions in your field, it is also about the type of conversation you are having and how you want to bring others into it.

e FORMATTING AND HANDING IT IN

If you are a diligent student, you will have checked the formatting rules long before you reach the stage of finishing touches. Believe me, it can be a very nasty surprise to discover that there is a 20,000 word limit when you have just proudly finished polishing your 50,000 words of perfect prose. But even diligent students (understandably enough) are not likely to remember all of those formatting rules while they are struggling to put their life's work on paper, so it is a good idea to check them one more time now that you have checked and double-checked your writing and references.

Some things in particular to look for in those guidelines are rules about margins, spacing, typeface, and binding. Most people just work in the default settings of their word processors, but universities might have very particular rules for how they want the text to look. It is normal, for example, to demand double-spacing or 1.5 spacing, for footnotes and endnotes as well as the main text. The guidelines might request wider margins than the normal settings on your word processor. There are usually very specific requirements for font size (usually 12 point), and sometimes even typeface (for example, Times Roman for body text and Helvetica for titles and headings). And you might be asked to make a specific type of cover page and get it bound in a particular way, or perhaps submit electronically.

 SAMIR ▬▬▬▬▬▬▬▬▬▬▬▬▬▬▬▬▬▬▬▬▬▬▬▬

Since I had already written a Master's thesis, I was sure I knew how they wanted it, but there were quite a few differences between this one and the last one. The total number of pages was different, they wanted the references done differently, and even the kind of

English they wanted was different. And although I used reference managing software, I still had to format all the references manually afterwards because my university used a style that was not predefined in my software.

Finally, make sure you completely understand the procedure: how many copies you should make, where you should hand them in, and what happens next (such as what kind of oral defence you should prepare for). Some universities are very good at keeping you informed about the next steps, others seem to enjoy keeping you guessing. Your peers and supervisor can be essential at this stage to help you understand what you can expect. The main thing is that when you have finished checking and re-checking, making sure that you are giving them your thesis in the way they expect, you can now lean back. You've followed the rules, handed it in, and now it's time to let your words take over.

'When you reach the top, keep climbing.'

Most of the work of writing a thesis should go into the effort you make to design a good research project, carry it out, think critically about what you've found, and tell your story in a way that makes sense to the person reading it. It is understandable that when you finish doing all that you will feel like you've reached the top of the mountain and now deserve a rest. But your thesis journey is not over until you've added those finishing touches – polished your prose, made sure you've followed all the guidelines set by your university, and submitted your work. And then, who knows? Maybe after you've defended your work, it will form the basis of a journal article, or perhaps a doctoral project. Climb one step at a time, but keep climbing.

Finding your path: Points for reflection

How will you make sure that the reader is clear about the purpose of each section of your thesis?
- To what extent do you need to summarize each chapter at the end, or provide an overview at the beginning?
- What other signposting strategies will you use throughout the thesis?
- How will you ensure that your title and headings accurately convey what you want them to?

What steps do you need to take to make sure your language is as polished as it can be?
- What are the key words in your work that you should use consistently?
- What kind of help can you get to check your writing?

What kind of style guide do you need to follow?

What style challenges do you have in your work (e.g., non-standard references or foreign terms)? How will you handle them?

What are the procedures you need to follow to submit your work?

REFERENCES AND FURTHER READING

American Psychological Association (APA) (2010) *Publication Manual of the American Psychological Association*, 6th edn. APA style is the most commonly used style in the social sciences. The manual provides an excellent reference for most aspects of style, including formatting of references.

Becker, Howard (1986) *Writing for Social Scientists: How to Start and Finish Your Thesis, Book, or Article*, 2nd revd edn. Chicago, IL: University of Chicago Press. Chapter 7 'Getting it out the door' discusses the more psychological aspects of fiddling with the details before submission.

Booth, Wayne C., Colomb, Gregory G., and Williams, Joseph M. (2008) *The Craft of Research*, 3rd edn. Chicago, IL: University of Chicago Press. Chapter 17 provides an excellent guide to thinking through how to revise your writing and edit for clarity.

Modern Language Association of America (2016) *The MLA Handbook for Writers of Research Papers*, 8th edn. New York: MLA. A shorter and easier to use version of the previous handbooks, this book explains MLA style specifically for students.

Murray, Rowena (2011) *How to Write a Thesis*, 3rd edn. Maidenhead: Open University Press. Throughout the entire book, but particularly in Chapter 7 on revising, Murray talks about things like signalling, signposting, and things to think about in revising.

Preston, Gina (2006) 'Understanding submission and examination processes', in Alan Bond (ed.), *Your Master's Thesis: How to Plan, Draft, Write and Revise*. Abergele: Studymates. Preston goes into detail about the kinds of things you need to think about when you are ready to hand in your work.

Reid, Natalie (2010) *Getting Published in International Journals: Writing Strategies for European Scientists*. Oslo: Norwegian Social Research (NOVA). Reid provides detailed, sentence-level advice on how to revise and tighten your language, especially for those with English as a second language.

Rekdal, Ole Bjørn (2014) 'Academic citation practice: A sinking sheep?', *Portal: Libraries and the Academy*, 14(4): 567–585. Rekdal provides a highly engaging discussion about the purpose of referencing and citations – and what happens to the nature of scholarship when authors take short cuts.

Single, Peg Boyle (2010) *Demystifying Dissertation Writing: A Streamlined Process from Choice of Topic to Final Text*. Sterling, VA: Stylus. Chapter 10 provides a good discussion of revising at both the organizational and content levels.

Sword, Helen (2012) *Stylish Academic Writing*. Cambridge, MA: Harvard University Press. Using her own research as a point of departure, Sword shows how different disciplines have different styles of writing.

University of Chicago Press (2010) *The Chicago Manual of Style (CMS)*, 16th edn. Chicago, IL: Chicago University Press. Although perhaps used more in the humanities than the social sciences, CMS nevertheless contains a lot of information about complex style issues – such as how to style words in foreign languages.

BIBLIOGRAPHY

American Psychological Association (APA) (2010) *Publication Manual of the American Psychological Association*, 6th edn. Washington, DC: American Psychological Association.

Becker, Howard (1986) *Writing for Social Scientists: How to Start and Finish Your Thesis, Book, or Article*, 2nd revd edn. Chicago, IL: University of Chicago Press.

Bloch, Joel (2012) *Plagiarism, Intellectual Property and the Teaching of L2 Writing*. Bristol: Multilingual Matters.

Boice, Robert (1990) *Professors as Writers: A Self-Help Guide to Productive Writing*. Stillwater, OK: New Forums Press.

Bolton, Gillie (2014) *Reflective Practice: Writing and Professional Development*, 4th edn. London: Sage.

Bond, Alan (ed.) (2006) *Your Master's Thesis: How to Plan, Draft, Write and Revise*. Abergele: Studymates.

Booth, Wayne C., Colomb, Gregory G., and Williams, Joseph M. (2008) *The Craft of Research*, 3rd edn. Chicago, IL: University of Chicago Press.

British Education Research Association (BERA) (2011) *Ethical Guidelines for Educational Research*. www.bera.ac.uk/researchers-resources/resources-for-researchers (last accessed 19.05.16).

Bui, Yvonne N. (2009) *How to Write a Master's Thesis*. London: Sage.

Cresswell, John W. (2003) *Research Design: Qualitative, Quantitative, and Mixed Methods Approaches*, 2nd edn. Thousand Oaks, CA: Sage.

Curry, Mary Jane and Lillis, Theresa (2013) *A Scholar's Guide to Getting Published in English: Critical Choices and Practical Strategies*. Bristol: Multilingual Matters.

Elbow, Peter (1998) *Writing with Power: Techniques for Mastering the Writing Process*, 2nd edn. New York: Oxford University Press.

Few, Stephen (2012) *Show Me the Numbers: Designing Tables and Graphs to Enlighten*. Burlingame, CA: Analytics Press.

Goldberg, Natalie (2005) *Writing Down the Bones: Freeing the Writer Within,* expanded edn. Boston, MA: Shambhala Publications.

Graff, Gerald and Birkenstein, Cathy (2014) *They Say, I Say: The Moves that Matter in Academic Writing*. New York: W.W. Norton & Company.

Harwood, Nigel and Petrić, Bojana (2017) *Experiencing Master's Supervision: Perspectives of International Students and their Supervisors*. London: Routledge.

Hennink, Monique, Hulter, Inge, and Bailey, Ajay (2011) *Qualitative Research Methods*. London: Sage.

Jesson, Jill K., Matheson, Lydia, and Lacey, Finona M. (2011) *Doing Your Literature Review: Traditional and Systematic Techniques*. London: Sage.

Kamler, Barbara and Thomson, Pat (2014) *Helping Doctoral Students Write: Pedagogies for Supervision*. London: Routledge.

Kellogg, Ronald T. (1994) *The Psychology of Writing*. New York, NY: Oxford University Press.

Kirton, Bill (2011) *Brilliant Dissertation: What You Need to Know and How to Do It*. Harlow: Prentice Hall.

Lee, Anne (2008) 'How are doctoral students supervised? Concepts of doctoral research supervision', *Studies in Higher Education*, 33(3): 267–81.

Lunenburg, Fred C. and Irby, Beverly J. (2008) *Writing a Successful Thesis or Dissertation: Tips and Strategies for Students in the Social and Behavioral Sciences*. Thousand Oaks, CA: Corwin Press.

Miller, Tina, Birch, Maxine, Mauthner, Melanie, and Jessop, Julie (eds) (2002) *Ethics in Qualitative Research*. Thousand Oaks, CA: Sage.

Modern Language Association of America (2016) *The MLA Handbook for Writers of Research Papers*, 8th edn. New York: MLA.

Murray, Rowena (2011) *How to Write a Thesis*, 3rd edn. Maidenhead: Open University Press.

Murray, Rowena (2013) *Writing for Academic Journals*, 3rd edn. Maidenhead: Open University Press.

Murray, Rowena and Moore, Sarah (2006) *The Handbook of Academic Writing: A Fresh Approach*. Maidenhead: Open University Press.

National Committees for Research Ethics in Norway (2006) *Guidelines for Research Ethics in the Social Sciences, Law and the Humanities*. Oslo: National Committees for Research Ethics in Norway. www.etikkom.no/en/ethical-guidelines-for-research/guidelines-for-research-ethics-in-the-social-sciences—humanities-law-and-theology

Nygaard, Lynn P. (2015) *Writing for Scholars: A Practical Guide to Making Sense and Being Heard*, 2nd edn. London: Sage.

Nygaard, Lynn P. (2015) 'Publishing and perishing: An academic literacies framework for investigating research productivity', *Studies in Higher Education*, open access.

Paltridge, Brian and Starfield, Sue (2007) *Thesis and Dissertation Writing in a Second Language: A Handbook for Supervisors*. London: Routledge.

Petre, Marian and Rugg, Gordon (2010) *The Unwritten Rules of PhD Research*, 2nd edn. Berkshire: Open University Press.

Reid, Natalie (2010) *Getting Published in International Journals: Writing Strategies for European Scientists*, Oslo: Norwegian Social Research (NOVA).

Rekdal, Ole Bjørn (2014) 'Academic citation practice: A sinking sheep?', *Portal: Libraries and the Academy*, 14(4): 567–585.

Ridley, Diana (2012) *The Literature Review: A Step-by-Step Guide for Students*, 2nd edn. London: Sage.

Roberts, Carol M. (2010) *The Dissertation Journey: A Practical and Comprehensive Guide to Planning, Writing, and Defending Your Dissertation*, 2nd edn. Thousand Oaks, CA: Corwin Press.

Robson, Colin (2011) *Real World Research*, 3rd edn. West Sussex: John Wiley and Sons.

Shon, Phillip Chong Ho (2015) *How to Read Journal Articles in the Social Sciences: A Very Practical Guide for Students*, 2nd edn. London: Sage.

Silvia, Paul J. (2007) *How to Write a Lot: A Practical Guide to Productive Academic Writing*. Washington, DC: American Psychological Association.

Single, Peg Boyle (2010) *Demystifying Dissertation Writing: A Streamlined Process from Choice of Topic to Final Text*. Sterling, VA: Stylus.

Swales, John (1990) *Genre Analysis: English in Academic and Research Settings*. Cambridge: Cambridge University Press.

Swedberg, Robert (ed.) (2014) *Theorizing in Social Science: The Context of Discovery*. Redwood City: Stanford Social Sciences.

Sword, Helen (2012) *Stylish Academic Writing*. Cambridge, MA: Harvard University Press.

Thody, Angela M. (2006) *Writing and Presenting Research*. London: Sage.

Toulmin, Stephen E. (2003) *The Uses of Argument*, updated edn. Cambridge: Cambridge University Press.

University of Chicago Press (2010) *The Chicago Manual of Style (CMS)*, 16th edn. Chicago, IL: Chicago University Press.

Wellington, Jerry (2010) *Making Supervision Work for You: A Student's Guide*. London: Sage.

Willis, Jerry W. (2007) *Foundations of Qualitative Research: Interpretive and Critical Approaches*. London: Sage.

Yau, Nathan (2011) *Visualize This: The FlowingData Guide to Design, Visualization, and Statistics*. Indianapolis, IL: Wiley Publishing.

INDEX

Figures are indicated by page numbers in bold.